# SMITHSONIAN CONTRIBUTIONS TO ANTHROPOLOGY

VOLUME 10

# The Native Polity of Ponape

Saul H. Riesenberg

SMITHSONIAN INSTITUTION PRESS
City of Washington 1968

*A Publication of the*

SMITHSONIAN INSTITUTION

United States National Museum

LIBRARY OF CONGRESS CARD 68–29128

United States Government Printing Office, Washington, 1968

For sale by the Superintendent of Documents, U.S. Government Printing Office
Washington, D.C. 20402 - Price $4.25

# Preface

A large part of the material presented in this work was obtained in the course of fieldwork on Ponape from July 1947 to January 1948. This fieldwork was sponsored by the Pacific Science Board of the National Research Council, with support by the Office of Naval Research. It was part of the CIMA Project (Coordinated Investigation of Micronesian Anthropology), and the preliminary report I submitted is partially incorporated in the present work. Other materials obtained on the same field trip have been published elsewhere and still others remain to be published. In 1953–54, during a year of leave from teaching duties at the University of Hawaii and while in the position of Staff Anthropologist to the High Commissioner of the United States Trust Territory of the Pacific Islands, I was on Ponape in the course of other duties several times, for periods ranging from a few days to a month, and took the opportunity to add to my field materials. In January to March 1963, I was again at Ponape performing other fieldwork under a grant from the National Science Foundation, and during that period was able to fill some additional lacunae in my notes.

I have made use of the unpublished field notes of Dr. J. L. Fischer of Tulane University, and of the letters, journals, and other documents of the American Board of Commissioners for Foreign Missions in the Houghton Library at Harvard University, and have drawn on the rich knowledge of Father Hugh Costigan, S.J., a missionary stationed on Ponape since 1947. To these institutions and individuals and to my Ponapean informants and friends, too numerous to mention here by name, I wish to express my enormous debt of gratitude.

I also wish to thank George Robert Lewis, Scientific Illustrator, Office of Anthropology, for preparing the line drawings and maps from my pencil sketches and Dr. Clifford Evans, my colleague, for kindly allowing me to use photographs taken by him during our joint field trip to Ponape in 1963 for Plates 5b, 6a, b, 7b, 8a–d, 9a, b, 10b, 11a, b, and 12a–d.

Standard Ponapean orthography as developed by Drs. Paul Garvin, Isidore Dyen, and John L. Fischer and as taught nowadays with some modifications in Ponapean schools has been followed in this work. It is as follows:

1. Vowels are roughly as in Spanish except for the digraph *oa,* a low back vowel.
2. Consonants are roughly as in English except that there is generally no aspiration, and presence or absence of voicing is of no phonemic significance. The exceptions are:
    a. *t* is a retroflex alveolar stop.
    b. *d* approximates English *t.*
    c. *ng* is a digraph for a velar nasal.
    d. *s* is about midway between English *s* and *sh,* and is sometimes heard as English *ch, ts,* and almost *j.*
    e. *pw* and *mw* each represent single phonemes, pronounced approximately as written but with lip rounding beginning before closure.
3. *h* represents no phoneme and is used only as a sign of phonemic length of the vowel preceding it.
4. Those consonants that can occur doubled (*m, mw, n, ng, l, r*) are written by repeating them, except for double *mw,* which is written *mmw,* and double *l,* which is written *nl* when this is its etymological derivation (but there is no difference in pronunciation between *nl* and *ll*).

*Smithsonian Institution*
*Washington, D.C.*

SHR

# Contents

# Tables



# Illustrations

## FIGURES



## PLATES

# The Native Polity of Ponape

298-818—68——2

# Introduction

## THE PHYSICAL SETTING

The island of Ponape lies at 6°54′ north latitude and 158°14′ east longitude, near the eastern end of the archipelago that comprises the Caroline Islands. Ponape and the nearby atolls of Pakin and Ant constitute the Senyavin group. Kusaie, the next major island to the east and last of the Caroline chain, is 307 nautical miles distant; and Truk is 383 miles to the west. Ponape is about midway between Honolulu and Manila, 2,685 and 2,363 miles distant, respectively.

The land area of Ponape as usually given is 334 square kilometers (129 square miles). Except for a few coastal plains and lower slopes, most of the island is ruggedly mountainous with several ranges and high peaks, the highest rising to 791 meters (nearly 2,600 feet), the highest peak in the Carolines. The mountain tops are often covered with cloud and mist. The island interior consists largely of basalt, with some andesite and other volcanic rock. The lower slopes and level areas are mostly sand and gravel. Here and there, most spectacularly on Sokehs Island, are high cliffs of columnar basalt, with columnar talus at their bases. Streams and waterfalls abound. The streams are very active after every rainfall and deposit alluvium in great flats.

The main island is roughly circular in outline. About 20 square miles of its area consists of coastal mangrove swamp; there are few beaches. Surrounding the island is an encircling reef, distant from the coast about 2 miles on the average and broken here and there by passages between the lagoon and the open sea. Where the reef rises above sea level, some 15 coral islets are formed. The lagoon between the main island and the encircling reef is of varying depth and contains many heads of live coral that may rise close to the water surface. It occupies about 98 square miles of water and includes in it 23 small islands of the same volcanic materials as the main island. Also in the lagoon are a number of alluvial islands lying close to the shore and, in the east, off Temwen Island, some 90 artificial islets are grouped together that contain the well-known archeological ruins of Nan Madol. All of these smaller islands together occupy an area of about 5 square miles.

Ponape, like the rest of the Carolines, is in the doldrum belt. This belt swings north May to July and south August to November, accompanied by stormy weather and heavy rain. The trade winds blow from the east December to April and move around more to the south the rest of the year. Typhoons are much less common than in western Micronesia.

Relative humidity is high; the monthly averages are 79 to 91 percent and are lowest in March and April. Rainfall is very heavy and is rather uniform throughout the year, though somewhat less in January to March. The annual average precipitation is 178 inches. The monthly temperature means are from 78° to 82° F., the extremes are 68° and 92° F.

The extensive mangrove swamps that line much of the low shore consist of *Sonneratia, Rhizophora, Bruguiera, Lumnitzera, Xylocarpus, Heritiera,* and also *Nypa* palm. Strand vegetation occurs largely on the reef islands and where the land of the main island starts to rise inland of the mangroves. Behind the strand and mangroves is a narrow strip of coastal plain vegetation, originally primary rain forest but now mainly occupied by single dwellings or small clusters of buildings and by cultivated areas. (Very few localities on Ponape can properly be called villages.) The cultivated areas contain coconut groves, banana, breadfruit, citrus, sweet potatoes, manioc, aroids (*Cyrtosperma, Alocasia,* and *Colocasia*), and a few other cultivated plants of less importance, as well as such trees as *Ficus, Calophyllum, Terminalia,* ivory nut palm, *Pandanus, Macaranga, Morinda,* and *Hibiscus,* with some grasses and undergrowth.

The rain forest is very dense and rich. Ponape has the most extensive native forests in Micronesia. Uninterrupted jungle covers most of the interior and reaches to the coast in a few places. The forest covers most of the steep slopes and summits and some lowlands. The lower primary forests contain large trees, palms, climbers, ferns, orchids, and other epiphytes. On the slopes where rain forest has been destroyed there are mixed coconut and breadfruit groves, also bananas, *Alocasia,* and some shrubbery. The montane rain forests consist of scrubby, mossy woods on the steep slopes and ridges, where the soil is thin. Tree ferns, *Exorrhiza* and *Ponapea* palms, *Freycinetia,* and many stunted broad-leaved trees bearing epiphytes predominate. On the high open crests are dwarfed shrubs, dwarfed *Exorrhiza,* tree ferns, dense growths of *Pandanus,* or open bogs. Grassland is rare.

According to Baker (1951) some 39 species of birds occur on Ponape, including sea birds, migratory shore birds, and land and fresh water birds. Among the species are a heron, a duck, seven of the snipe-sandpiper family, six gulls and terns, two doves and a pigeon, a lory, an owl, a kingfisher, two flycatchers, two starlings, three white-eyes, and two weaver finches. Insects are numerous but comprise only a small number of genera. The only land reptiles are a few species of lizard. There were only three mammals, aboriginally: rats, bats, and dogs; pigs were introduced in very early postcontact times, and some are now feral, as are the deer brought in during German times. In contrast, the lagoon is rich in fishes, mollusks, crustacea, and other marine fauna, including two kinds of turtles.[1]

## DISCOVERY AND EARLY HISTORY

Ponape's first European visitor was Pedro Fernandez de Quiros, commanding the *San Geronimo,* the last seaworthy vessel of the four that had comprised the Mendaña expedition. Alvaro de Mendaña had died in the Santa Cruz Islands, and Quiros, the first pilot, took command. On December 23, 1595, he sighted Ponape while en route to Guam and Manila. The description he gives is brief and he did not land; he only saw a few canoes and established no communication, other than by gestures, with the distant natives (Markham, 1904). But the name Quirosa, which the island thus received, became attached by mistaken cartographers to Truk instead of to Ponape.

Two earlier sightings of Ponape may possibly have occurred, by Loyasa in 1526 and Saavedra in 1528 (Navarrete, 1827, pp. 99–100, 468). But the meager description appears to apply to low, coral islands, not to Ponape. Equally doubtful sightings are those of Musgrave in 1793, Ibargoita in 1801, and Dublon in 1814 (Hambruch, 1932 I, p. 78). But a Ponapean legend very circumstantially tells of a ship that came to Kiti, its men having skins of iron and one man in black wearing a cross. The visitors could be killed only by spearing them in the eyes. Evidently this is a memory of some unrecorded European voyage, probably Spanish. Another story tells of the removal by the Sou Kiti (a high chief's title) of a small brass cannon from some foreign ship that visited Kiti. The cannon was kept until 1839, when Captain Blake of HMS *Larne* carried it off to Hong Kong (Blake, 1924). It bore a Spanish coat of arms, according to the missionary L. H. Gulick (1862, p. 175); evidence of French or Chinese origin, according to Rosamel (Hambruch, 1932 I, p. 118). In the 1830s, whaler and trader captains, rummaging in the ruins of Nan Madol and elsewhere for supposed treasure, found various European objects, including two silver crucifixes, coins, and a pair of dividers (L. H. Gulick, 1862, p. 175; A. Gulick, 1932, p. 88; Maigret, 1837–38).

The second visitor, after Quiros, for whom we have good documentation did not arrive at Ponape until September 10, 1825. He was Capt. John Henry Rowe (*Hobart Colonial Times,* May 25, 1827; *Sydney Gazette,* June 15, 1827). He also did not land. His vessel was chased by five canoes; this was his only contact with the natives. He gave the name John Bull's Island to his discovery, after the name of his bark.[2]

It is not clear who the next visitors were. In a note in an Australian newspaper of February 1835 (Lhotsky, 1835), there is a reference to a Mr. Ong of New South

[1] The foregoing is compiled from Bascom, 1965; Baker, 1951; Fischer, 1957; Gressitt, 1954; Hambruch, 1932; and Glassman, 1952.

[2] I am much indebted to Mr. Harry Maude and to Mrs. Honore Forster of Australian National University for providing me with this information concerning Capt. Rowe, for details of Australian history that affect the veracity of O'Connell's story (discussed later in this section), and for drawing my attention to several Australian newspaper accounts.

Wales who "some years back" was at Ponape and remained several months. A brief description of the Nan Madol ruins is given. The same article states that the island was discovered "very lately" by HM Sloop of War *Raven;* I have been unable to learn anything more of a voyage to Ponape by such a vessel, despite search of various archives. One can only guess what "some years back" might mean. Equally indefinite is the "discovery" by Captain Harper. According to Alick Osborne, who arrived at Ponape on December 20, 1832, in the ship *Planter,* the island, which he calls Harper's Islands, "was discovered by Captain Harper, in the ship *Ephemina,* bound from Sydney to Canton about six years ago . . ." (Osborne, 1833, p. 34). This would make the date of Harper's visit about 1826. But the captain of Osborne's ship, L. Frazer (1834, p. 74), refers to the island as his own original discovery and names it William the Fourth Group. (The name William the Fourth is sometimes applied to Ant atoll, as is also the name Frazer's. Ant is only 8 miles from Ponape and in the same Senyavin group, but Frazer's description is not of an atoll but a volcanic island and must be of Ponape.) Ong uses the name Ascension for Ponape, as did Capt. J. H. Eagleston of the bark *Peru* (Eagleston, 1832–33) when he sighted the island on January 3, 1832; it was already on Eagleston's charts under that name. It is uncertain who first called it Ascension Island, but it quickly became established in the literature and was used by nearly all later visitors.

The first description of the island and natives of any length is by the Russian, Capt. F. Lutké (or Lütke), whose vessel, the *Senyavin,* gives its name to the group consisting of Ponape, Ant, and Pakin (Lutké, 1835–36). He was at Ponape only 5 days (January 14–19, 1828). His boats attempted to land but could not make the shore because of the throngs of canoes that pressed about them and the show of hostility. But natives came aboard, some trading occurred, a short vocabulary was compiled, and a map was made. F. H. von Kittlitz, a member of the expedition, wrote a supplementary account (Kittlitz, 1858). The two reports together provide the first real knowledge of Ponape.

That others visited Ponape about the same time as or before Ong, Rowe, Frazer, Osborne, Lutké, and Kittlitz is apparent from the article published in 1836 by a Dr. Campbell [3] who arrived on the cutter *Lambton* about the end of 1835. (The *Lambton* was the next year to participate in the infamous *Falcon* affair, which resulted in a war between two parties of Ponapeans, one of them allied with the survivors of the *Falcon* and the crews of the *Lambton* and two other ships, and in the overthrow of the ruling line of chiefs of one of the tribes. This incident is described later in this work.) Campbell says that the island "has been occasionally visited during the last nine years by the masters of ships engaged in the whale fishery, for the purpose of refreshment . . ." (Campbell, 1836), which would put the beginning of these visits in about 1826. James F. O'Connell, the allegedly shipwrecked Irish sailor who was rescued from Ponape in 1833, makes remarks that lead to similar conclusions; he refers to a song celebrating "the barking of a dog on board some vessel which had visited them," he asked the natives "why they stole from vessels," he refers to "bits of iron hoop, an officer's coat, and other articles" on nearby Pakin, to traditions of guns, to fowl descended from a pair presented to one of the chiefs by people with moustaches who arrived in "a big canoe with one stick" about 40 years before, etc. (O'Connell, 1836, pp. 175, 178, 181, 192, 201). This "big canoe" is interpreted by O'Connell to refer to a Spanish or Portuguese schooner; but Rosamel (*in* Hambruch, 1932 I, p. 117) refers to traditions of a Chinese junk that was wrecked at Ponape about 1810 and which brought the first fowls, and an identical remark is in one of L. H. Gulick's letters.

When O'Connell arrived is not certain. On the basis of his remark that he left Australia "in or about the year 1826" both Fischer (1957, p. 24) and Hambruch (1932 I, p. 77) conclude that he was already on Ponape when Lutké arrived in January 1828. However, I am inclined to agree with the Reverend L. H. Gulick (1859, p. 131), the missionary to Ponape in the 1850s, when he says that "so much of the irreconcilably and egregiously incorrect is mingled with O'Connell's narrative . . . concerning everything connected with the whole island . . ." that very little of what he reports can be trusted. His story of his adventures in Australia before he came to Ponape and in the Philippines and China afterward is full of improbabilities, exaggerations, anachronisms, and outright falsehoods. Even his name appears to be a pseudonym. Although he denies it, he was probably an escaped Sydney convict. By his own account he stayed at Ponape for something over 5 years; since he was rescued in November 1833, this would put his arrival in 1828. He names the ship he sailed on as the bark *John Bull,* under Captain Barkus, which he says foundered after striking on a reef; after 4 days in an open boat he and five shipmates made Ponape. However, Barkus and the *John Bull* (the same vessel previously mentioned as under Captain Rowe when he discovered Ponape in 1825) did not sail on their final voyage from Sydney until May 13, 1830, and the bark was seen by another vessel off Japan in August of that year (*Sydney Gazette,* May 15 and November 13, 1830). Moreover, a newspaper report of 1837 states that the

[3] Campbell's article was republished in *The Polynesian,* July 11, 1840, where Francisco Michelena y Rojas, the Venezuelan traveler who was at Ponape in 1841, evidently saw it. He proceeded to plagiarize from it, almost verbatim, in his own account of Ponape (Michelena y Rojas, 1843) as though he were the original author. The story is told in detail in Riesenberg, 1959.

bark and crew were the victims of some Europeans and "other savages" 7 or 8 years before at Pleasant Island, a good 800 miles from Ponape, a distance hardly likely to have been covered in 4 days in a boat (*Sydney Herald,* September 4, 7, and 28, 1837; *The Friend,* May 1853, p. 38). The missionary Sturges, writing in the early 1850s, flatly states that O'Connell ran away by swimming ashore from a ship that was lying off Kiti.

O'Connell says he saw no ships or other white men, apart from his five companions, all the time he was at Ponape, until Captain Knight of the Salem brig *Spy* rescued him in November 1833. But Knight (1925, p. 200) reports that O'Connell told him that "a Botany Bay ship left the coast only ten days before, after obtaining upwards of seven hundred pounds of shell and in consequence I should find it much scarcer than usual," implying that a regular commerce in tortoise shell with trading vessels already existed; also, "a lot of whites came off with a quantity of shell which I purchased. These fellows had been put into the canoes of the natives by the Botany Bay whalers as they passed the island and undoubtedly were convicts. . . ." Knight (1834, letter) states that when he was at New Zealand, earlier in 1833, he inquired of various English whaling captains as to where was the best place to trade for shell; "one and all were united in saying that Ascension was the best island for shell in the Pacific." Evidently, then, Ponape was already well known. O'Connell is silent about the Sydney bark *Nimrod,* which lay in harbor with the *Spy,* and whose captain told Knight that he himself had left nine white men at Ponape, apparently on an earlier voyage. (This unnamed captain had replaced Captain McAuliffe, who had been killed a few days before at Pingelap. *Sydney Gazette,* April 8 and May 8, 1834; *Sydney Morning Herald,* May 8, 1834.)

This same *Nimrod,* a whaler, then under a Captain White, had, according to Gulick (1858b, p. 34), anchored at Kiti in November 1832, on an earlier voyage, a month before Osborne and Frazer arrived in the *Planter.* In the same month another Sydney whaler, the *Albion,* Capt. John Evans, also stopped at Kiti. James (1835, p. 74), whose brief description of Ponape is dated December 1833, must also have been at Ponape before O'Connell's rescue, but O'Connell mentions none of these visitors.

From this time on the whaling and trading vessels came in increasing numbers, and very soon a large colony of beachcombers, escaped convicts, and ship's deserters became established ashore. The log of the ship *Eliza,* Captain Winn, on October 30, 1834, already refers to several white men in canoes coming off to the ship. Rosamel's 1840 report of the voyage of the French corvette, *La Danaïde* (published in Hambruch), states that between 1834 and 1840 some 47 vessels had visited Ponape, nearly all of them whalers: two were English, the rest American. There are no further statistics until the Protestant missionary period, beginning in 1852, but in that year Gulick reports the arrival of 29 vessels. In the next 4 years the tabulations are 33, 42, 23, and 19 vessels, respectively, 146 in all, of which all but 11 were whalers (Gulick, 1853, p. 19). Campbell states that in 1835 25 foreigners were living ashore and that a short time before there had been 40. Blake (1924, p. 668) gives a census of over 30 whites and Negroes in 1839; Michelena y Rojas (1843) mentions 40–50 Europeans in 1841; Cheyne (1852, p. 110) reports upwards of 60 foreign residents in 1846, "chiefly bad characters"; the report of the Swedish frigate *Eugenie* (*in* Hambruch, 1932 I, p. 148) gives a total of 30 in 1852. The missionary sources (letters and various issues of *The Friend*) count 150 in 1850, 60–80 in 1852, 60–70 in 1855, and 25–30 in 1857. By 1871, according to Mahlmann (1918, p. 56), after the decline of the whaling industry and before the Spanish established their colony, the foreign population had fallen to two missionaries and 12 beachcombers.

The effects of these acculturative influences were enormous. But they did not all stem from foreigners. The brig *Harmony* (*Nautical Magazine,* 1838, p. 138), at Ponape in October 1835, signed on as a crewmember a Ponapean boy of 16. Campbell, who was at Ponape the same year, reports that one native had already been to Hawaii and had returned. The cutter *Lambton* in 1835 and 1836 took at least one Ponapean as a crewmember to Sydney and back to Ponape (Blake, 1924, p. 18). Soon Ponapean sailors were plying the Pacific and some were reaching New England ports, and many returned to their home island.

Most of the foreigners attached themselves to chiefs, as did O'Connell, who married his protector's daughter. Blake (1924, p. 668) describes the situation in 1839 in these terms: the European seamen reside

> with Chiefs or petty Chiefs under their immediate protection, to whose tribe they are considered to belong and whose people become as it were their working attendants or slaves, pulling them in their Canoes, fishing for turtle for them, collecting shell, etca., in short doing whatever may be required for them; the only compensation they receive being occasional small payments in pieces of tobacco. The chief perhaps receives nothing for a long period; but, on the arrival of a ship when trading is carried on, he is presented, in return for his protection and the services of the people of his tribe, with one or two muskets, Axes, adzes for making Canoes, powder or a portion of Tobacco, or whatever he may most desire; and this seems to be the sort of tenure by which the white men hold their settlement in the Island. When the Chiefs have once engaged to protect, they have in general shewn great fidelity to the White men . . .

There was another hold on the foreigners, for among the letters of the missionary L. H. Gulick is one dated in 1853 that says it was a common habit to rob a white man of all he had if he attempted to leave the tribe for another tribe. In another letter Gulick remarks that the foreigners were quite at the mercy of the chiefs, so far as their property was concerned; the chief expected at least half of all the earnings from a foreigner under his protection. Commerce with the ships was almost entirely in their hands. Mahlmann, who was on Ponape from 1868 to 1871, says (1918, p. 58) that the chiefs "were always very eager to have a white man to do the bartering for them. They did not give them any pay, but treated them like their own sons; gave them houses to live in, and supplied them with everything the island produced, including wives."

The first missionary arrived on December 13, 1837. He was Father L. Maigret, later to become Bishop of Honolulu (A. Gulick, 1932, p. 89; Jore, 1953, p. 33; Yzendoorn, 1927, pp. 117–120; Maigret, 1837–38; Maigret, 1839). With him had sailed another priest, Father Bachelot, but he died aboard the ship and was buried upon arrival at Ponape. In their company were a number of Mangarevans and Tahitians, some of whom remained behind and left descendants on Ponape. Maigret sailed away again, after an unsuccessful 7 months, on July 29, 1838. (I mention these details because in the accounts by Fischer (1957) and Hambruch (1932) there are errors of dating and names.) The American Board of Commissioners for Foreign Missions, a Protestant organization with headquarters in Boston, sent a group of missionaries in 1852; they established themselves at Ponape permanently, and a wealth of information about the island is contained in their letters and journals deposited in the Houghton Library at Harvard University.

The later history of Ponape is admirably set forth in detail by Hambruch (1932), Bascom (1965), and Fischer (1957) and need not be recounted here. Though the Spanish had some claim to the Caroline Islands, it was only in 1886 after a dispute over sovereignty with Germany that they really began to exert political authority. In consequence of the Spanish-American War, Germany, in 1899, purchased the islands, together with all the Marianas except Guam. The Japanese occupied them in 1914 and the Americans in 1945. The natives of Ponape often refer to events in their past as having occurred, for example, "in German times," "before the Spanish," and so on. For this reason it will be convenient in this work when precise dates of particular events are not determinable to refer, as Bascom does, to the following historical periods:

| | |
|---|---|
| Native period | Before 1825 |
| Pre-Spanish period | 1825–86 |
| Spanish period | 1886–99 |
| German period | 1899–1914 |
| Japanese period | 1914–45 |
| American period | Since 1945 |

## POPULATION

The early estimates of the number of natives of Ponape are highly unreliable, since they are based on brief encounters with the people in a few localities. The Ponapeans often say that the population was once much greater than it is today, and they may be correct, for abandoned dwelling sites can be found in many places in the interior of the island, which is completely uninhabited today (see Plate 1a). A list of estimates from various sources is given in Table 1. It would seem from the estimates that soon after European contact a population decline began, dramatically accelerated in 1854 in consequence of the smallpox epidemic of that year; the decline continued until about the turn of the century, when more accurate figures began to be compiled and a reversal of the trend commenced.

I have not compiled later figures because the official German and Japanese tabulations for the period up to World War II do not usually distinguish between Ponapeans and natives of other islands. The out-islanders began to arrive about 1906 and were considerably augmented in 1912. Most of them, especially from the Mortlock Islands, were resettled on Ponape by the administration in consequence of destructive typhoons in their home islands. The 1911–12 figure of 3,190, given in Table 1, is composed only of Ponapeans, the census showing in addition 585 Central Carolinians and 279 Melanesian soldiers, but later figures are unreliable in this matter. The official Japanese figures compiled by Bascom (1965, p. 7) show a fairly steady increase from 4,165 "natives" in 1920 to a maximum of 5,905 in 1939, with some decrease thereafter until 1946, but they are affected by the forced labor drafts that involved movement of Ponapeans and natives of other islands both to and from Ponape.

My own census (Table 2), conducted in November and December of 1947, with native assistance, shows a total population of 5,628, of which 4,451 were Ponapean and 1,177 were natives of other Pacific localities. (In 1963 the population was nearly 10,000.) Nearly 700 of the non-Ponapeans were natives or descendents of natives of the Mortlock Islands; most of them live in the six villages on Sokehs Island. The only other community, inhabited by both Ponapeans and out-islanders, is the town of Kolonia, where the successive foreign admin-

TABLE 1.—*Population of Ponape from Native Period to 1914*

| Source | Date of estimate | Population estimate |
|---|---|---|
| Sturges, 1855 letter | Native period | 20 or 30, 000 |
| Lutké, 1835–36 | 1828 | 2, 000 |
| James, 1835 | 1833 | 1, 000 |
| Campbell, 1836 | 1835 | 5–6, 000 |
| Hale, 1846 (from Punchard, verbal) | 1835 | 15, 000 |
| Hale, 1846 | 1838–42 | 7, 500 |
| Rosamel (*in* Hambruch, 1932 I) | 1840 | 20, 000; more likely 15, 000 |
| Michelena y Rojas, 1843 | 1841 | 7–8, 000 |
| Cheyne, 1852 | 1844 | 7–8, 000 |
| Hernsheim, 1884 | 1845? | 15, 000 |
| Gulick, 1852 letter | 1852 | no less than 10, 000 |
| The Friend, June 1853 | 1853 | 10, 000 |
| Doane, 1855 letter | 1854 (before smallpox) | 10, 000 |
| Sturges, 1855 letter | 1854 (before smallpox) | 10, 000 |
| Sturges, 1854 letter | 1854 (after smallpox) | less than 5,000 |
| Sturges, 1855 letter | 1855 | less than 5, 000 |
| Sturges, 1855 letter | 1855 | a little more than 4, 000 |
| Gulick, 1855 letter | 1855 | about 5, 000 |
| Doane, 1855 letter | 1855 | 6–8, 000 |
| Doane, 1855 letter | 1855 | 5, 000 |
| Gulick, 1858a | 1857 | 5, 000 |
| Mahlmann, 1918 | 1858 | 2, 000 |
| Novara voyage (*in* Hambruch, 1932 I) | 1858 | 2, 000 |
| Mahlmann, 1918 | 1868–71 | 2, 300 |
| Hernsheim, 1884 | 1875? | less than 2,000 |
| Finsch, 1880 | 1880 | 2, 000 |
| Miguel, 1887 | 1885 | 5–6, 000 |
| Gomez, 1885 | 1885? | 6, 000 |
| Moss, 1889 | 1887 | 2, 500 |
| Yanaihara, 1940 | 1891 | 1, 705 |
| Pereiro, 1895 | 1895 | nearly 5,000 |
| Christian, 1899 | 1896 | 5, 000 |
| Bennigsen, 1900 | 1899 | 4, 000 |
| Reichstag, 1902 | 1900–01 | 3, 165 |
| Reichstag, 1904 | 1902–03 | 3, 266 |
| Reichstag, 1905 | 1903–04 | 3, 279 |
| Kolonialamt, 1911 | 1909–10 | 3, 500–4, 000 |
| Fritz, 1912 | 1910 | 3, 200 |
| Kolonialamt, 1913 | 1911–12 | 3, 190 |
| Bascom, 1965 | 1914 | 4, 401 |

istrations have had their centers. The rest of the population is scattered in single houses or in groups of a few dwellings along the shores and coastal plains of the main island and on some of the lagoon islands.

The census figures of Table 2 are broken down into subtotals showing populations by clan (or by place of origin for the out-islanders) and tribe. The natives of Ponape, like most of the Carolinians, all belong to exogamous, matrilineal clans (*dipw* or *sou*) whose

TABLE 2.—*Population of Ponape, 1947*

| | Tribe | | | | | |
|---|---|---|---|---|---|---|
| | Uh | Madol-enihmw | Kiti | Sokehs | Net | Total |
| Ponapeans, by clan name: | | | | | | |
| 1. Pwuton | 32 | 1 | – | – | 11 | 44 |
| 2. Lasialap | 250 | 56 | 81 | 11 | 50 | 448 |
| 3. Sounrohi | – | – | 1 | 1 | – | 2 |
| 4. Dipwinmen | 29 | 99 | 264 | 50 | 35 | 477 |
| 5. Ledek | 12 | 31 | 15 | 5 | 12 | 75 |
| 6. Dipwilap | 78 | 27 | 65 | 42 | 184 | 396 |
| 7. Sounkawad | 60 | 124 | 281 | 67 | 251 | 783 |
| 8. Dipwinluhk | 56 | 100 | 36 | – | 22 | 214 |
| 9. Dipwinwai | 48 | 134 | 135 | 24 | 75 | 416 |
| 10. Liarkatau | 74 | 1 | 7 | – | 11 | 93 |
| 11. Lipitahn | 28 | 12 | 49 | – | 32 | 121 |
| 12. Sounsamaki | 7 | – | 26 | 13 | 25 | 71 |
| 13. Dipwinpahnmei | 143 | 229 | 117 | 4 | 61 | 554 |
| 14. Sounmaraki | 20 | 48 | 2 | – | – | 70 |
| 15. Nahniek | 36 | 7 | 66 | 4 | 36 | 149 |
| 16. Sounpelienpil | 13 | 2 | 20 | 1 | – | 36 |
| 17. Dipwinpehpe | 4 | 24 | 233 | 17 | 18 | 296 |
| 18. Sounpwok | 8 | 110 | 65 | 3 | 12 | 198 |
| 19. Unknown | – | 8 | – | – | – | |
| TOTAL | 898 | 1, 013 | 1, 463 | 242 | 835 | 4, 451 |
| Out-Islanders, by island of origin: | | | | | | |
| Palau | – | – | – | – | 2 | 2 |
| Yap | – | – | – | 21 | 5 | 26 |
| Truk | 8 | 14 | 21 | 3 | 27 | 73 |
| Mortlocks | – | 17 | 12 | 605 | 30 | 664 |
| Nukuoro | – | – | – | 1 | 5 | 6 |
| Kapingamarangi | – | 2 | – | 1 | 35 | 38 |
| Ngatik | – | 21 | – | 28 | 2 | 51 |
| Mokil | – | 25 | – | 105 | 2 | 132 |
| Pingelap | 4 | 23 | – | 85 | 14 | 126 |
| Kusaie | 4 | 3 | – | – | 1 | 8 |
| Marshalls | – | – | – | 1 | 4 | 5 |
| Gilberts | – | 4 | – | 3 | 3 | 10 |
| Saipan | 8 | 12 | – | 9 | 1 | 30 |
| Philippines | 1 | – | – | – | 1 | 2 |
| Malaya | – | – | – | – | 1 | 1 |
| New Guinea | 1 | – | – | 2 | – | 3 |
| TOTAL | 26 | 121 | 33 | 864 | 133 | 1,177 |
| GRAND TOTAL | 924 | 1, 134 | 1, 496 | 1, 106 | 968 | 5, 628 |

members live in all five of the tribes. The 18 clans are nearly all subdivided into sub-clans (*kaimw* or *keinek*), which may or may not correspond to the conventional definition of the lineage; but these are not tabulated separately.

The clans listed in Table 2 differ somewhat from those

given by Hambruch (1932 II, pp. 25–69) and Bascom (1965, p. 19). Bascom's Souniap, Dipwinpwehk, and Dipwinwehi are extinct. He also shows three divisions of the Dipwinmen clan, which here are lumped together. Hambruch's material on Ponapean clans, put together from his notes by Eilers after his death and in part evidently misinterpreted by her, lists as Ponapean two Mortlock or Truk clans, Sapwinipik and Sorr.

I have not attempted to list the sub-clans, for several reasons. For one thing, it is very seldom that any two informants will completely agree on the number, names, and relative seniority of the sub-clans within a clan. Sometimes a man will insist that a sub-clan whose name was obtained from another man does not exist, or is only a branch of another sub-clan, or is a synonym for it. Some of the names appear to apply to groups of descent units on a level between clan and sub-clan; two such intermediate levels may exist among the Dipwinmen. In many clans there is one named group that, it is said, can intermarry with the other groups, which by the usual rule of exogamy ought to cause it to be defined as a separate clan, yet is not so regarded by its members. And among the 18 clans I have listed are a few that are often said to be only subdivisions of others; for example, clan 14 is frequently given as part of clan 13, clans 3 and 16 as part of clan 4. All of this is to be expected in an evolving, viable society whose unilinear kinship groups continue to ramify, and my list of 18 is to be regarded as necessarily a rather arbitrary one.

In the distribution of non-Ponapeans to island of origin, native classificatory ideas were followed in compiling Table 2. This no doubt has resulted in a number of errors. For example, a person born on Ponape of an out-islander mother is classed according to origin of the mother, even though the father is Ponapean; but if the mother was Ponapean and the father an out-islander, he is listed under his Ponapean clan. A number of clans are shared among Ponape, Mokil, Ngatik, and Pingelap; and some clans in the Mortlocks, Truk, and elsewhere, though known by different names, are equated with Ponapean ones. It is thus very probable that there has been inconsistent treatment in classification to island of nativity. The fact that natives of the Gilbert Islands and Gilbertese descendants live on Pingelap and Ngatik is also a complicating factor; some of the people classed as Gilbert Islanders are probably natives of Pingelap and Ngatik, and vice versa. Also, descent in the two Polynesian outliers, Nukuoro and Kapingamarangi, and in the Gilberts has a patrilineal bias and true clans are lacking, in contrast to the other Micronesian islands where matrilineal, exogamous clans exist; when intermarriages occur, clan affiliation of the children is often in doubt.

Reference to clan membership throughout this work will usually be by use of the numbers preceding the clan names given in Table 2.

# The Tribes

Ponape, as it is presently constituted politically, is divided into five independent states or tribes (*wehi*):[4] Uh, Madolenihmw, Kiti, Sokehs, and Net (Figure 1). Each of them is headed by two principal chiefs, known respectively as Nahnmwarki and Nahnken. The tribes are organized on a feudal basis and subdivided into a number of sections (*kousapw*) whose heads (*kaun* or *soumas*) are appointed by and formerly held their fiefs as vassals under the principal tribal chiefs. The sections are further subdivided into farmsteads (*peliensapw*), occupied by separate households whose relation to the section heads was likewise a feudal one. In theory all the land formerly belonged ultimately to the Nahnmwarki and Nahnken, who received regular tribute and whose rule was absolute.

## THE TITLES

Each of the two principal chiefs, the Nahnmwarki and the Nahnken, in each of the five tribes is the first of a series of ranked titleholders. In theory the two series of titles are the same in each tribe; actually they vary, for reasons to be discussed. The first 12 titles of each series are considered the most important, but the lists of titles obtained from informants often contain many more than 12; one Net man recited a series of 210 such titles. Following Bascom, the series of chiefs headed by the Nahnmwarki (the *pali soupeidi*) will be referred to as the A-line; the series headed by the Nahnken (the *pali nahnken*) as the B-line. If the Nahnmwarki is considered A1, the other titles then follow, A2, A3, A4, etc., and for convenience will usually be referred to thus rather than by title. Similarly, the Nahnken is B1, and is followed by B2, B3, B4, etc. The A- and B-lines may also, for convenience in reference, be called respectively the royalty and the nobility but without implying the European connotations of these terms. The lists of A and B titles for each tribe are given in Tables 3 and 4.

[4] Commonly called districts by the present Trust Territory administration.

Most of the titles given in Tables 3 and 4, as well as the many lower ones not listed, are purely honorific. Their translations are often suggestive of special functions (e.g., Watchman of the Mountain, Gatherer of the Banana Fields, etc.), sometimes religious in nature (e.g., Lord of Thinking of Idehd, Idehd being the artificial island among the cluster known as Nan Madol where according to legend a sacred eel was once kept and fed; Sapawas and other place names that occur in the titles are also localities at Nan Madol). But such functions have long lapsed; the few titles that still confer on their bearers particular duties or privileges are discussed later.

In these titles I translate the honorific words Nahn as Lord and Isoh as Honored One. These are arbitrary translations, since they have no specific meanings, and any English honorific would serve as well instead. Other terms, as Watchman, Steward, etc., are fairly specific. Sou is given as Master; it has the implication of agency, similar to the -er ending in English.

Madau I have translated in some titles as ocean, in others as thinking. Both are correct, the choice in each case was that made by informants. I have given Sed as sea to distinguish it from Madau; Sed probably means

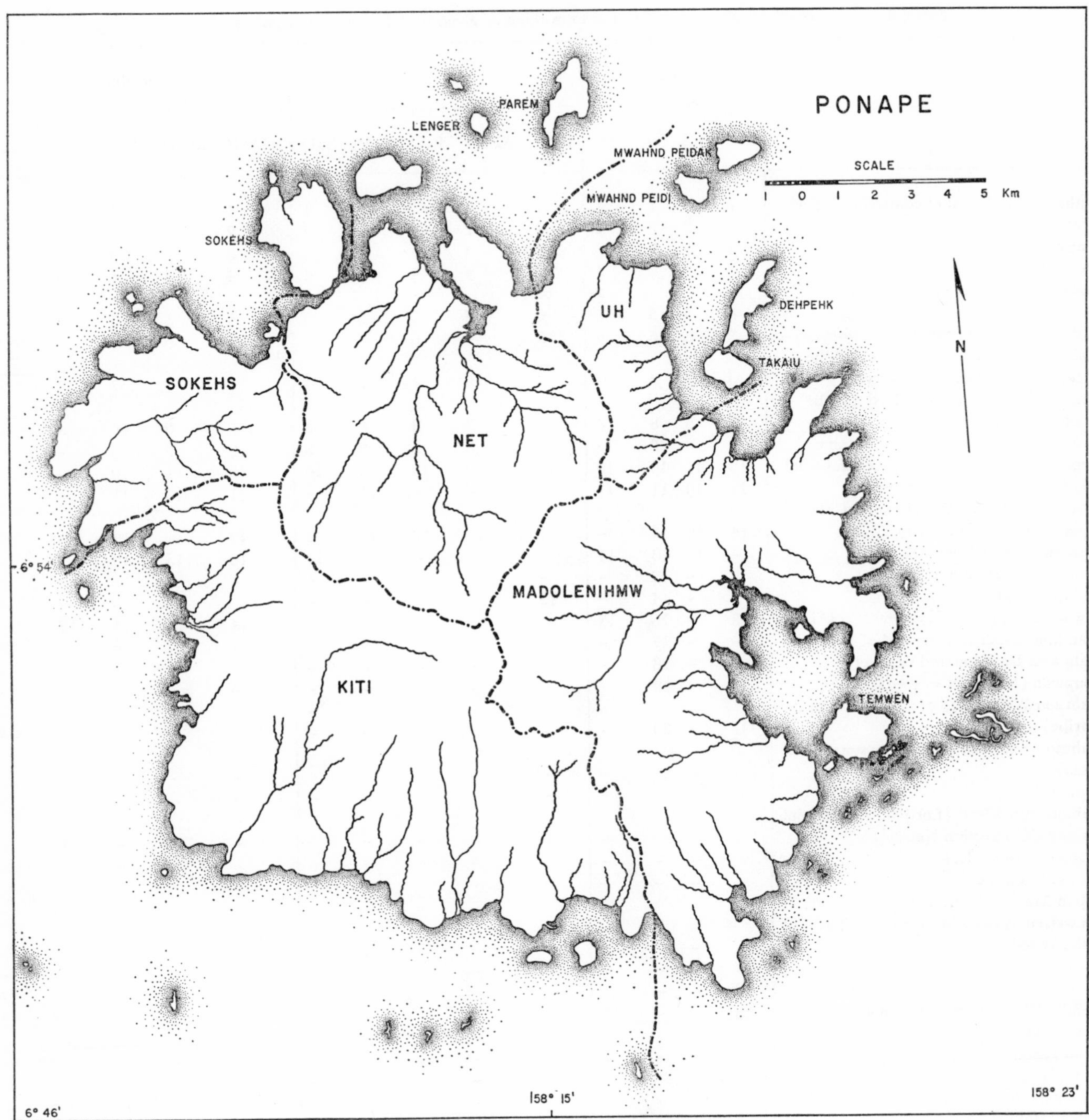


FIGURE 1.—Map of Ponape showing the five independent tribes.

more exactly the water inside the reef. Ririn I have consistently translated as ladder; Fischer gives it as gate, but my informants insist it refers to the ladder that stood at the entranceway to the artificial island known as Pahn Kedira; it is not the ordinary word for ladder and is not used in any other case I know of except in the legend of a canoe descending from heaven, containing the god Luhk, which was suspended in the air and was reached by such a ladder.

The translation of Lempwei as successful side refers to a side in competition against another side. It could also be translated as a successful person who is outside of one's hearing.

The *Pei* in Pohnpei (Ponape: "on" or "above the altar") and in titles is translated as altar for convenience. It actually means any ancient stone structure, including burial chambers, house foundations, and ruins, usually with religious significance but not necessarily.

Table 3.—*A-line of titles* (numbered according to ranking as given by informants and published sources)

| | General | | | | Uh | | | | | Madolenihmw | | | | |
|---|---|---|---|---|---|---|---|---|---|---|---|---|---|---|
| | Ch | HaI | Lu | HaII | A2U | A2Uw | B1U | SoA* | BaU | A11M* | B1MI | Wa* | BaM | Hah |
| Nahnmwarki (Lord of controlling titles) | 1 | 1 | 1 | 1 | 1 | 1 | 1 | 1 | 1 | 1 | 1 | 1 | 1 | 1 |
| Wasai | 2 | 2 | 2 | 2 | 2 | 2 | 2 | 2 | 2 | 2 | 2 | 2 | 2 | 2 |
| Dauk | 3 | 3 | 3 | 3 | 3 | 3 | 3 | 3 | 3 | 3 | 3 | 3 | 3 | 3 |
| Noahs (Spray of the waves?) | 4 | 4 | 4 | 4 | 4 | 4 | 4 | 4 | 4 | 4 | 4 | 4 | 4 | 4 |
| Nahnawa (Lord of endearment; Dear lord) | 6 | 5 | 5 | 5 | 6 | 5 | 5 | 5 | 5 | 5 | 5 | 5 | 5 | 5 |
| Nahnipei (Lord of the altar) | 7 | 6 | 6 | 6 | 5 | – | 6 | 6 | 6 | 6 | 6 | 6 | 6 | 6 |
| Nahn Kiroun Pohn Dake (Lord of the husbanders above the reserve) | 8 | 7 | 7 | – | – | 6 | 7 | 7 | 7 | 7 | 7 | 7 | 7 | 8 |
| Nahlik Lapalap (Great lord of the exterior) | 10 | 9 | 8 | 8 | 8 | 7 | 8 | 8 | 8 | 8 | 8 | 8 | 8 | 10 |
| Nahnid Lapalap (Great lord of the eel) | 9 | 8 | 9 | 9 | 9 | 8 | 9 | 9 | 9 | 9 | 9 | 9 | – | 7 |
| Lempwei Lapalap (Great successful side) | 13 | 11 | 10 | 10 | 10 | 9 | 10 | 10 | 10 | 10 | 11 | 10 | 9 | 11 |
| Soudel (Master of the ——) | 12 | 10 | 11 | 11 | – | – | – | 11 | – | 11 | 10 | 11 | – | 9 |
| Oundolen Ririn (Watchman of the mountain of the ladder) | 14 | 12 | 15 | – | 11 | 10 | 12 | 12 | 12 | 12 | – | 12 | – | – |
| Nahntu (Lord of ——) | – | 13 | 13 | 14 | – | – | – | – | 11 | 13 | 13 | 13 | 11 | – |
| Isohlap (Great honored one) | – | – | 12 | – | – | – | – | – | – | – | – | – | 10 | – |
| Kulap (Great ——) | – | – | 14 | – | 12 | – | – | – | – | – | – | – | – | 14 |
| Mwarekehtik (Little Nahnmwarki [Al]) | 15 | – | 16 | 13 | – | – | – | – | – | 14 | 14 | 14 | 12 | – |
| Kanikihn Sapawas (Steward of Sapawas) | – | – | 17 | – | – | – | – | – | – | – | – | – | – | – |
| Nahnawa Iso (Honored dear lord) | – | – | 18 | – | – | – | – | – | – | – | – | – | – | – |
| Soupwan (Master of ——) | – | – | 19 | – | – | – | – | – | – | – | – | – | – | – |
| Nahnsou Wehi (Lord of the masters of the tribe) | 11? | – | 20 | – | – | – | – | – | – | – | – | – | – | – |
| Nahnsou Sed (Lord of the masters of the sea) | – | – | 21 | – | – | – | – | – | – | – | – | – | – | – |
| Sapwetan | – | – | – | – | – | – | – | – | – | – | – | – | – | – |
| Nahmadoun Oare (Lord of thinking of Oare [Kiti Section No. 15]) | – | – | – | – | – | – | – | – | – | – | – | – | – | – |
| Kiroun (Husbander) | – | – | – | – | – | – | – | – | – | – | – | – | – | – |
| Kaniki (Steward) | – | – | – | – | – | – | – | – | – | – | – | – | – | – |
| Lepen Madau (High one of the ocean) | – | – | – | – | – | – | – | – | – | – | – | – | – | – |
| Souwel en Wasai (Master of the forest of the Wasai [A2]) | – | – | – | – | – | – | – | – | – | – | – | – | – | – |
| Nahn Pohnpei (Lord of Ponape) | – | – | – | – | – | – | – | – | – | – | – | – | – | – |
| Oun Pohnpei (Watchman of Ponape) | 17 | – | – | – | – | – | – | – | – | – | – | – | – | 17 |
| Oundol (Watchman of the mountain) | 18 | – | – | 12 | – | – | – | – | – | – | 12 | – | – | 13 |
| Sou Madau (Master of the ocean) | – | – | – | – | 13 | – | – | – | – | – | – | – | – | 12 |
| Nahn Kirou (Lord of the husbanders) | – | – | – | 7 | 7 | – | 11 | – | – | – | – | – | – | – |
| Nahnkei (Lord of ——) | – | – | – | – | – | – | – | – | – | – | – | – | – | 15 |
| Luhennos (Remainder of the Noahs [A4]) | – | – | – | – | – | – | – | – | – | – | – | – | – | 16 |
| Lepen (High one) | – | – | – | – | – | – | – | – | – | – | – | – | – | 18 |
| Ou (Watchman) | 16 | – | – | – | – | – | – | – | – | – | – | – | – | 19 |
| Nahniau (Lord of the mouth) | – | – | – | – | – | – | – | – | – | – | – | – | – | – |
| Oaron Pwutak (Gatherer of the boys [boys=A2's title of address]) | – | – | – | – | – | – | – | – | – | – | – | – | – | – |
| Kaniki Ririn (Steward of the ladder) | – | – | – | – | – | – | – | – | – | – | – | – | – | – |
| Lepen Ririn (High one of the ladder) | – | – | – | – | – | – | – | – | – | – | – | – | – | – |
| Sou Wene (Master of Wene) | 5 | – | – | – | – | – | – | – | – | – | – | – | – | – |

*Numbers in these columns are used in the text for reference purposes.

TABLE 3.—*A-line of titles* (numbered according to ranking as given by informants and published sources)—Continued

| | Kiti | | | Sokehs | | | | | Net | | | |
|---|---|---|---|---|---|---|---|---|---|---|---|---|
| | A6K* | Le | BaK | B2S | A1b | Kw | BaS* | HaS | B2NI | B1N* | A1N | BaN |
| Nahnmwarki (Lord of controlling titles) | 1 | 1 | 1 | 1 | 1 | 1 | 1 | – | 1 | 1 | 1 | 1 |
| Wasai | 2 | 2 | 2 | 2 | 2 | 2 | 2 | 2 | 2 | 2 | 2 | 2 |
| Dauk | 3 | 3 | 3 | 3 | 3 | 3 | 3 | 3 | 3 | 3 | 3 | 3 |
| Noahs (Spray of the waves?) | 4 | 4 | 4 | 4 | 4 | – | 4 | 6 | 4 | 4 | 4 | 4 |
| Nahnawa (Lord of endearment; Dear lord) | 5 | 5 | 5 | 5 | 6 | – | 5 | – | 5 | 5 | 5 | 5 |
| Nahnipei (Lord of the altar) | 6 | 6 | 6 | 6 | – | – | – | 8 | 6 | 6 | 6 | 6 |
| Nahn Kiroun Pohn Dake (Lord of the husbanders above the reserve) | 8 | 7 | 8 | 7 | – | – | 6 | – | 7 | 7 | 7 | 7 |
| Nahlik Lapalap (Great lord of the exterior) | 7 | 8 | 7 | 8 | 8 | 4 | 7 | 10 | 8 | 8 | 8 | 8 |
| Nahnid Lapalap (Great lord of the eel) | 9 | 9 | 9 | 9 | 9 | – | 8 | – | 9 | 10 | 9 | 10 |
| Lempwei Lapalap (Great successful side) | 14 | 11 | – | 10 | 10 | – | 9 | – | 10 | 9 | 10 | 9 |
| Soudel (Master of the ———) | 13 | 10 | 10 | – | – | – | – | – | 11 | 11 | 11 | 11 |
| Oundolen Ririn (Watchman of the mountain of the ladder) | 11 | – | 11 | – | – | – | – | – | – | – | 15 | – |
| Nahntu (Lord of ———) | – | – | – | – | – | – | – | – | 12 | 12 | 14 | – |
| Isohlap (Great honored one) | – | – | – | – | – | – | – | – | 13 | 13 | 12 | – |
| Kulap (Great ———) | 15 | – | – | – | – | – | – | – | 14 | 14 | 13 | – |
| Mwarekehtik (Little Nahnmwarki [A1]) | – | – | – | – | – | – | – | 9 | 15 | 15 | 16 | 12 |
| Kanikihn Sapawas (Steward of Sapawas) | – | – | – | – | – | – | – | – | – | – | – | – |
| Nahnawa Iso (Honored dear lord) | – | – | – | – | – | – | – | – | – | – | – | – |
| Soupwan (Master of ———) | – | | – | – | – | – | – | – | – | – | – | – |
| Nahnsou Wehi (Lord of the masters of the tribe) | – | – | – | – | – | – | – | – | – | – | – | – |
| Nahnsou Sed (Lord of the masters of the sea) | – | – | – | – | – | – | – | – | – | – | – | – |
| Sapwetan | – | – | – | – | 5 | – | – | – | – | – | – | – |
| Nahmadoun Oare (Lord of thinking of Oare [Kiti Section No. 15]) | – | – | – | – | 7 | 6 | – | 5 | – | – | – | – |
| Kiroun (Husbander) | – | – | – | – | – | 5 | – | – | – | – | – | – |
| Kaniki (Steward) | – | – | – | – | – | 7 | 12 | – | – | – | – | – |
| Lepen Madau (High one of the ocean) | – | – | – | – | – | 8 | 10 | 7 | – | – | – | – |
| Souwel en Wasai (Master of the forest of the Wasai [A2]) | – | – | – | – | – | – | 11 | – | – | – | – | – |
| Nahn Pohnpei (Lord of Ponape) | 10 | – | – | – | – | – | – | – | – | – | – | – |
| Oun Pohnpei (Watchman of Ponape) | 12 | – | 12 | – | – | – | – | – | – | – | – | – |
| Oundol (Watchman of the mountain) | – | 12 | – | – | – | – | – | – | – | – | – | – |
| Sou Madau (Master of the ocean) | – | – | – | – | – | – | – | – | – | – | – | – |
| Nahn Kirou (Lord of the husbanders) | – | – | – | – | – | – | – | – | – | – | – | – |
| Nahnkei (Lord of ———) | – | – | – | – | – | – | – | – | – | – | – | – |
| Luhennos (Remainder of the Noahs [A4]) | – | – | – | – | – | – | – | – | – | – | – | – |
| Lepen (High one) | – | – | – | – | – | – | – | – | – | – | – | – |
| Ou (Watchman) | – | – | – | – | – | – | – | – | – | – | – | – |
| Nahniau (Lord of the mouth) | – | – | – | – | – | – | – | 4 | – | – | – | – |
| Oaron Pwutak (Gatherer of the boys [boys=A2's title of address]) | – | – | – | – | – | – | – | 11 | – | – | – | – |
| Kaniki Ririn (Steward of the ladder) | – | – | – | – | – | – | – | 12 | – | – | – | – |
| Lepen Ririn (High one of the ladder) | – | – | – | – | – | – | – | 13 | – | – | – | – |
| Sou Wene (Master of Wene) | – | – | – | – | – | – | – | – | – | – | – | – |

*Numbers in these columns are used in the text for reference purposes.

TABLE 4.—*B-line of titles* (numbered according to ranking as given by informants and published sources)

| | General | | | Uh | | Madolenihmw | | | | | |
|---|---|---|---|---|---|---|---|---|---|---|---|
| | HaI | Lu | HaII | SoA* | BaU | A1IM | B1MI* | B1MII | Wa | BaM | Hah |
| Nahnken (Lord of ———) | 1 | 1 | 1 | 1 | 1 | 1 | 1 | 1 | 1 | 1 | 1 |
| Nahlaimw (Lord of ———) | 2 | 2 | 2 | 2 | 2 | 2 | 2 | 2 | 2 | 2 | 2 |
| Nahnsau Ririn (Lord of the masters of the ladder) | 4 | 3 | 4 | 3 | 3 | 3 | 3 | 3 | 4 | 3 | 3 |
| Nahnapas (Lord of ———) | 3 | 4 | 3 | 4 | 4 | 4 | 4 | 4 | 3 | 4 | – |
| Nahmadaun Idehd (Lord of thinking of Idehd) | 5 | 5 | 5 | 6 | 6 | 7 | 5 | 6 | 5 | 5 | 5 |
| Souwel Lapalap (Great master of the forest) | – | 7 | 7 | 5 | 5 | 6 | 6 | 7 | 6 | 6 | 4 |
| Lepen Ririn (High one of the ladder) | 6 | 6 | 6 | 9 | 7 | 5 | 7 | – | 7 | 7 | 8 |
| Ou Ririn (Watchman of the ladder) | 7 | 9 | 8 | 8 | 8 | 9 | 8 | 5 | – | 8 | 7 |
| Nahn Pohnpei (Lord of Ponape) | – | 10 | 11 | 10 | 9 | 13 | 10 | 10 | – | – | 9 |
| Oun Pohnpei (Watchman of Ponape) | – | 11 | 9 | – | 12 | 12 | 9 | 9 | – | – | – |
| Kaniki Ririn (Steward of the ladder) | – | 8 | 13 | 12 | – | 10 | 11 | 11 | – | 9 | 13 |
| Nahnku (Lord of ———) | – | 12 | – | – | – | – | – | – | – | – | – |
| Kaniki (Steward) | – | 13 | 12 | – | – | – | – | – | – | – | – |
| Kiroulikiak (Husbander of ———) | – | – | – | – | – | – | – | – | – | – | – |
| Oun Sapawas (Watchman of Sapawas) | – | 14 | – | – | – | – | – | – | – | – | – |
| Isohlap (Great honored one) | – | – | – | 11 | – | – | – | – | – | – | 6 |
| Soulikin Soledi (Master of the exterior of ———) | – | – | – | – | – | – | – | – | – | – | – |
| Lempwei Lapalap (Great successful side) | – | – | – | – | – | – | – | – | – | – | – |
| Lepen (High one) | – | – | – | – | – | – | – | – | – | – | – |
| Nahnipei Ririn (Lord of the altar of the ladder) | – | – | – | – | – | – | – | – | – | – | – |
| Sou Madau (Master of the ocean) | – | – | – | – | – | – | – | – | – | – | – |
| Ou (Watchman) | – | – | 10 | – | – | – | – | 8 | – | – | – |
| Kulap (Great ———) | – | – | – | – | – | – | – | – | – | – | – |
| Nahn Kirou (Lord of the husbanders) | – | – | – | – | – | – | – | – | – | – | – |
| Nahnkei (Lord of ———) | – | – | – | – | – | – | – | – | – | – | – |
| Nahmadaun Pehleng (Lord of thinking of "Under Heaven" [Kiti Section No. 35]) | – | – | – | – | – | – | – | – | – | – | – |
| Soupwan (Master of ———) | – | – | – | – | – | – | – | – | – | – | – |
| Oundol (Watchman of the mountain) | – | – | – | – | – | – | – | – | – | – | – |
| Nahnsou (Lord of the masters) | – | – | – | – | – | – | – | – | – | – | – |
| Soulik (Master of the exterior) | – | – | 14 | – | – | 8 | 13 | 13 | – | – | 11 |
| Kiroun (Husbander) | – | – | – | 7 | – | – | – | – | – | – | – |
| Soulikin Dol (Master of the exterior of the mountain) | – | – | – | – | – | – | – | – | – | – | – |
| Nahntu (Lord of ———) | – | – | – | – | – | – | – | – | – | – | 12 |
| Mwarekehtik (Little Nahnmwarki [A1]) | – | – | – | – | – | – | – | – | – | – | – |
| Soulikin Sapawas (Master of the exterior of Sapawas) | – | – | – | – | – | – | – | – | – | – | – |
| Lempwei Ririn (Successful side of the ladder) | – | – | – | – | 10 | – | – | – | – | – | – |
| Nahnsohmw en Ririn (Lord of ——— of the ladder) | – | – | – | – | 11 | – | – | – | – | – | – |
| Nahnsaumw en Wehi (Lord of ——— of the tribe) | – | – | – | – | – | 11 | 12 | 12 | – | 10 | – |
| Kanikihn Sapawas (Steward of Sapawas) | – | – | – | – | – | 14 | 14 | 14 | – | – | – |
| Nahn Kirou Ririn (Lord of the husbanders of the ladder) | – | – | – | – | – | – | – | – | – | 11 | – |
| Nahnid Lapalap (Great lord of the eel) | – | – | – | – | – | – | – | – | – | 12 | – |
| Oundolen Ririn (Watchman of the mountain of the ladder) | – | – | – | – | – | – | – | – | – | – | 10 |
| Oaron Maka (Gatherer of the banana fields) | – | – | – | – | – | – | – | – | – | – | 14 |
| Kiroun Dolehtik (Husbander of "Little Mountain" [Sokehs Section No. 18]) | – | – | – | – | – | – | – | – | – | – | – |
| Sou Maka (Master of the banana fields) | – | – | – | – | – | – | – | – | – | – | – |

*Numbers in these columns are used in the text for reference purposes.

TABLE 4.—*B-line of titles* (numbered according to ranking as given by informants and published sources)—Continued

| | Kiti | | | Sokehs | | | | Net | | | | |
|---|---|---|---|---|---|---|---|---|---|---|---|---|
| | A6K | Le* | BaK | B2S | A1b | BaS* | HaS | B2NI | B1N* | B2NII | A1N | BaN |
| Nahnken (Lord of ———) | 1 | 1 | 1 | 1 | 1 | 1 | 1 | 1 | 1 | 1 | 1 | 1 |
| Nahlaimw (Lord of ———) | 2 | 2 | 2 | 2 | 2 | 2 | 3 | 2 | 2 | 2 | 2 | 2 |
| Nahnsau Ririn (Lord of the masters of the ladder) | 3 | 3 | 3 | 3 | 5 | 3 | – | 3 | 3 | 3 | 3 | 3 |
| Nahnapas (Lord of ———) | 5 | 4 | – | 4 | 4 | 4 | 4 | 4 | 4 | 4 | 4 | 4 |
| Nahmadaun Idehd (Lord of thinking of Idehd) | 4 | 5 | 4 | 5 | – | 5 | – | 5 | 5 | 5 | 5 | 5 |
| Souwel Lapalap (Great master of the forest) | 6 | 6 | 5 | 6 | 6 | 6 | 7 | 6 | 6 | 6 | 6 | 6 |
| Lepen Ririn (High one of the ladder) | 8 | 8 | 7 | – | 9 | – | – | 7 | 7 | 7 | 7 | 7 |
| Ou Ririn (Watchman of the ladder) | 9 | 9 | 8 | – | – | – | – | 8 | 8 | 8 | 10 | 8 |
| Nahn Pohnpei (Lord of Ponape) | – | 12 | 9 | – | – | 12 | – | 10 | 10 | 12 | – | 10 |
| Oun Pohnpei (Watchman of Ponape) | – | – | – | – | – | – | – | 11 | 11 | 11 | – | 11 |
| Kaniki Ririn (Steward of the ladder) | 11 | 10 | 10 | – | – | – | – | 9 | 9 | 9 | 12 | 9 |
| Nahnku (Lord of ———) | – | – | – | – | – | – | – | 15 | 15 | – | 14 | – |
| Kaniki (Steward) | – | – | – | – | – | – | – | – | – | – | 16 | – |
| Kiroulikiak (Husbander of ———) | – | – | – | – | – | – | 5 | – | – | – | – | – |
| Oun Sapawas (Watchman of Sapawas) | – | – | – | – | – | – | – | – | – | – | – | – |
| Isohlap (Great honored one) | 7 | 7 | 6 | 7 | – | – | – | – | – | – | – | – |
| Soulikin Soledi (Master of the exterior of ———) | – | – | – | – | 3 | – | 2 | – | – | – | – | – |
| Lempwei Lapalap (Great successful side) | – | – | – | – | 7 | – | – | – | – | – | – | – |
| Lepen (High one) | – | – | – | – | 8 | 9 | – | – | – | – | – | – |
| Nahnipei Ririn (Lord of the altar of the ladder) | – | – | – | – | 10 | – | – | – | – | – | – | – |
| Sou Madau (Master of the ocean) | – | – | – | – | – | 7 | – | – | – | – | – | – |
| Ou (Watchman) | – | – | – | – | – | 8 | – | 12 | 13 | – | 9 | – |
| Kulap (Great ———) | – | – | – | – | – | – | 9 | – | – | – | – | – |
| Nahn Kirou (Lord of the husbanders) | – | – | – | – | – | 10 | – | – | – | – | – | – |
| Nahnkei (Lord of ———) | – | – | – | – | – | 11 | 6 | – | – | 10 | 8 | – |
| Nahmadaun Pehleng (Lord of thinking of "Under Heaven" [Kiti Section No. 35]) | – | – | – | – | – | – | – | 13 | 17 | – | – | – |
| Soupwan (Master of ———) | – | – | – | – | – | – | – | 14 | 14 | – | 15 | – |
| Oundol (Watchman of the mountain) | 10 | – | 12 | – | – | – | – | – | 12 | – | – | 12 |
| Nahnsou (Lord of the masters) | – | – | – | – | – | – | – | – | 16 | – | – | – |
| Soulik (Master of the exterior) | – | – | – | – | – | – | 8 | – | – | – | 11 | – |
| Kiroun (Husbander) | – | – | – | – | – | – | – | – | – | – | 13 | – |
| Soulikin Dol (Master of the exterior of the mountain) | 12 | 11 | 11 | – | – | – | – | – | – | – | – | – |
| Nahntu (Lord of ———) | 13 | – | – | – | – | – | – | – | – | – | – | – |
| Mwarekehtik (Little Nahnmwarki [A1]) | 14 | – | – | – | – | – | – | – | – | – | – | – |
| Soulikin Sapawas (Master of the exterior of Sapawas) | 15 | – | – | – | – | – | – | – | – | – | – | – |
| Lempwei Ririn (Successful side of the ladder) | – | – | – | – | – | – | – | – | – | – | – | – |
| Nahnsohmw en Ririn (Lord of ——— of the ladder) | – | – | – | – | – | – | – | – | – | – | – | – |
| Nahnsaumw en Wehi (Lord of ——— of the tribe) | – | – | – | – | – | – | – | – | – | – | – | – |
| Kanikihn Sapawas (Steward of Sapawas) | – | – | – | – | – | – | – | – | – | – | – | – |
| Nahn Kirou Ririn (Lord of the husbanders of the ladder) | – | – | – | – | – | – | – | – | – | – | – | – |
| Nahnid Lapalap (Great lord of the eel) | – | – | – | – | – | – | – | – | – | – | – | – |
| Oundolen Ririn (Watchman of the mountain of the ladder) | – | – | – | – | – | – | – | – | – | – | – | – |
| Oaron Maka (Gatherer of the banana fields) | – | – | – | – | – | – | 10 | – | – | – | – | – |
| Kiroun Dolehtik (Husbander of "Little Mountain" [Sokehs Section No. 18]) | – | – | – | – | – | – | 11 | – | – | – | – | – |
| Sou Maka (Master of the banana fields) | – | – | – | – | – | – | 12 | – | – | – | – | – |

*Numbers in these columns are used in the text for reference purposes.

Key to Tables 3 and 4

SOURCES

| | |
|---|---|
| A1N | Chief A1 of Net |
| A2U | Chief A2 of Uh |
| A2Uw | Wife of Chief A2 of Uh |
| A6K | Chief A6 of Kiti |
| A11M | Chief A11 of Madolenihmw |
| Alb | Alberto of Sokehs |
| B1U | Chief B1 of Uh |
| B1MI | Chief B1 of Madolenihmw, October 4, 1947 |
| B1MII | Chief B1 of Madolenihmw, October 28, 1947 |
| B1N | Chief B1 of Net alone |
| B2NI | Chiefs B1 and B2 of Net together |
| B2NII | Chief B2 of Net alone |
| B2S | Chief B2 of Sokehs |
| Ba U, Ba K, Ba M, Ba N, Ba S | Bascom's various lists for Uh, Kiti, Madolenihmw, Net, and Sokehs (Bascom 1965, pp. 22-25) |
| Ch | Christian, p. 325 |
| Hah | Hahl, 1901, pp. 6–7 |
| HaI | Hambruch, 1932 II, p. 10 (applies to all tribes except Net) |
| HaII | Hambruch, 1932 II, pp. 11–12 (applies to Uh, Madolenihmw, and Kiti) |
| HaS | Hambruch, 1932 II, pp. 12–13 |
| Kw | Kwan of Sokehs |
| Le | Chief Lependeleur of Kiti |
| Lu | Luelen of Kiti (from a manuscript written in the 1920s & 1930s by Luelen, now in the hands of the B6 of Kiti) |
| SoA | Chief Soulik of Awak, Uh |
| Wa | Warren Kehoe of Madolenihmw |

It will be noted that the lists vary from one another to some extent. Some of these variations are no doubt due to use of truncated forms by some informants; for example, A2U fails to give Nahn Kiroun Pohn Dake in position A7 as most informants do but gives instead Nahn Kirou; the latter is also a legitimate but lower title, but is at the same time an abbreviated form of the A7 title, which is probably what was intended. Similarly B1MI, Hah, and Le give Oundol as A12 or A13 and omit to mention Oundolen Ririn in that approximate position as other informants do.

But more significant is the factor of political manipulation. Supposedly the series originated anciently in Madolenihmw, after the legendary defeat of the Saudeleur dynasty by the hero Isohkelekel, who became the first Nahnmwarki, and the other tribes later copied the new system. Disruption of the original order has come about through maneuvering for position, as discussed later in this work. Some 21 of the titles listed are found in both tables. This is due in greatest part to the fact that high-born persons during their early careers may move freely from one line to the other; this also is discussed later. In this connection, informants are apt often to think of the holder of a title rather than of the title per se in listing its position; thus the title now held by a young member of the royal clan, who will eventually have a high A-tide but presently has a lower B-title, may sometimes be listed in the A-line; and vice versa. Finally, the factors of uncertainty, poor memory, and ignorance must also enter, as witness, for example, the two different lists given by both B1 of Madolenihmw (B1MI and B1MII) and B2 of Net (B2NI and B2NII) on different dates.

For purposes of reference throughout this work the columns in both tables headed by asterisks are to be used. They have been chosen for this purpose as probably most reliable, but in some instances arbitrarily. Reference will usually be made to a title in the following text only by letter and number, except for titles that are not listed in the tables.

## CLANS AND CLASSES

The exogamous and matrilineal clans of Ponape for the most part have no clan chiefs. They are subdivided into sub-clans, which are ranked by seniority within the clan, and the senior man of each (the *meseni en keinek*) is its chief. The clans and their subdivisions are dispersed over the whole island, as is seen in Table 2.

In theory, and perhaps in fact in earlier days, the first 12 titles of the A-line in any tribe are held by the 12 senior males of a particular clan, and of a particular sub-clan within that clan. The first 12 titles of the B-line similarly belong to another clan and sub-clan. Usually these are different in each of the five tribes, making 10 ruling sub-clans in all (actually the number is not 10, for reasons to be explained later). The royal and noble classes, who are the A and B titleholders, are thus, with exceptions to be described, equivalent to the ruling sub-clans, which may therefore also be referred to as the A and B or royal and noble sub-clans.

The functions of the sub-clan chief are less political than economic or social. But when his sub-clan is the royal or the noble sub-clan in one of the five tribes he is normally the A1 or the B1 of that tribe.

In each tribe the ideal was that the two ruling sub-clans intermarried exclusively, hence all high chiefs carried royal blood on one side and noble blood on the other. Infant betrothal, which once insured such intermarriage, has fallen into disuse in modern times, and the proper type of marriage is still preferred by only limited groups.

Although the two sub-clans that in each tribe tend to monopolize the higher titles compose the royalty and nobility, if a man of a different sub-clan or clan has, by means to be discussed, achieved a high title, he is also regarded as royal or noble. All other persons are commoners (*aramas mwahl*), including people whose sub-clans are royal or noble in one tribe but who, for reasons generally having to do with landownership, are living in another tribe where their sub-clans do not rule.

O'Connell makes reference to a caste of slaves known as "nigurts," a statement that Hambruch and Eilers apparently accept uncritically. No authorities before or after O'Connell mention "nigurts"; where they employ the term "slave," it is apparent that what is meant is "commoner." Because O'Connell describes his slaves as darker in skin than the upper castes and suggests Negrito affinities, Hambruch and Eilers connect them with the legendary small dark aborigines of Ponape called *liet;* and this in turn is connected with the terms for male servant and female servant (*ladu* and *lidu*). It is difficult, however, to take these speculations seriously. If one accepts the aboriginal *liet,* one might also accept other legendary races of beings, including a species of flying cannibal. Informants, none of whom recognized the term *nigurt,* suggest that O'Connell's dark race was composed of fishermen, who spend more time in the sun than other persons and to whom as a class is ascribed a lack of ambition to achieve titles.[5]

In any event, a slave caste has not existed on Ponape since white contact. Commoners may have had a very low status formerly, but they were never considered chattels of the chiefs, and they were free to take up residence in any locality where they could receive a grant of land. Their status corresponded much more closely to that of a feudal peasant than to that of slave. As for servants, these were usually dependent relatives or persons who had been banished from their own homes and had taken refuge with their friends elsewhere. There was no sort of traffic in commoners or servants and no taking of prisoners of war for purposes of enslavement.

Essentially, then, there are three social strata: royalty, nobility, and the great mass of commoners. But within these strata, and within each clan and sub-clan, status is finely graded. The sub-clans of each clan are in a ranked series; most clans are considered to be descended from a legendary woman or female animal, the daughters of whom became the eponymous ancestresses of the sub-clans, which are ranked according to the relative ages of those daughters. Within the sub-clan every man is graded according to seniority of descent, and titles are distributed roughly according to the same standard. Actually, then, no two men have the same rank. Even two men holding the same title in different tribes are not equal, for the tribes are likewise graded, Madolenihmw holding the highest position, followed in order by Uh, Kiti, Sokehs, and Net. Nor are heads of sections on the same level, for various sections have superior status.

Commoners, that is the people belonging to sub-clans other than the two ruling ones, fall roughly into one class but with minor gradations, since the holders of the lesser tribal titles, section head titles, and lesser section titles all count as commoners too. Within each commoner clan grading proceeds again according to seniority, and section titles are handed out with some respect to such seniority. The commoner clans themselves are not graded with reference to each other, but they are treated differentially. Some clans, such as clan 10, are few in number and scattered, hence they are handled somewhat more cavalierly than others; formerly they might not get land from the Nahnmwarki or from the section head, and they are ignored when it comes to distribution of food at feasts. Since they possess no great titles and own no section, it is easy for the chiefs to give them the harder tasks to do. But such clans might rise in the scale by feats of war. Thus, in Net, clan 5 was formerly held to be higher than in Uh, because a member was a great warrior of Net once and was killed in an ancient war and the clan once possessed section 15 of Net. Now that a member of clan 5 has become Nahnken of Uh the clan has risen in position in that tribe too.

The royal sub-clans, which hold or should hold the A1 titles and most of the other titles in the A-line, are nowadays as follows:

| | |
|---|---|
| Uh................ | Clan 2, sub-clan Sounpasedo |
| Madolenihmw....... | Clan 13, sub-clan Inenkatau, also called Upwutenmai |
| Kiti................ | Clan 4, division Dipwinmen dondol, sub-clan Lipohnroahlong |
| Sokehs............. | Clan 7 (sub-clans bear no names) |
| Net................ | Clan 7 (sub-clans bear no names) |

The noble or B-line sub-clans are:

| | |
|---|---|
| Uh................ | Clan 5, sub-clan Isoh |
| Madolenihmw....... | Clan 9, sub-clan Upwutenut, or Clan 2, sub-clan Sounlehdau |
| Kiti................ | Clan 11, sub-clan Lipeitato |
| Sokehs............. | Clan 6, sub-clan Tingalongal |
| Net................ | Clan 6, sub-clan Lukelapalap |

[5] If we may take O'Connell's orthographic rendering of "kalek" (a type of dance) into "gurlic," and "isak" (gourd bottle) into "ajurk," as examples of how an Irish sailor would have heard and pronounced Ponapean words more than 100 years ago, it is possible to make "naikat" out of his "nigurt," meaning "my people here," referring to servants and dependents. Hale (1846, p. 83), who interviewed O'Connell, writes "nigurt (*naikat*)" as though correcting his pronunciation, which tends to validate my speculation.

The royal and noble status of these clans and sub-clans is of varying antiquity. The clan 7 conquest of Sokehs and Net, which appears to have been two or three generations before white contact, overthrew clan 4 and clan 2, respectively, as the Sokehs and Net royal lines. The noble line of Sokehs was formerly clan 12, and that of Net was clan 9. In Uh clan 5 has provided the B1 for only one generation; a member of clan 8 was B1 previously, and the previous B1, in Hahl's time (1901), belonged to clan 9; but according to tradition clan 1 is the "rightful" noble class. Before Kiti became a united tribe, shortly before white contact, Wene, nowadays Kiti's eastern part but at that time independent, had as its royal line the senior sub-clan, Liesenpahlap, of a branch of the Dipwinmen dondol ("clan of the black bird"). Then the second ranking sub-clan, Liesenpal, overthrew it (according to legend, with the aid of the god Isopau) and took over the A-titles. Then followed a series of wars that resulted in the unification of Wene and Kiti proper and the ousting of the ruling sub-clan of the latter, the Sounkiti, which belongs to another division of clan 4. The Liesenpal continued to rule all Kiti until its members became extinct, with Nahnmwarki Paul; his successor, Sigismundo, and the present A1, Benito, have belonged to another sub-clan, Lipohnroahlong, which ranks third after the Liesenpahlap and Liesenpal.

In one tribe, Madolenihmw, two sub-clans are eligible to provide the Nahnken and the other titleholders in the B-line, because a woman from each of them was a wife of Isohkelekel, the semilegendary hero who became the first Nahnmwarki. The women of these two noble sub-clans therefore provide more possible traditional marriage partners for the men of the A-line than in the other four tribes, where there is only one noble sub-clan. In another tribe, Net, clan 6 has provided only the last two Nahnkens, clan 9 the previous two; clan 6 is held to be the noble clan, but clan 9 is by many regarded as of equal status. But in none of the five tribes can the Nahnmwarki come from more than one sub-clan, as long as there are survivors thereof, at least in theory. Today, though a tendency to marry between the two lines persists and some parental pressure to make a traditional alliance continues, missionary and other influences have encouraged young people to make their own decisions, and marriage of both royalty and nobility with commoners is frequent. In the tribe of Net, where the royal clan is clan 7 and the noble clan is clan 6, all but one of the first 15 titleholders on the A side belong to the proper clan (that is to say, had clan 7 mothers) but only six of them had clan 6 fathers. Of the nine royal men whose fathers came from other clans, one had a father of clan 9 (the former noble clan), hence was the offspring of a marriage regarded as almost proper; but the other eight fathers were commoners.

In other words, less than half the marriages in the parental generation followed the ideal pattern of A-B marriage. On the B side, of the first 15 titles, five holders belong to clan 6, three to clan 9, one is a man whose mother is from the Mortlock Islands but whose Mortlock clan is equated with clan 9, and the other six belong to other clans; while only seven of these 15 nobles had clan 7 (or royal) fathers; thus again most of the marriages in the parental generation were not of the traditional type.

In Madolenihmw the royal clan is clan 13 and the two noble clans are clans 2 and 9. The last seven A1's (all of them of clan 13) and the clan affiliations of their wives are as follows:

| | |
|---|---|
| Moses (the present A1) | married a woman of clan 18 |
| Alexander | married a woman of clan 18 |
| Solomon | married a woman of clan 6 |
| Hezekiah | married a woman of clan 18 |
| Paul | married a woman of clan 9 |
| Luhkenmweiu | 2 wives, 1 of clan 2, 1 of clan 9 |
| Luhkenkidu | 10 wives, all of clan 9 |

It is evident therefore that since the time of Paul, the first Christian Nahnmwarki of Madolenihmw, during the 1890s, marriages of the traditional type have been in abeyance.

## GRADES OF CHIEFS

A number of terms are in use that have to do with social position, levels of chieftainship, and degree of ceremonial deference. They and their literal or near-literal English translations are:

| | |
|---|---|
| *soupeidi* | Those Who Face Downwards |
| *mwohnsapw* | First of the Land |
| *oloiso* | Royal (or Honored) Men |
| *seriiso* | Royal (or Honored) Children |
| *ipwin pohn warawar* | Born Upon the Ditch |

The line headed by the Nahnmwarki, which I am calling the A-line, is commonly referred to as the *pali soupeidi,* literally the Side of Those Who Face Downwards. This expression, *pali soupeidi,* is used in contrast to the expression *pali nahnken,* that is to say the Side of the Nahnken, which means the entire line of titles that I am calling the B-line. The A1 and B1 are thus contraposed as Soupeidi and Nahnken instead of Nahnmwarki and Nahnken.

Yet the word *soupeidi* does not have the meaning of A1. It derives from the fact that certain persons customarily sit in the place of honor on the main platform of the community house, looking down toward the mass of people, who sit on the lower, side platforms and in the central, ground-level area. The Nahnmwarki is not the only one who sits here and faces the people; his wife, the Nahnken, and the Nahnken's wife also have their places on the main platform; and certain other men may likewise occupy the place of honor, as will be described later. At a formal feast most of the men of the A-line (and not those of the B-line) must actually be employed in the central area and never, except in the absence of anyone higher in the line than they, have the chance to sit on the main platform looking down, in spite of the fact that it is the A-titled men who are called the Side of Those Who Face Downwards. Perhaps the literal meaning of the word has been extended to these potential occupants of the seats of honor.

Though the whole A-line is called *pali soupeidi,* the Side of Those Who Face Downwards, the word *soupeidi* by itself is used with several other connotations. By some it is applied only to the A1, B1, and their wives, who are the ones who most commonly occupy the place of honor at feasts, and thus its usage coincides with its literal meaning. One informant uses the term to mean all persons eligible by blood to become A1 or B1. Several apply it to chiefs A1–A4 and B1–B4; another restricts it to chiefs A1–A4 (making A5–A12 Royal Men and B1–B4 the Side of the Nahnken); still another definition is that any A-line chief who is in the same sub-clan as the Nahnmwarki is one of Those Who Face Downwards, but A1–A4 are the first class of Those Who Face Downwards. Chief B1 of Net says that until he attained the title of B4 he was not one of Those Who Face Downwards but was a Royal Child. Yanaihara (p. 183) uses the term to include A1–A8 and B1–B3 (but omits Nahnpei, who is usually regarded as A6).

As an example of the confusing usage current today, Chief B1 of Madolenihmw in a single interview gave the following definitions of the term *soupeidi:*

1. All members of clan 13 (the A clan of Madolenihmw).
2. A1 and all fellow members of his sub-clan.
3. A1, A2, A3, and their sub-clans (in Madolenihmw the present A1 belongs to the second sub-clan of clan 13, the A2 to the third, the A3 to the first), as well as members of the fifth sub-clan of clan 13 (the fourth being extinct).
4. A1 to A4, men from A5 to A12 being Royal Men.
5. A1 to A14, men below A14 being commoners.

He thus omits all holders of B titles from the category.

Other informants give explanations combining various of these definitions, and many use the term simply to mean those in authority, much as we in slang refer to the "big shots" or the "brass."

The word *mwohnsapw,* meaning literally the First of the Land, is likewise used in different ways. The expression First of the Land is interpreted by Ponapeans as designating those persons entitled to first fruits. By some it is used in this literal meaning and thus includes not only Nahnmwarki and Nahnken but section chiefs. Others restrict it to Nahnmwarki and Nahnken; some say it means chiefs A1–A4 and B1–B4; still others define it as equivalent to the A-line; and several informants agree with Hambruch in making it include both lines. (In this connection it should be pointed out that Eilers, who wrote up Hambruch's notes after his death, badly misconceives the facts, and her classifications and her discussion of the relative positions of the two lines and of the commoners must be disregarded.) One definition is that Those Who Face Downwards and the First of the Land mean the identical people, but that the first expression is used in connection with the community house and the second with the land and first-fruit offerings.

I have translated the word *seriiso* as Royal Children (almost any English honorific for *-iso* would do instead of Royal; in other connections I have used the words Honored One and Sir). Its primary reference is to people who are children of men of the A-line, and most people agree that as applied it is equivalent to the B-line. But some informants exclude the B1 from this definition, and one man regards as Royal Children only those B-line titles below B4, calling B1–B4 only Side of the Nahnken. The Nahnken of Madolenihmw, who does not extend the expression Those Who Face Downwards to anyone in the B-line, including the Nahnken, uses the term Royal (*isoh*) for Nahnken, B2, and B4, and calls only B3 and chiefs lower than B4 Royal Children. Yanaihara (p. 183) applies Royal Child to the Souwel Lapalap (whose position he does not give, but who in my tables is usually B5 to B7) and the next seven titles in the B-line. As is discussed below, not only are children of A-titled men Royal Children but so are children of B-titled men when they are not members of the royal clan; and the expression has certain further extensions.

Most informants agree, except those who stand to lose by so doing, that the expression Royal Children is properly applicable to a clan (which is therefore the clan holding the B-titles) only when they are literally such children, that is, when their fathers (and sons) are Royal Men because their women regularly marry the A-titled men.

O'Connell (1836, pp. 125–128), describing conditions in 1833, refers to two classes of people besides "slaves," and calls them Moonjobs and Jerejohs, obviously my *mwohnsapw* or First of the Land and *seriiso* or Royal Children. Though his description is ethnocentric and artless, it is apparent that they are my A and B lines:

> The whiter race upon the islands of Bonabee are divided into two classes—the *Moonjobs,* composed of chiefs and their blood

connections, and the *Jerejohs*, or free whites. The negroes form one caste, and are known under the name *Nigurts* . . . Jerejohs and Moonjobs intermarry with each other, but seldom or never with the Nigurts . . . (and) the issue takes the rank of the mother.

In L. H. Gulick's vocabulary (1872), obtained in the 1850s, the word *monjap* (again my *mwohnsapw* or First of the Land) is defined as "a chief of the highest order (to be distinguished from *jerijo*): synonym of *jopeti*." *Jerijo* (my *seriiso* or Royal Child) is given as "a son of a *monjap*; a chief of that order." *Jopeti* (my *soupeidi* or Those Who Face Downwards) is "a chief (in some tribes a chief that in others would be called *monjap*)." Like O'Connell, and also like some of my informants, he contraposes the First of the Land and the Royal Children as the A and B lines respectively. He evidently equates Those Who Face Downwards also with the A-line. If a difference between tribes in the designation for the A-line really existed in the 1850s, such was not the case in 1947 and later. In 1947 any contrast between A and B was in all five tribes usually made not in terms of First of the Land versus Royal Children but of Those Who Face Downwards versus Royal Children.

A rarer term is *oloiso,* literally Royal Men. This unmistakably means the A-line. But informants disagree on whether it includes all A-titles. One man, for example, says that it means only the titles from A7 down; another makes it include chiefs below A4 only. Yanaihara (p. 183) interprets it to mean A9–A16.

Although the A and B lines of titles, and the terms Royal Men and Royal Children which are by most people applied to these respective lines, are identified with the royal and noble sub-clans, the terms are often extended to members of other sub-clans (or clans) who reach high position in either line. In Net, for example, the present B2 does not belong to the noble clan but is properly a commoner, being a member of clan 2; yet he is known as Royal Child by reason of his high title. In this instance we have to do with a Royal Child in a literal sense, for his father was a member of clan 7, the royal clan; but even if he were commoner on both sides he would, according to many informants, still be so designated.

If pressed on these matters, Ponapeans will often say that people whose fathers belong to the A-clan but whose mothers are commoners are Royal Children, yet not "real" ones. (They are also called *ipwihpw en soupeidi,* that is, Born of Those Who Face Downwards, meaning born of men of the A-line.) There appears to be a conflict in their minds between the literal meaning of the term and the feeling that its application ought to be limited to the B-clan. Perhaps the conflict has arisen only since precontact times, when, supposedly, intermarriage between the royal and noble sub-clans was exclusive and Royal Children could presumably have been born only of B-clan mothers; but since high-ranking men were polygamous, often taking secondary wives from commoner clans, and with the supplanting of ruling clans by other clans through war and other means to be discussed, it is difficult to believe that there ever was a time when such a state of affairs prevailed.

Such Royal Children as belong today to commoner clans cannot, at least in theory, rise to the position of B1. The aforesaid B2 of Net, it is said, can never become B1. In the tribe Kiti such a man cannot advance beyond B3, because the title of B2 is reserved, for certain historical reasons, to members of clan 9.

In actual practice, as we will see in the chapter on Promotion and Succession, limitations to political advancement imposed by rules connected with descent are circumvented and the rules are manipulated in many ways.

The children of a man of A-title are then all Royal Children, regardless of the clan of the mother. But the children of men of the B-line, themselves Royal Children, may be either Royal Men or Royal Children. They are Royal Men if the mother is a member of the royal (A) clan, Royal Children if she is a member of a commoner clan. Alternatively, if it is desired to make a distinction between such Royal Children and "real" Royal Children, they may be called Born of Those Who Face Downwards (*ipwihp en soupeidi*) or Born of Royal Children (*ipwihp en seriiso*). In the next generation, a commoner child of a man who is Born of One Who Faces Downwards or of one who is Born of a Royal Child is still reckoned as a sort of Royal Child. He is called Fruit of *Cyrtosperma* of Those Who Face Downwards (*wahn mwahng soupeidi*), Fruit of *Cyrtosperma* of the Nahnken (*wahn mwang nahnken*), or Fruit of *Cyrtosperma* of Clan ______ (the blank representing the name of the clan of the A-line or B-line grandfather). Informants disagree on whether such diluted Royal Children remain such after the royal or noble grandparent dies; some say they do only if married to royalty or nobility themselves.

For children of a Nahnmwarki or Nahnken there are two terms. All children born to either of these chiefs before they have been promoted to the highest titles are known as *tiekepe*. (The term *tiekepe* is also used to mean true children as distinguished from adopted children.) But children born after the father's accession to the title of Nahnmwarki or Nahnken are Born Upon the Ditch (*ipwin pohn warawar;* referring to the chasm which separates the men of highest honor from all others). One who is Born Upon the Ditch has great honor, receives more deference than anyone else, and sits in the highest position in the community house, above his elder brothers, if any, who are *tiekepe*. As to the question of which receives the higher title, my information is conflicting. The usual statement is that as a principle *tiekepe,* because of their seniority by birth, receive higher titles. The present

Nahnken of Kiti, son of a former Nahnmwarki, is the only regnant person who is Born Upon the Ditch; but, it is said, if he had had an older brother who had been born before the father became Nahnmwarki, the brother would have preceded him as Nahnken. The distinction then is one that affects deference patterns but not the titles themselves. Nevertheless, in Kiti where the maintenance of this principle is of vital concern to the noble clan (clan 11) the question is not settled (see p. 37).[6]

A man would normally go ahead of his older brother only if the two had different mothers and if the mother of the elder was a commoner, the mother of the younger a member of the royalty or nobility.

A commoner may be Born Upon the Ditch; this term was applied to Henry Nanpei whose father, Nahnku, was a Nahnken but whose mother belonged to a commoner clan. He was honored very highly by Paul, the Nahnmwarki of Kiti, who constantly deferred to him and gave him one of his own additional titles, Rohsa. Some of the power wielded today by Oliver, son of Henry, who is also Rohsa, derives from the honor inherited thus second-hand.

Some informants use as equivalent to Born Upon the Ditch the term Royal Child, thus adding still another definition to that already overburdened term. They distinguish children born to a Nahnmwarki, Royal Children of Those Who Face Downwards, from those born to a Nahnken, Royal Children of the Nahnken, and both of these from children born to a lesser A-chief or to a Nahnmwarki before his promotion to that title, Born of Those Who Face Downwards, and those born to a lesser B-chief or to a Nahnken before he became Nahnken, Born of the Nahnken.

## THE TITLE SERIES IN NET

In discussing the lines of chiefs, the tribe of Net must be considered separately from the other four tribes. The series of A and B titles in Net as given in Tables 3 and 4 have been imitated only recently from the other tribes. Net did not have Nahnmwarki and Nahnken titles until the German Governor Kersting made the change in late German times. The higher titles of the two older lines as remembered by a living informant are:

| *A* | *B* |
|---|---|
| 1. Lepen Net (A1) | 1. Nahnsoused (A2) |
| 2. Soulik en Daun | 2. Krou en Rohi (B1) |
| 3. Soukoahng (A3) | 3. Madau en Rohi (A4) |
| 4. Soulik en Popat | 4. Luwehrei (A6) |
| 5. Soulik en Sokele | 5. Nahmadaun Kipar (A5) |

Hambruch gives a quite different and longer series; in the foregoing list the parenthetical letters and numbers suffixed to some titles refer to the positions of those titles in Hambruch's series.

Several informants who gave shorter lists give the title Nahnsoused as A2 instead of B1, as does Hambruch. (I have assumed its equivalence with Hambruch's title Nansau en Not.) One informant, the present A1 of Net, gives the title I have listed as A2 as an alternative title of the A1. And some say that there was only a single line of titles in Net, not distinct A and B series, in contrast to the other tribes, until German times.

O'Connell, writing in 1836, says, "My father-in-law was Ahoundel-a-Nutt (Oundol en Net), chief of the island of Nutt, and the most powerful chief on . . . Bonabee." Modern informants agree that O'Connell greatly exaggerated the political position of his wife's father and that the title is actually far down in the series (see Tables 3 and 4), at least in the modern lists.

Several copies of a manuscript relating the legendary and recent history of Ponape exist today in the hands of various Ponapeans. It was written during the 1920s and 1930s by a native of Kiti named Luelen (Llewellyn), who is no longer living. Hereafter I shall refer to his valuable work as the Luelen manuscript. It indicates as the ruler of an area called Tipwen Dongalap in ancient times the Lepen Net "or" the Soukoahng; the meaning of the conjunction can only be guessed. The title Lepen Net

[6] These remarks, based on my 1947 notes, need to be modified by information given me by Father Hugh Costigan in 1966. The B1 of Madolenihmw, Sali by name, died in 1959 or 1960. The A1, Moses, had a son, John, who was Born Upon the Ditch. John, the 8th of his children, had the title of B8. Moses did not want to promote the B2 to B1 but wished instead to elevate his own oldest son, Christian, who was B6. (The B2 referred to here was a member of clan 18, having succeeded the one mentioned on p. 37. He was a cross cousin of Moses and the son of Alexander, Moses' predecessor as A1 and his mother's brother.) At the promotion feast Moses arose, with the traditional cup of kava, made a speech that dwelled on Ponapean customs concerning those Born Upon the Ditch, then called his son John up, gave him the cup, and proclaimed him B1. John, in his twenties, was a victim of tuberculosis (he died soon after). He made a speech that mentioned his own inadequacies, inexperience, and illness, then he called on his brother, Christian, gave him the cup, and said that Christian would be B1 instead of him. All of this had been rehearsed ahead of time. The A1 would have found it a delicate and difficult matter to promote the B6 to B1 ahead of the B2, but by using the device described here he got around the problem. It would therefore appear that someone who is Born Upon the Ditch can actually go ahead of an older brother, at least in Madolenihmw.

is given as A1 and Soukoahng as A3 in both my list and Hambruch's. Elsewhere the same manuscript lists the rulers of Downwind Wenik as the Lepen Net, the Soukoahng, and the Wasai of Sokehs. Tipwen Dongalap is the ancient name for the part of modern Net between the Net estuary and modern Uh, an area still regarded as Net proper and which is sometimes the area meant instead of all Net when the word Net is used today. Wenik in relatively recent times was equivalent to modern Uh but more anciently had a wider extent. Downwind Wenik is variously defined but often seems to refer to a former political unit consisting of the western part of Uh (known as Awak), all of Net, and at least part of Sokehs. (Upwind Wenik was made up of the eastern part of Uh and part of Madolenihmw.) It may be that the Soukoahng at one time ruled independently over part of these territories and that as boundaries shifted he became subordinate to the Lepen Net.

At the time the changeover to the present series (of Table 3 and 4) was ordered by Kersting, so that Net titles would be comparable to those of the other four tribes, the title of Nahnsoused was held by a man named Paulino. In the readjustment that the chiefs of Net undertook, the then Lepen Net, Nicholas, became Nahnmwarki and Paulino became Nahnken. This would indicate that there were already two lines of titles, that Lepen Net corresponded to A1 and Nahnsoused to B1, so that in the minds of the Net people the change to Nahnmwarki and Nahnken was only a substitution of equivalent titles. Further, the Lepen Net was a member of clan 7, as the members of the A-line of Net are still, while Paulino belonged to clan 9, suggesting that he was not in the A-line.

Nevertheless at a more remote time, holders of the title Nahnsoused do seem to have belonged to clan 7. The succession as remembered by informants, beginning with the present B1, was as follows:

1. Joseph. Clan 6, sub-clan Lukelapalap. Nahnken.
2. Augustino. Clan 6, sub-clan Lukelapalap. Nahnken.
3. Paulino. Clan 9, sub-clan Sounmwerekerik. Nahnsoused, later Nahnken.
4. Maximino. Clan 9, sub-clan Sounmwerekerik. Nahnsoused.
5.–10.[7] Members of clan 7. Nahnsoused.

The fact that the earlier Nahnsouseds belonged to clan 7 would suggest that informants who maintain that there was only one line of titles are correct and would tend to support the placing of the title Nahnsoused in the A-line by Hambruch, who obtained his list when the older system was still in effect. Nevertheless both Hambruch and I recorded two lines of titles. Possibly in the time of the earlier Nahnsouseds clan 7, or two sub-clans thereof, monopolized the title of both lines.

If such were the case a most peculiar situation would have existed. In the other four tribes men of the A-clan ideally marry women of the B-clan, and men of the B-clan marry women of the A-clan; thus, with matrilineal descent, it is assured that a man and his grandson are in the same line, while his father and son are in the opposite line. If one clan held both lines of titles such alternation of generations would not be necessary, but clan incest would be required. Precisely this is strongly indicated in the clan myths. Informants insist that clan 7, the Soun Kawad, was unique among all the clans in that its members once regularly intermarried with each other. Enough statements are available to indicate that there may be some foundation to this scandalous charge, and members of the clan are reluctant to talk about it. A common saying is "there are no taboos against crossing the mountains of the Soun Kawad clan" (*sohte pelen kot nahnahn* Soun Kawad); the reference is to the story that members of this clan, before their conquest of Net and Sokehs, lived in the mountains by themselves and married each other. The traditional origin of the clan, which may have some historical validity, is at Marakei in the Gilbert Islands, where true exogamous clans are lacking and where there is a patrilineal bias in contrast to the strict matrilineal rule of Ponape. (Other clans in Ponape also have traditions that their founders were women who arrived from other islands.) If a group of Gilbertese coming to Ponape were regarded by Ponapeans as composing a single clan, they would eventually come to conform to the prevailing exogamy, but there might be a period of adjustment while they continued to intermarry before the practice became established.

The clan 7 traditions also tell of a series of adventures terminating in their conquest of Sokehs and Net. Supposedly they took over the existing titles of these two tribes. It would thus have been possible for two groups of people in clan 7, or two sub-clans thereof, to array themselves in Net as the two intermarrying lines of titles which in the other tribes were composed of men of two different clans. Clan 7 is also the one Ponapean clan whose sub-clans are not named, and the exact affiliation by sub-clan of any dead chief is difficult to recall, since affiliation of living persons in clan 7 is given either with reference to the present senior man of the sub-clan or by number in order of seniority of the sub-clans (the numbers given in the terminology used in counting the successive hands of a stalk of bananas of the variety called *uhtmwot*). In other tribes it is often possible, when an informant is unsure to which line a title belongs, to place it in one line or the other by recollection of the clan of its holder, but this would be impossible if one clan held both sets of titles. Hence, one can understand the confusion in the minds of living informants as to whether there was in Net one line or two up to the time of Maximino, the first B1 who was not a member of clan 7.

[7] Incumbent No. 8 or 9 was involved in the wars between Wene, Kiti proper, and Pehleng, discussed later in this work.

# Subtribes

## THE SECTIONS AND OTHER SUBDIVISIONS

Each tribe is divided geographically and politically into a number of *kousapw,* referred to by the American administration as sections. On a miniature scale they parallel the organization of the tribe. Corresponding to the A and B lines of titles there are, in most sections, two lines of section titles, which will be referred to as the X and Y lines. The chief of each section (*kaun* or *soumas*), who will in this work be designated for convenience as the X1, heads the X-line, just as the Nahnmwarki, the A1, heads the A-line of titles in the tribe. Likewise, the Y1 of the section corresponds to the B1 of the tribe, although he is of little importance politically compared to the B1. The X and Y lines, like the A and B lines, are referred to by the natives as *pali soupeidi* and *pali nahnken* respectively. A man may hold a tribal title and a section title simultaneously.

The titles of a typical section, that of Enipeinpah (*eni* or *ani:* ghost; *pein:* female; *pah:* lower) or section 16 in Kiti, are as follows:[8]

| *X-line* | *Y-line* |
|---|---|
| 1. Kroulikiak | 1. Serihnei |
| 2. Souan en Enipein | 2. Kanikin Enipein |
| 3. Oun Pohnpein Enipein | 3. Nahnawahn Enipein |
| 4. Nahlik en Enipein | 4. Nahnkrou en Enipein |
| 5. Nahnsahun Enipein | 5. Isohlap en Enipein |
| 6. Luwen Saped en Enipein | 6. Lepen Madau en Enipein |
| 7. Leperirin Enipein | 7. Loampwein Enipein |
| 8. Kaniki Ririn Enipein | 8. Nahnsahum en Enipein |
| 9. Kroun en Pohnial en Enipein | 9. Sidin Enipein |
| 10. Kanikin Semwei en Enipein | 10. Lepen Enipein |
| 11. Isohwa en Enipein | 11. Luwennos en Enipein |
| 12. Aron Krou en Enipein | 12. Nahnpohnpein Enipein |

It will be noted from Tables 3 and 4 that the A and B series (except until recently in Net) with minor differences are essentially the same in each of the five tribes. However, the X and Y series of the various sections are hardly ever similar. And while it is possible to use the title Nahnmwarki as alternative to A1 in any tribe (and other titles and other letter-number combinations similarly) no titles could be used in connection with all the X1's (or other X or Y chiefs).

The sections generally form strips or wedges of land extending from the coast into the interior; few of them are entirely inland (Figure 2). A list of the sections and their chiefs in each tribe follows; the sections are arranged as nearly as possible in clockwise order around the island, beginning with those of Uh in the north. (The numbers preceding the section names will usually be used hereafter instead of the names when the sections are referred to, in order to avoid wearying the reader with native words.)

[8] In this and the following tables of titles some apparent inconsistency in spelling will be noted. Thus in some instances (e.g., X10, Y2, Y3, Y7) when the first word of the title ends in a vowel the following word "en" (meaning approximately "of") is absorbed by a process of sandhi, but not in the case of others (e.g., Y4, X11). Also, when a word ends in "n" it sometimes is followed by "en" (e.g., X2, X9), sometimes not (e.g., X7). The head of section 2 of Kiti is Nahnkrou en Rehntu, but the head of section 8 is Nahnkroun Posain. This is no doubt due to individual variation among speakers, and even inconsistency in the same speaker under different conditions, but since there are other titles in which the difference seems to be important (e.g., the head of section 19 of Kiti is Krou en Wein, but the Y1 of section 1 of Uh is Kroun en Awakpah), all titles are recorded as heard, even when what may be the same term is heard differently from different informants.

UH

| Section | Title of Chief X1 | Title of Chief Y1 |
|---|---|---|
| 1. Awakpah | Soulik en Awakpah | Kroun en Awakpah |
| 2. Awakpowe | Soulik en Awakpowe | Kroun en Awakpowe |
| 3. Metipw en Awak | Soulik en Metipw | Soumadau en Metipw |
| 4. Metipw en Uh | Soulik en Metipw | Soumadau en Metipw |
| 5. Kipar | Luwen en Kipar | Nahmadau en Kipar |
| 6. Souna | Oun Souna | Soulik en Souna |
| 7. Nan Uh [9] | | |
| 8. Pahlap | Reteng en Pahlap | Soumaka en Pahlap |
| 9. Dien | Luwen en Dien | Soumadau en Dien |
| 10. Saladak | Soumadau en Saladak | Nahnkroun en Saladak |
| 11. Rohi | Soulik en Dianso | Soumaka en Rohi |
| 12. Takaiehu | Kehlahk en Takaiehu | Soumadau en Takaiehu |
| 13. Dehpehk | Souwen en Dehpehk | Soumadau on Dehpehk |
| 14. Mwahnd peidi | Lepen Mwahnd | Soulik en Mwahnd |
| 15. Mwahnd peidak | Soudel en Mwahnd | Lepen Mwahnd |

Sections 12–15 are islands within the lagoon, the others are on the mainland of Ponape.

Awak was formerly a single section and was split into sections 1–3 in a quarrel over succession of its chief. Under the Japanese, sections 4 to 9 were combined and called by the name of section 7. (Bascom's list evidently reflects this condition, since he omits my sections 3–6, 8, and 9.) Then the B3 of Uh, who was a commoner but had received his title because he was a policeman under the Japanese, complained that he was not being respected and threatened to leave Uh; so Nan Uh was split into Uh Kaieu (Uh No. 1) and Uh Keriau (Uh No. 2), the former consisting of sections 8 and 9 and half of section 7, the latter of the remainder, and the B3 was made X1 of one of these. Supposedly Uh is now reconstituted as it was in pre-Japanese times.

But it is not certain that this series of sections of Uh represents a condition of much antiquity. The missionary L. H. Gulick, writing in the 1850s (unpublished records of the American Board of Commissioners for Foreign Missions), lists as place names for the "Wanega tribe" (Wanega or Wenik here equivalent to Uh) the following: Takaiu I. (my section 12), Tapak I. (my section 13), Mantapeiti (my section 14), Mantapeta (my section 15), Salatuk (my section 10), Uh, and Awak. The sequence of names is Gulick's. Presumably Awak corresponds to my sections 1 to 3, and Uh to my sections 4 to 9, so possibly the Japanese organization is a reflection of a former condition. Gulick's list corresponds exactly with the "Uanik" list given in the Luelen manuscript, except that the latter adds also Roi (my section 11). It may be that the other Uh sections are therefore of a recent origin.

[9] The present Luwen en Pwudoi acts as X1, but the title bears no relationship to the job; Nan Uh is the capital (*nanwei*) of Uh and has no proper X1 title.

Awak is often mentioned in 19th-century literature as a semi-independent entity.

A list of sections circulated in mimeograph form by the Ponape District Office of the American administration, dated December 29, 1954, gives the same Uh series as mine but omits my sections 5 and 8.[10]

MADOLENIHMW

| Section | Title of Chief X1 | Title of Chief Y1 |
|---|---|---|
| 1. Alohkapw | Lepen Alokapw | Soumadau en Alokapw |
| 2. Ipwitek | Soumadau en Ipwitek | Nahnkroun Ipwitek |
| 3. Kinakapw | Soumadau en Kinakapw | Lepenken en Kinakapw |
| 4. Areu | Saudepe en Areu | Soulik en Areu |
| 5. Ohwa | Lepen Ohwa | Soulik en Ohwa |
| 6. Mesihsou | Soumadau en Mesihsou | Soulik en Mesihsou |
| 7. Lukoap | Soumadau en Lukoap | Sou Lukoap |
| 8. Metipw | Lepen Madau en Metipw | Soumadau en Metipw |
| 9. Dolopwail | Salapat en Dolopwail | Oun Dolopwail |
| 10. Kepinne | Luwennos en Kepinne | Soumadau en Kepinne |
| 11. Takaiuh | Kehlak en Takaiuh | Soulik en Takaiuh |
| 12. Edielleng | Soule en Edielleng | Soumadau en Edielleng |
| 13. Kitamw | Soumadau en Kitamw | Soulik en Kitamw |
| 14. Lehdau | Lep Lehdau | Nahno en Lehdau |
| 15. Elieluwi | Souwen en Peitik | Soumadau en Pahlap |
| 16. Diadi | Soumadau en Diadi | Soulik en Diadi |
| 17. Pohnauleng | Soukeperoa | Sipwin Lewetik |
| 18. Sapwehrek | Soulik en Sapwehrek | Soumadau en Sapwehrek |
| 19. Keprohi | Koaroahm en Keprohi | Soumadau en Keprohi |
| 20. Tamworohi | Luwennos en Tamworohi | Soumadau en Tamworohi |
| 21. Lehiak | Soulik en Lehiak | Nahnkroun Lehiak |
| 22. Nanwei [11] | | |
| 23. Temwen | Ninakap | Sihpw |
| 24. Enipoas | Oun Enipoas | Soumadau en Enipoas |
| 25. Akahk | Kanikin Akahk | Soumadau en Akahk |
| 26. Wapar | Lepen Wapar | Soumadau en Wapar |
| 27. Lohdpowe | Soulik en Lohd [12] | Kroun en Lohd |
| 28. Lohdpah | Lepen Sehd [13] | Soumadau en Lohd |

[10] Father Hugh Costigan tells me (1966) that there is now a new section, Kepin Awak, which split off from section 2 because of dissatisfaction with the head. Its X1 is Soulik en Kepin Awak, its Y1 is Kroun en Kepin Awak.

[11] Nanwei is the seat of the Nahnmwarki of Madolenihmw and has no proper X1; chief A11 of the tribe acts as head presently. (Information in 1966 is that A11 was deposed because of failure to offer first fruits and because of eating a turtle instead of presenting it to the A1. He was followed by Luwen Madolenihmw and then by Luwennos en Ririn.)

[12] Father Costigan says (1966) that the Soulik en Lohd has become inactive but retains his title. The X1 is now Kaniki en Wehi.

See footnote on following page.

Sections 21, 22, and 23 constitute the island of Temwen.

A number of former political subdivisions exist between the tribal and section levels in Madolenihmw. They are Enimwahn (sections 1–9), Sapwalap (sections 10–18), Nanwei (sections 19–23), and Lepinsed (sections 24–28). The term Nanwei sometimes applies only to section 22, sometimes to sections 21–23 (the island of Temwen), suggesting shifting political boundaries at various times. These four areas, which comprise all of Madolenihmw, have historical significance, but today their names are only geographical terms. Several titles that contain these names still exist but they have no political relationship to the areas concerned. Among them are Sou Sehd and Lepen Sehd, corresponding to the area of Lepinsed; and Lepen Enimwahn, similarly related to Enimwahn. (The title of Lepen Sehd, whose holder today is the X1 of section 28, and that of Lepen Enimwahn are said by some informants to be recent creations of Moses, the present A1 of Madolenihmw, but the latter title is listed in Luelen's manuscript, which antedates Moses' accession to authority, and the former is probably a revival of a temporarily lapsed title.)

Two other titles in Madolenihmw are of special significance and are above X1 level. One is Kroun en Lehdau, the holder of which is traditionally overlord of sections 12, 13, and 14 (nowadays also 10 and 11), an area called Lehdau (also the name of section 14 alone). The other is Lepen Moar, its holder having a similar relationship to sections 15 and 16 (plus 17 and 18 in more recent times), an area known as Senipehn. The Kroun en Lehdau, though holding his fief under the Nahnken, belongs always to the clan of the Nahnmwarki. The Lepen Moar holds his under the Nahnmwarki but always belong to another clan, clan 7; for traditional reasons he has a particularly high status and may sit alongside the Nahnmwarki at feasts. At some time in history the holder of this last title appears to have had both Lehdau and Senipehn as his fiefs.

Gulick's list of place names for the "Matalinim tribe" omits my sections 1, 2, 3, 7, 12, 13, 15, 19, 21, and 22, and counts my sections 27 and 28 as one; following Lohd (27 and 28) he has "Nantiaiti" and "Nantamaroi" as additional sections, which he marks on his accompanying map as west of Lohd, at the Madolenihmw-Kiti border. (Both are now reckoned as part of section 28.)[14] No doubt the discrepancies reflect the splitting and recombinations of political divisions referred to later in this work.

Cabeza Pereiro (maps facing pp. 198 and 240) shows the easternmost section of Uh, No. 11 (which he writes "Roy"), as the first, northwesternmost section, of "Metalanim," west of my section 1, Alohkapw. His map of Madolenihmw omits my sections 2, 4, 7, 21, and 22, and counts my sections 27 and 28 as one. On another map he shows the names of sections 4 and 7 as names of capes, but in the proper location. Between sections 6 and 8 he has Tien (today in section 8), and between sections 14 and 15 he has "Chacorrorriau" (Sekeren riau, "second landing place"), which is a former section, now part of section 15.

Luelen's manuscript gives as the ancient organization of Madolenihmw the areas Enimwahn (comprising sections 1–9, in agreement with my informants except for section 2, which was split off from section 12 in German times), Lehdau (sections 13 and 14), Senipehn (sections 15, 16, and the above-mentioned Sekeren riau), Lepinsed (no sections named), and a group of apparently unaffiliated sections (Nos. 17–20, 27 and 28 as one, and "Lauatik"; the last is nowadays defunct but its name is contained in the Y1 title of section 17 in the above list). Elsewhere Leulen seems to regard Senipehn as equivalent to the above-mentioned Sapwalap, and at an apparently earlier stage in history he considers Madolenihmw to have four parts: Enimwahn, Senipehn, Lepinsed, and "Uanik," as though the latter, which is usually held to be the same as modern Uh, was once in Madolenihmw. (Indeed, he gives the northwest boundary of ancient Madolenihmw as the Sokele River, which would include not only Uh but Net proper, and he joins the rest of Net to Sokehs.)

Bascom's list of sections is identical to mine. The Ponape District Office list of 1954 adds "Nankepira" (Nankeperoa) to my 1947 list as a section between my numbers 17 and 18. (This section has seceded from section 17, and both the X1 and Y1 went with it.) It also shows two new sections, Nansalohi (between my 14 and 15) and Nanpahlap (between my 26 and 27). These two were split off in 1951 as resettlement areas for immigrants from Pis and Losap respectively, the two communities on Losap atoll southeast of Truk, in an attempt to relieve them of overpopulation.

The Japanese set up a new organization consisting of six major divisions called *pwihn,* as follows:

1. Sections 1–5
2. Sections 6–9
3. Sections 10–14
4. Sections 15–18
5. Sections 24–28
6. Sections 19–23

Footnotes continued from previous page.

[13] Father Costigan's information is that about 1950 the Lepen Sehd asked to be relieved as X1 because of age and chose as his successor the Lepen Sapw, but retained his own title. Then when he died a clansmate of his who was not a resident of section 28 became Lepen Sehd, so it would appear that the X1 title in section 28 has changed.

[14] One of my 1947 informants also gave me Nan Tamworohi as a section.

298-818—68——3

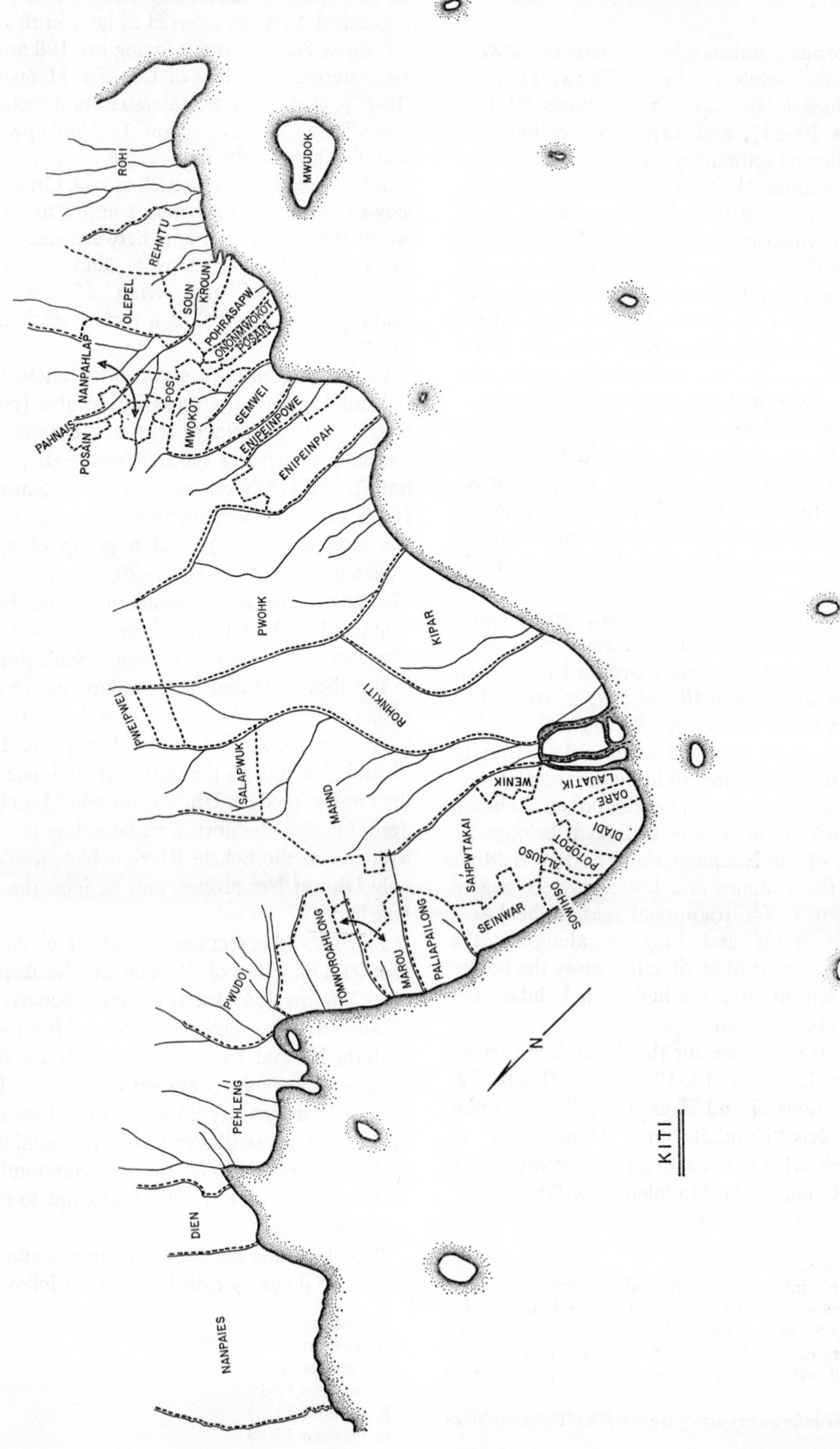


FIGURE 2.—The tribe of Kiti and its sections.

There are no *pwihn* titles, but various chiefs were made heads of the *pwihn:* e.g., in *pwihn* 1 the head is Nahmadau en Pahlap, in *pwihn* 2 he is chief A3.[15]

The Madolenihmw sections were divided in ownership between the Nahnmwarki and the Nahnken. To the Nahnmwarki traditionally belong sections 1–5, 8–9, 11, 15–24, and 26–28. To the Nahnken belong the others. Only some of the X1's belong to the same clans as the Nahnmwarki and Nahnken. Bascom's compilation of X1 titles for Madolenihmw (unlike his list for Uh, where those titles he gives are the same as mine) is rather different from those of page 22. Only 12 of the 28 titles are the same in both lists.

KITI

| *Section* | *Title of chief X1* |
|---|---|
| 1. Rohi | Souwen en Rohi |
| 2. Rehntu | Nahnkrou en Rehntu |
| 3. Mwudok | Soulik en Mwudok |
| 4. Sounkroun | Soulik en Paleidi |
| 5. Olepel | Lepenmadau en Olepel |
| 6. Pohrasapw | Ounwene en Pohrasapw |
| 7. Ononmwakot | Nahnawahn Ononmwakot |
| 8. Pohsein | Nahnkroun Pohsein |
| 9. Kepinne | Soulik en Kepinne |
| 10. Nanpahlap | Soulik en Pahlap |
| 11. Pahnais | Nahmadau en Kepinne |
| 12. Pehs | Oun Rolong |
| 13. Mwakot | Soulik en Mwakot |
| 14. Semwei | Karohm en Semwei |
| 15. Enipeinpowe | Soulik en Semwei |
| 16. Enipeinpah | Kroulikiak |
| 17. Pwohk | Souwen en Pwohk |
| 18. Kipar | Kanikin Kipar |
| 19. Rohnkiti | Krou en Wein |
| 20. Pweipwei | Riting en Pweipwei |
| 21. Salapwuk | Saum |
| 22. Mahnd | Kasa |
| 23. Wenik | Lepen Wenik |
| 24. Lauatik | Sihpwen Lauatik |
| 25. Oare | Soulik en Kepinne |
| 26. Diadi | Nahmadaun Diadi |
| 27. Poatoapoat | Kaniki en Akahk |
| 28. Alauso | Nahnsahu en Ileu |
| 29. Sewihso | Nahnsahu en Sewihso |
| 30. Seinwar | Soulik en Seinwar |
| 31. Paliapailong | Nahmadaun Paliapailong |
| 32. Marahu | Soulik en Marahu |
| 33. Tamworoahlong | Soulik en Lohd |
| 34. Pwudoi | Luwen en Pwudoi |
| 35. Pehleng | Nahmadau en Pehleng |
| 36. Dien | Nahnsahused en Pehleng |
| 37. Nanpaies, or Paies | Soukoahng en Paies |

Some informants list Sahpwtakai as a section; others include it in section 27. Here is the former seat of the Nahnmwarki of Kiti. Today it is inhabited by only one family.

Gulick's list of the 1850s is rather different. He gives sections 1, 2, and 3 as I have them, then come Wana (no doubt my Wene, discussed below) and Palikatau, which seem to include my sections 4–13. This is close to my informants' definition of Wene as comprising sections 1–13. Then come five names that match 14 to 19 of my list (except that 15 and 16 together are called Anapen), after which follow my 22, 26, 32, 33, 34, and 35. Between 22 and 26 he has Rai, and between 26 and 32 he has Palui, Tianipo, Sakaruntu, and Iun.

Bascom's list is the same as mine except for his omission of section 37. The Ponape District list includes the aforementioned Sahpwtakai, which some informants regard as nowadays part of section 27, and another section called Peil between sections 17 and 18; it omits my section 9, as does also the Japanese map copied as Figure 2, where it is apparently included as part of section 10.

It will be noted that I have not given a list of Y1 titles for the sections of Kiti, and for those of Sokehs and Net that follow. My information for these tribes is in this matter contradictory and fragmentary, and by the time I was working in these three areas I began to have doubts whether the idealized pattern of two lines of titles in each section, as expressed by informants, had much validity, as I will discuss later. Sometimes an informant seemed to be searching for a title to give me in order to fit it artificially into the scheme, and I am certain that many of the alleged Y1 titles I obtained are only the titles possessed at the time by men who occurred to my informants as being prominent in their sections.

In 11 of the 37 sections Bascom's X1 titles differ from mine, and Father William McGarry's[16] in five. In two of these instances Bascom and Father McGarry agree, and I have therefore deferred to them in the foregoing list; these are in section 14, where my own information was that Mad Semwei was X1, and section 3, where I had Nahnsoused en Mwudok; in the last case, Father McGarry writes that a minority of his informants agreed with me. He also says that until quite recently sections 4 and 6 were one, with Soulik en Paleidi as X1, and that in 1963 the Nahnmwarki, being unable to discover what the proper X1 title of section 6 should be, made one up, Soulik en Porasapw. It is probably for reasons of this kind that information about such titles is often contradictory.

As in Madolenihmw, political divisions larger than the sections once existed. As given to me by informants they are:

| | |
|---|---|
| Wene........................ | Sections 1–13 |
| Lukoap........................ | Sections 14–19 |
| Kepihleng (Kiti proper)........ | Sections 20–34 |
| Lehnpwel..................... | Sections 35–37 |

[15] By 1966, according to Father Costigan, with the résettlement of people from Pingelap in addition to those from Losap atoll already mentioned, there were five new sections, and these are reckoned now as a seventh *pwihn*.

[16] Correspondence with Father McGarry, missionary at Ponape

Wene and Kiti are terms still used for the two major halves of modern Kiti, and people describe themselves as belonging to one or the other, but the other names are of only historical interest.

Luelen's manuscript gives several similar lists of political divisions, which apparently apply to different periods of history. One of these lists adds "Pasau" to the foregoing four areas and substitutes Pehleng (the modern name of section 35) for Lehnpwel. Another list consists of Wene, Kepihleng, Lehnpwel, and Ant; the last is the atoll 8 miles off Kiti that nowadays is reckoned as part of section 19. A third list is the same as the last except for the substitution of the name Kiti for Kepihleng, its equivalent, but subsumes all four areas under Onohnleng, which is almost always regarded by modern informants as the same as Wene only. A fourth list gives Wene, "Puasa," Ant, and Deleur—the last is a name otherwise applied to the ancient seat of the Saudeleurs at Temwen Island in Madolenihmw but also nowadays to a locality in Wene. Still a fifth list gives only three areas: Wene, Kiti, and Pehleng.

What is now the tribe of Kiti apparently came into being in precontact times, in consequence of a series of wars between Wene, Kiti proper (Kepihleng), and Pehleng. The date of these events is suggested from the information, given by several informants and by Luelen's manuscript, that there have been 22 Nahnmwarkis since the time of the wars. (Other informants say there have been only 19.) The last six of these men, beginning with the present incumbent, were Benito, Sigismundo, Paul, Mikel (or Mensile), Hezekiah, and Luhkenmweimwahu (or Penena). It was either Luhkenmweimwahu or his predecessor who is referred to by L. H. Gulick as having died shortly after his arrival in Ponape from Hawaii in 1852. This would work out roughly as an average of a 15- or 20-year reign for the last six Nahnmwarkis, and application of this formula to the earlier 16 incumbents would make the total span of time about 330 to 440 years. However, this seems far too long a time. Another line of evidence suggested by remarks of Gulick concerning a war which occurred a generation or two before 1852 would place it about 1800, if it is the same war. The Soulik en Semwei, who was 63 years old in 1947, informed me that when he was a small boy he had seen the son of a certain well-known participant in the final battle (one Mahsohr, referred to elsewhere), this man then being quite old; the war, therefore, could hardly have occurred very long before 1800. He also said that the war occurred in the lifetime of his great-grandmother, who had already lived through the reigns of 12 successive rulers; if one assumes she was about 80 years old, the average reign of a precontact chief was about 7 years, and the last 16 Nahnmwarkis before 1852 occupied a period of 112 years, putting the war in about 1740 (or about 1760 if one figures 19 instead of 22 Nahnmwarkis since the war).

In the time before these wars Wene was ruled by a kind of priest-king with the title of Soukisehnleng ("Master of part of heaven"), commonly abbreviated to Soukise. He was regarded as the highest priest of all Ponape and was the leader of a cult and of religious practices different from those elsewhere on Ponape. It is not altogether clear whether he headed a single line of titles in Wene or whether two lines existed; the latter is more likely. Luelen's manuscript gives the four senior titles of Wene, in order, as Soukise, Sou Wene, Madau, and Sohmw, and indicates that they all belonged to the ruling clan, hence would have been one line. My own informants give the first three of these titles in the same order. In another place, in telling the story of the conquest of Kiti proper by Wene, Luelen describes how the holders of the same three titles, Soukise, Sou Wene, and Madau, after the victory took the new titles of Nahnmwarki, Wasai, and Dauk (A1, A2, and A3), while another titleholder, Soumadau en Ponta, became Nahnken (B1),[17] which would suggest that two clans were involved and that two lines of titles already existed in Wene, their holders taking equivalent titles of the conquered land. Hambruch (1932 II, p. 133) also says that the Soumadau en Ponta was the equivalent of the Nahnken. He names the Kroun Tamw instead of the Sou Wene as A2 or Wasai, and elsewhere (1932 II, p. 38) he gives Soukise, Sou Wene, Madau, and Soumadau en Ponta, in that order, as the four highest titles of a single ruling clan, which would make the last equivalent of A4, not B1, contrary to Luelen, my informants, and those of Father McGarry. The fact that the title Soumadau en Ponta was held at one time by a man of clan 17 and later (as now) by clan 11, while Soukise and his line were members of clan 4, increases the probability that two lines of titles did actually exist in Wene.

Besides these titles there was a group of ranked priests who did not belong to the foregoing series (see the section on priestly titles to follow and the lists of titles in Hambruch, 1932 II, pp. 132–133).

In the aforesaid war, Pehleng (or Lehnpwel) first attacked Kepihleng (or Kiti proper). At that time Kepihleng was ruled by the Soun Kiti, a sub-clan of clan 4, its senior member was the Soukiti, and the Soukiti was therefore the highest chief of Kepihleng. Pehleng's high chief, Nahmadau en Pehleng, a member of clan 17, overcame Kepihleng and apparently assumed the title of Nahnmwarki, a title either not previously used in Kiti or else a secondary title that had belonged to the Soukiti. Wene was under another sub-clan of clan 4, and its high chief,

[17] Father William McGarry has written me that his information is that Soukise, Sou Wene, Madau en Ne, and Kroun en Ne became Nahnmwarki, Wasai, Dauk, and Nohs (A1, A2, A3, A4) respectively while Soumadau en Ponta became Nahnken (B1).

Soukise, was appealed to on the ground of clan solidarity. He thereupon, in concert with a high chief of Net, the Nahnsoused, marched against Kepihleng, overthrew clan 17 in a battle at Sahpwtakai, and took the title of Nahnmwarki as already described; all of Kiti now became united into one tribe and Pehleng was reduced to a section within Kiti, the situation that exists today. The Nahnsoused of Net was rewarded for his help in the war with the title of Soukiti and the fief of section 32, both of which were returned to Kiti only much later.

Just before Soukise's conquest of Kepihleng he sent messengers, according to Luelen, to sections 14–19 to invite them to join him in the battle, which they did. My informants refer to these sections as Lukoap ("middle place") and from the context it would appear that they were semi-independent at the time. The five different lists of geographical units given by Luelen, as mentioned earlier, suggest that political alliances varied in composition from time to time, and Lukoap appears as an entity in only one of them. Some informants give only sections 17–19 as comprising Lukoap, and Luelen's account of the war, which uses antique names for all six sections, has "Pasaulap" for section 14 and "Pasautik" for section 15, probably the "Pasau" or "Puasa" of two of the five lists, set off against Lukoap, suggesting again a condition of fluid boundaries.

In Kiti proper, after the war and until German times, all of the sections adhered to the Nahnmwarki as his fiefs, except for sections 25 and 31, which were under the Nahnken. Some of these sections were directly under other high chiefs who in turn were enfeoffed under the Nahnmwarki; thus section 32 came under the chief A7, section 27 was under the A3, sections 28 and 29 belonged to the A2, section 21 to the Saum, and sections 30, 33, and 34 were provinces of the Soukiti, a title that continued in use in Kiti as well as in Net though its holder was no longer A1. The other sections served the Nahnmwarki directly. (See page 30 for a discussion of change of allegiance of some of these sections.) Wene was also divided between the Nahnmwarki and Nahnken, the former holding sections 1, 4–7, and 12, the latter sections 2, 8–11, and 13.[18] To the high chief of section 35 (Pehleng) two other sections, 36 and 37, had owed allegiance, as already noted; after the Kiti war his title (Nahmadau en Pehleng) was given to chief B2 (or Nahlaimw), who held the three sections in fief to the Nahnmwarki; the B2 to this day holds both titles Nahlaimw and Nahmadau en Pehleng. (This is the reason for my earlier remark, p. 18, concerning the B2 title in Kiti.) In Lukoap, after incorporation into the tribe of Kiti, sections 14–16 came under the Nahnmwarki, the others under the Nahnken.

SOKEHS

| *Section* | *Title of chief X1* |
|---|---|
| PALIKIR (the mainland of Sokehs) | |
| 1. Nanipil | Soulik en Sokele |
| 2. Tomwara | Soulik en Tomwara |
| 3. Palikir | Lepen Palikir |
| 4. Iohl | Krou en Wehn |
| 5. Likie | Noahs Palikir |
| 6. Oumoar | Nahmadaun Oare |
| 7. Sekere | Lepen Sekere |
| 8. Pohnmal, or Nanpohnmal | Soulik en Kepin |
| 9. Nankui | Kroun en Sokele |
| SOKEHS ISLAND | |
| 10. Peitie | Soukoahng Peitie |
| 11. Utui | Nahmadaun Oare |
| 12. Sekerelap | |
| 13. Mwalok | Soumadau en Sokehs |
| 14. Lupwur, or Lup | Mwarekehtik en Sokehs |
| 15. Naneir | |
| 16. Denpei | |
| 17. Tamworohi, or Nanimwinsap en Epwel | Lempweilapalap en Sokehs |
| 18. Dolehtik | Kroun en Dolehtik |
| 19. Roio | Nahnken en Sokehs |
| 20. Ipwal | Nahlaimw en Sokehs |
| 21. Soledi | Oun Sokehs |
| PAKIN ATOLL | |
| 22. Pakin | Souni |

This list of sections and section chiefs is given as it existed before the Sokehs rebellion against the Germans in 1911, following which there was a wholesale expulsion to Palau and elsewhere; the exiles were not permitted to return until Japanese times, when they found their lands, especially on Sokehs Island, occupied by out-islanders who had been settled in Sokehs by the Germans. The organization of Sokehs had meantime been considerably changed. Today section 1 is in Net. Sections 3–5 in 1947 constituted modern Palikir section (which some informants reckon as two sections, Palikirpah and Palikirpowe), but the 1954 Ponape District list shows section 5 separately. Section 6 is now part of section 7. Section 9 is now part of section 8. (Section 8 itself was once part of a section called Kepin, a name preserved in the title of its X1 as given in the foregoing list.) Sokehs Island (sections 10–21) is divided into six villages of out-islanders. Sections 10–14 constitute the modern village of Pingelap, which takes its name from the atoll where its inhabitants originated. Similarly, sections 15–17 are the modern Mokil village, named after that atoll. From the atoll of Ngatik came the settlers of Ngatik village, made up of former section 18 and part of sections 19 and 20. Three more villages are composed of islanders from

[18] This is in contradiction to Bascom (1965, p. 66) who says that the Nahnmwarki owned all of Kiti proper, the Nahnken all of Wene.

Lukunor atoll and from Te and Satawan in Satawan atoll, all in the Mortlock group; Lukunor village comprises part of sections 20 and 21, Te village part of sections 19 and 20, and Satawan village part of section 21.

Bascom's list (1965, p. 25) of 28 Sokehs sections differs so markedly from mine that it is well to give my informants' interpretation of his section names. His sections 1, 2, 3, 4, 5, 8, 10, 11, 12, 14, 15, 17, 22, and 27 correspond respectively to my numbers 16, 15, 14, 13, 12, 21, 20, 19, 17, 8, 7, 6, 4, and 2. But according to my informants, 12 of his sections are only farmsteads, No. 6 is in my section 11, No. 9 in my 21, No. 16 in my 7, Nos. 18–19 in my 5, Nos. 20–21 and 23 in my 4, Nos. 24–25 in my 3, and Nos. 26 and 28 in my 2. Hambruch (1932 I, p. 321) gives a list of 12 sections only for Sokehs Island; he omits my sections 11, 12, and 18 (which he regards as farmsteads) as well as 19 and 20, but he lists five others.

It will be noted that the X1's of sections 13, 14, 17, and 19–21 are represented as having tribal titles (see Tables 2 and 3), as shown by the inclusion of the word "Sokehs" in their titles. These could hardly be section titles. A man may have both a section title and a tribal title, as will be seen later, but in this list of Sokehs section titles there is no doubt some confusion in the minds of informants; the events following upon the rebellion of 1910–11 have probably dimmed their memories and they apparently remember better the highest tribal chiefs living in a section than the possessors of the section X1 titles. Since a man may have both a section title and a tribal title, it is probable that informants have remembered only the latter as of the time of the rebellion.

It is not clear how the tribal area was divided between the highest chiefs of the A and B lines. (I do not refer to A1, or Nahnmwarki, here because Sokehs for a long period of time was ruled by the Wasai, a title which is A2 in the other tribes. The reason for this is a legendary one. Today there is a Nahnmwarki.) Clan 7 traditionally supplies the holders of the higher titles of the A-line, clan 6 those of the B-line. The X1's of sections 1, 6, 8, 9, 11, 15, and 22 belonged to clan 7, those of sections 2, 10, 12, 17, and 19 to clan 6; however, in view of the situation in the other tribes, this is not necessarily a clue to the division of Sokehs between the two highest chiefs. As for the other sections, the X1 of section 21 belonged to clan 4, sections 18 and 20 to clan 5, sections 3–5 to clan 9, section 13 to clan 13, and section 7 to clan 17; section 14 fell under either clan 4 or 12, it is not clear which. Section 16 was the A2's seat and had no hereditary X1.

Gulick's list of place names in the "Jekoits tribe" mentions, besides "Jekoits" Island, only "Tomora" (my section 2) and "Paliga" (my section 3). The last of these, Palikir, in Gulick's day was much larger than today and at one time apparently included all of what is now the mainland part of Sokehs and was politically independent.

NET

| *Section* | *Title of chief X1* |
|---|---|
| 1. Parem | Lepen Parempei |
| 2. Lenger | Lepen Lenger |
| 3. Dolonier | Krou en Doaroapoap |
| 4. Pohrakied | Nahnawa en Mesenieng |
| 5. Ninseitamw | |
| 6. Mesenieng | Nahlaimw en Metipw |
| 7. Nanipil | Soulik en Sokele |
| 8. Eirike | Soumadau en Sapwalap |
| 9. Meitik | Lepen Paremkep |
| 10. Kahmar | Sou Kahmar |
| 11. Pahnimwinsapw | Sou Net |
| 12. Paliais | Soulik en Ais |
| 13. Nanpohnsapw | Soulik en Sapawas |
| 14. Ninsoksok | Soulik en Ninsoksok |
| 15. Tamworohi | Madau en Rohi |
| 16. Leprohi | Nahmadaun Ided |
| 17. Sekerenkauki | Nahnapas en Net |
| 18. Lukapoas | Soukoahng |
| 19. Areke | Krou en Rohi |
| 20. Pohnpeil | Soulik en Net |
| 21. Peile | Nahnsahu en Ileu |
| 22. Pohnmanga | Luwehrei Net |
| 23. Dolokei | Koaroahm en Dolokei |

Sections 1 and 2 are islands. Section 7 formerly belonged to Sokehs. Most of section 6 is now the site of the town of Kolonia and is not usually reckoned as under Net. A former farmstead in section 6, Komwonlaid, is today sometimes considered a section. Section 4 was also formerly part of section 6. Section 23 is sometimes considered as two sections, Dolokeipowe and Dolokeipah.

The Net sections as in other tribes were anciently grouped into larger divisions. Sections 7–10 are collectively known as Sapwalap and were under the X1 of section 7. Sections 11–13 were under the X1 of section 12. Sections 15–17 were headed by the X1 of section 15. Sections 18–21 and a section called Leptohmara, consisting of modern sections 22 and 17, were under the X1 of section 19 (though overlordship of section 17 could not have been held simultaneously with that of the X1 of section 15). Informants distinguish Net proper, meaning the Net peninsula, from the rest of Net as including sections 12 to 23 (some say 14 to 23).

Bascom's list omits my sections 5, 11, and 22. The Ponape District Office list of 1954 omits my sections 4–5, 11–12, and 15–22, apparently lumping most of them under a section called Pali Pohn Net, or Net proper.

Gulick gives for the "Nut tribe," besides the island sections, only four on the mainland: Misinipali, Nut, Misiniung, and Deliniur. The last two, judging from his sketch map, apparently comprise everything west of the Dahu Sokele River and are identifiable under the names of my sections 6 and 3. "Nut," shown as the peninsula east of the river, corresponds fairly well with the native usage of the tribal name in its meaning of Net proper. Misinipali is unidentifiable, but is shown on the Uh border.

In Net the sections nowadays have been reduced to mere geographical significance. The functioning units for administrative and ceremonial purposes are the *pwihn,* artificial units into which the sections have been grouped. These are as follows:

1. Section 1
2. Section 23
3. Sections 15–22
4. Sections 11–14
5. Sections 7–9
6. Section 10
7. Sections 3–6 and Komwonlaid

Section 2 is not included because it is unoccupied and is used by the civil administration. It should be noted that while the section numbers as given here for Net and other tribes are of the writer's devising for use in reference, the *pwihn* numbers, as in Madolenihmw, are used by the natives.

## SECTIONS, SECTION CHIEFS, AND CLANS

The boundaries of the sections are very precisely known, and some appear to be very ancient. Nevertheless a process of splitting and of combination is apparent from the legendary and historical examples previously mentioned. The boundaries and names of many defunct political units are remembered, but when such areas are deserted and revert to wilderness they are no longer considered as sections. The various old sections that constitute modern Palikir (see the Sokehs list of sections) show the process of combination at work. A number of pairs of sections bear the same names, with suffixes *powe* (upper) and *pah* (lower), indicating splitting of one section into two. Chiefs' titles in full are usually composed of three parts, as will be seen upon inspection of the various lists: the title proper, followed by the word *en* (of), then a word which in section titles is most often a section name. The fact that in each list of section titles a number of titles appear in which the geographical names that form part of them are different from the names of the sections to which those titles today pertain suggests a continual history of political reorganization and recombinations. For example, the Soulik en Semwei is X1 not of Semwei (section 14 of Kiti) but of Enipeinpowe (section 15). The X1's of sections 11 and 25 in Kiti bear titles containing the name of section 9. In section 4 of Net the title of the X1 refers to section 6. The X1 and Y1 titles in section 15 and the Y1 title of section 17, in Madolenihmw, contain the names of ancient sections that have become depopulated and reverted to forest and are no longer considered as sections. And the X1 of section 8 of Net has as part of his title the name of the ancient area that includes the present-day sections 7–10.

Some present-day or former sections are known as *kap,* areas in the forest where everything reputedly grows well and where breadfruit remains ripe longer than elsewhere. Such a section is said always to belong to the same clan, though other sections may change clan affiliation from time to time. The areas covered by the ancient sections of Senipehn and Kepin in Sokehs are by some reckoned as *kap;* in Kiti, sections 9, 21, and 35 are so classed; in Net, section 7; in Uh, the hinterland of Awak; and in Madolenihmw, those sections in the area called Sapwalap that are under the Lepen Moar. (All of these are under clan 7, except Awak, which comes under clan 2.)

There are a number of differences between the political organizations of the tribe and the section. The clan affiliation of the X1 is less consistently the same from generation to generation than is that of the A1, and there is no attempt, at least nowadays, to reserve all the section titles in one line for a particular clan. The ideal is to have each clan and each family in the section represented in the series. For example, in the X-line of section 16 of Kiti only 5 of the first 12 titles (given on p. 21) are held by the clansmates of the X1. In the organization of section 15 of Kiti the titleholders by name are as follows:

| *X-line* | *Clan* | *Y-line* | *Clan* |
|---|---|---|---|
| 1. Cosmos | 16 | 1. Emereno | 15 |
| 2. Moses | 12 | 2. Jacques | 8 |
| 3. David | 15 | 3. Perna | 4 |
| 4. Ignace | 4 | 4. Petrigo | 16 |
| 5. Ignace | 16 | 5. Michael | 8 |
| 6. Luis | 15 | 6. Johannes | 8 |
| 7. Aleck | 12 | 7. Lucius | 8 |
| 8. Margarita | 16 | 8. Luciana | 8 |
| 9. Joseph | 15 | 9. Senio | 15 |

Five, instead of only the ideal two, clans are represented in the above rank order. (The total population of this section is 37 and is divided among seven clans.) It is obvious that the parallel with the tribal system has broken down, unless we suppose that it never was anything but a pale imitation. Since the issuance of individual deeds to land in German times, the X1 no longer holds all the land in fief to the Nahnmwarki; his family therefore is in no more advantageous an economic position than any other, except for the first fruits he may continue to receive through force of tradition, and is less likely to monopolize the higher titles than formerly. The population of a section is small enough that, in contrast to the tribe, every man and many women receive a title of some sort; for no unilineal kinship group can ordinarily fill even the most important titles in one line and members of other clans are necessarily drawn upon. Thus in Uh in 1947 the total population of one section (section 4) was only 7; the most populous section (section 2) had 138 men, women, and children. Moreover, since exclusive intermarriage of two clans does not exist on this political level, kinship bonds and the obligations to reward kinsmen with titles become dispersed over a number of clans. In the small population of a section nearly everyone is related to everyone else; so in section 15 of Kiti, X6, X9, Y5, and Y9 in the foregoing list of names are X1's grandsons; Y8 is his daughter; X8 and Y4 are children of his sister; and Y6 is a brother-in-law. As a result, there is less feeling that a line of titles belongs to a single clan than there is on the tribal level. Also, there is no objection to free movement between the two lines during a man's career of political promotions. Thus the present X1 of section 15 was formerly Y1. Nevertheless, the tradition persists in section 15 that clan 15 has some proprietary right here; only five members of this clan are now residing in the section, among a total population of 37, but all of them are included among the highest 18 titles as shown above.

Uh seems to be the most conservative tribe in keeping X1 titles in the same clan. The X1 titles of all but five sections in Uh are supposed to belong to the same sub-clan of clan 2 as do the A-line titles of the tribe. The exceptions are section 1, which belongs to clan 6; section 11, which has been under clan 11 but is now under clan 7; section 13, which should be under an X1 of clan 13 but has also had X1's of clans 8 and 9; and sections 2 and 5, which are under two different sub-clans of clan 2. In recent times section 8 has fallen under clan 5, section 9 under clan 10, section 12 under clans 13 and 15.

In the Y series of titles of Uh sections there is less regularity of inheritance. The Y1 titles of the 14 sections belong to eight different clans at present, no clan having more than three sections, and in only one section is it possible to find a Y1 title persisting as much as three generations in one clan.

Clan affiliation of successive X1's in Kiti is apparently less stable than in Uh. In the following list of Kiti sections the term "former," with reference to clan membership of the X1, applies to some unspecified period of time in the past, as remembered by one informant:

| *Section* | *Former Clan Affiliation of X1 (by clan number)* | *Present Clan Affiliation of X1 (by clan number)* |
|---|---|---|
| 1. | 4 | 4 |
| 2. | 11 | 18 |
| 3. | 4 | 18 |
| 4. | 4 | 4 |
| 5. | 4 | 4 |
| 6. | 4 | 7 |
| 7. | 11 | 18 |
| 8. | 11 | 18 |
| 9. | 11 | 18 |
| 10. | 4 | 11 |
| 11. | 11 | 18 |
| 12. | 17 | 17 |
| 13. | 4 | 17 |
| 14. | 4 | 4 |
| 15. | 15 | 16 |
| 16. | 15 | 4 |
| 17. | 13 | 13 |
| 18. | 4 | 4 |
| 19. | 13 | 18 |
| 20. | 16 | 18 |
| 21. | 8 | 18 |
| 22. | 7 | 7 |
| 23. | 7 | 17 |
| 24. | 7 | 2 |
| 25. | 4 | 6 |
| 26. | 13 | 17 |
| 27. | 4 | 4 |
| 28. | 7 | 17 |
| 29. | 4 | 17 |
| 30. | 4 | 4 |
| 31. | 7 | 16 |
| 32. | 4 | 6 |
| 33. | 9 | 7 |
| 34. | 2 | 2 |
| 35. | 17 | 9 |
| 36. | 9 | 7 |

It was previously remarked that various sections in Kiti were formerly held by the Nahnmwarki and Nahnken respectively, and each section was given in fief to an X1, directly or through subordinate chiefs. That the rule, or at least tendency, was for the Nahnmwarki and Nahnken to choose X1's of their own clans, namely clans 4 and 11, can be seen from the foregoing list. Thus sections 1, 4–6, 14, 27, 29, 30, and 32, which came under the Nahnmwarki all formerly had X1's of clan 4; sections 1, 4, 5, 14, 27, and 30 still do. Similarly sections 8, 9, 11, owned by the Nahnken, had X1's of clan 11.

In 25 out of the 36 Kiti sections listed above, the X1 now belongs to a different clan than formerly. Here, as in Uh and elsewhere, the causes are various, including dying out of the proper line, interference by the Japanese administration, and the issuance of private deeds of ownership and the institution of patrilineal inheritance of land by the German administration, which had the effect of releasing land ownership from direct connection with either clan membership or the political structure. Many of the Kiti sections shown as now under clan 18 are legally owned by Oliver Nanpei, the A6 of Kiti, the wealthiest man in Ponape and a member of that clan.

The clan affiliation of the X1's of the various sections of Sokehs has already been discussed.

Most informants agree that the X1 title should be inherited like that of A1, going first to younger brothers and then to eldest sister's sons in order of age; they attribute the deviations from this rule to the effect of the German administrative measures just mentioned. With the title went the land; chieftainship was inseparable from land ownership, as noted elsewhere. Several instances were collected of patrilineal inheritance in pre-German times, but it should be remembered that the influence of the missionaries was also directed toward this end. Some time before 1865 the then Nahnken of Kiti, Nahnku, who held about 10 sections of Kiti, left his land to his son, Henry Nanpei, instead of to the successor to his title, thereby founding the fortune of the Nanpei family. The Oliver Nanpei mentioned previously was Henry's son and heir. The Nahnken had married the half-Ponapean daughter of an Englishman, James Headley, who helped him to compose a written document formalizing the legacy, which was later accepted as valid by foreign administrations. That it was not challenged by later Nahnkens is a tribute to the strength of Nahnku who was in other respects as well an extraordinary personality, but it is also an indication of the weakening of matrilineal institutions. The chieftainship of section 26 of Kiti has been inherited patrilineally for at least seven generations, going from a man of clan 16 to one of clan 9, then in turn to a member of clan 4, 15, 7, 13, and now 17. On the other hand a number of sections have retained matrilineal inheritance of the X1 title, regardless of how the land was inherited; thus the title of X1 of section 30 of Kiti has gone to a man of clan 4 as far back as informants' memories served, and in section 15 of Uh it has remained in clan 2 for at least eight generations.

Perhaps related to the introduction of private deeds to lands by the Germans is the fact that a man may hold more than one section title simultaneously, having one "every place he works," i.e., wherever he holds lands or works lands for someone else. Thus the present X3 of section 16 of Kiti is also Y1 of section 15. Whether this might have occurred in pre-German times could not be determined.

The section organization is also different from the tribal political organization in that the division into two lines of titles is less clearly marked. The fact that two sub-clans do not tend to monopolize the two lines as they do in the tribe has already been pointed out. When clansmates find themselves in opposite lines the distinction between the lines becomes blurred. For a number of sections it was impossible to obtain lists of titles ranged in two series, and in a few cases the existence of a Y1 was denied; either the series have been forgotten or the dual system was never in effect in some areas. The minor role of the Y1 in many sections in contrast with that of the B1 in the tribe indicates that the division into two lines is not very significant politically in the section. Usually the section organization has the appearance of an imitation, but a weak one, of the tribal political system.

Yet exceptions are to be noted to these generalizations. For example, in section 2 of Uh the Y1 by far overshadows the X1 in importance and dominates in all situations. This is of course a function of the personalities of the two men involved and is parallel to the situation that sometimes occurs in a tribe involving the A1 and B1. It should also be pointed out that in the older sections the X1 title can sometimes be very important.

In the section the X1 may or may not belong to the royal or noble clans. In Madolenihmw, according to native theory, if a single man of clan 13 lives in a section that is under (and before the German division of the lands belonged to) the Nahnmwarki, himself of clan 13, that man will ordinarily be X1. An X1 of the same clan as the Nahnmwarki or Nahnken is in an advantageous position, for he has a freer hand in his section than an X1 who does not belong to one of the ruling clans. Before German times a section under an X1 of commoner clan affiliation reverted, upon death of the X1, to the Nahnmwarki to be reissued on feudal principles. Usually the assignment of the section and the awarding of the X1 title that went with it followed matrilineal principles, but these could be disregarded at the pleasure of the Nahnmwarki. If the X1 was of the Nahnmwarki's clan, however, such reversion did not occur, and inheritance proceeded along strictly matrilineal lines. In native thought, statements like "X1 A owns section 5" and "clan B owns section 5" are equivalent, with reference to pre-German times, if X1 A belongs to clan B; and "the Nahnmwarki owns section 5" means that ultimate title to the land resides in the Nahnmwarki, who grants it in fief to the X1. The Nahnmwarki would hardly disturb the normal rules of succession and inheritance among his own clansmates.

The principle that the X1 should be of the clan of the Nahnmwarki if the section concerned fell under the Nahnmwarki, and of the clan of the Nahnken if the section was in the part of the tribe belonging to the Nahnken, though sometimes observed more in theory than in practice, sometimes meant that a high-ranking tribal chief was not the X1 of the section in which he lived. At one time the A2, A3, and B2 of Net all lived in section 1 of Net, a section falling under the Nahnken, but a man of much lower tribal title, Oaron Mwar, was X1, and simultaneously held the section X1 title, Lepen Parem. This was because the section belonged to clan 9, the clan of the Nahnken, and all of the three tribal chiefs were members of other clans, while Oaron Mwar was the senior member of clan 9 living in section 1. Of all these chiefs only he had the right to banish a man from the section. Nevertheless, in such situations the X1 often defers to the opinions of the coresident tribal chiefs and frequently consults them.

Most informants use the terms *kaun* and *soumas* interchangeably to designate the X1 of a section. But a Net

298-818—68——4

informant says that the highest tribal titleholder residing in the section is the *soumas,* while the holder of the highest section title, the X1, is the *kaun.* A Kiti man, however, says exactly the opposite. A Sokehs man states that *kaun* is the proper term for the X1, but when the X1 is on a visit elsewhere or is ill and designates someone to take his place temporarily, the substitute is called *soumas.*[19]

Some of the section heads were virtually independent of the tribe. Sometimes this state of affairs resulted from the personal qualities of a particular X1 and persisted only as long as he held office; for example, when Paulino, later Nahnken of Net, was the X1 of section 2 of Net he had a free hand to receive offerings like a Nahnmwarki or a Nahnken; his status was like that of an independent baron in feudal times in Europe. In other sections there was a traditional semiautonomy; this was true of Awak in Uh and of Palikir in Sokehs. Some of the X1 titles are considered to be very high, even when held by commoners; the X1 of section 15 of Kiti, for example, belongs to a nonroyal clan but nevertheless is said to take precedence over chiefs below A2 and B2 in such matters as food distribution at feasts. The A4 of Kiti, who is the son of the A1's mother's sister's daughter and therefore ranks high in his sub-clan as well as in title, is also X1 of section 16, and informants say that it is his X1 title, Kroulikiak, that is the more important and entitles him to more honor. The present X1 of section 27 of Madolenihmw possesses simultaneously a tribal title but never uses it, regarding his section title as more important. The same is true of the X1's of sections 18, 24, and 25 of Madolenihmw; the first of these three men was recently offered a fairly high tribal title but refused it.[20]

## FUNCTIONS OF THE SECTION CHIEF

The X1 must keep an eye on the productive abilities of the various farmsteads of his section. He attends the Cookhouse Counting feasts (q.v.), since he must know how the crops are progressing. He counts all the food articles brought and may instruct the people of any farmstead to do better. One farmstead may be occupied by a family of only five people, another by 30, yet the first will try to do as well as the second; so the X1 may attempt to arrange with the more populated farmsteads to make larger offerings to the high chiefs at feasts, in order that demands on the smaller farmsteads will be less. If a man with a tribal title lives in the section, the X1 comes to him, reports on the difficulties of the small farmsteads, and secures advice.

The X1 was formerly charged with the keeping of those tribal properties (*kepwe en wehi*) not retained by the Nahnmwarki. Formerly each section annually made a tribal canoe (*wahr en wehi*). All of these canoes were delivered simultaneously, by the fourth month of the year, to the Nahnmwarki. Such of the canoes as were not retained by the Nahnmwarki were returned to the custody of the individual sections, but were called upon when needed for the tribe, as on the occasion of a visit in force to another tribe. If a section did not have its canoe ready by the designated time, it had to be destroyed and the people of the section did not attend the ceremony that was held then; an X1 might be demoted for such negligence.

Other objects made for the tribe but retained in the section included pit-breadfruit, sennit, sleeping mats, spears, and various other valuables. Nowadays only large yams and kava are placed in the category of tribal property. They are actually grown on the individually held land, but the concept persists that these goods belong to the Nahnmwarki, even though the land on which they are grown no longer belongs to him but has been issued under private deeds, and they are called for on the occasion of a visit by a Nahnmwarki of another tribe. The X1 would also be called upon to deliver balls of sennit and mats, kept for his Nahnmwarki, especially for such visits, to be distributed as gifts; the visiting Nahnmwarki who received the gifts would redistribute them to his own section heads to keep for him, and they might be returned to the original donor, often with interest, on a return visit.

Usually as many spears were kept in the section as there were male residents, and they were given out before a battle. The Nahnken and other chiefs would count the spears after the fight and thus would know who had fled the field; such flight was a great shame, and a coward might be put to death. The spears were kept in the house of the X1 and in the houses of any tribal chiefs who resided there.

[19] Hahl (1904, p. 10) defines *kaun* as "Obrigkeit, Herrschaft, Herrscher, Haupt" and *soumas* as "Häuptling (=erster in Stamm)."

[20] Father Costigan tells me (1966) that when the present A1 of Madolenihmw was A2 (he was A4 during my 1947 field trip) he was simultaneously X1 of section 8, where he had the title Soulik en Metipw, and it was the latter title that was called out in the food distribution at the section feasts, not his tribal title of Wasai (A2).

Chiefs' fiber kilts, differing from ordinary kilts in that each fiber was crimped along its length, and the loom-woven banana-fiber belts worn especially by men of high rank were made by the section women for the tribe; the Nahnmwarki would keep some for himself and retain others for gifts. Pit-breadfruit might be tribal or section property; each section made a pit near the house of the X1 and the contents were used on the occasion of a visit by the Nahnmwarki to the section or at a section festival; a similar pit was made for the Nahnmwarki from the breadfruit brought to him as offerings on various occasions. The people of each section made communally the three types of seines used in Ponape and deposited them at the home of the X1; the same was done with the communally built section canoe. Anyone might use these articles as he needed them. Today there are no section nets, but some section canoes are kept. The change is due to the encroachment of money economy on the native subsistence patterns; people prefer now to sell their catch, hence they use their own fishing apparatus, whereas formerly they used section property and divided the catch with the X1.

Just as the section heads were tenants (*kohwa*) of the tribal chiefs who owned the sections, or of other chiefs on intermediate levels who in turn held fiefs under higher chiefs, so the commoners were tenants of the X1. (A patch of ground in pre-German days might have several "owners," each holding it under another.) Whether a farmstead reverted to the X1 on its owner's death is not clear; there are many statements to the effect that farmsteads reverted directly to the Nahnmwarki; possibly the reversion to the X1 occurred only if he was a member of the same clan as the Nahnmwarki (or Nahnken, if it was the Nahnken who owned the section). In any case, matrilineal rules of inheritance were usually followed, with only occasional interference by the X1; even if a family died out, the land was not redistributed to other residents of the section but relatives were often brought in from elsewhere to occupy it. If a stranger came from elsewhere to take up residence, the X1 would consult with lesser titleholders in the section and they would decide upon a piece of land to give the man in tenancy. There was usually plenty of vacant land in the interior for this purpose, for Ponape at its maximum population in pre-contact times seems never to have been overpopulated. The stranger would then get a section title from the X1 and would offer first fruits to him.

## CAPITAL SECTIONS

Included in the lists of sections are some designated as *nanwei;* properly these are not sections at all and do not have hereditary X1's, for they are the seats of residence of the Nahnmwarki. There was no such permanent place of residence for the Nahnken, who might live anywhere. The *nanwei* might justifiably be referred to as the capital of the tribe. In Kiti the Nahnmwarki always lived in Sahpwtakai; the term *nanwei* here is used by some informants to include also sections 24 to 34, which constitute most of Kiti proper. In Wene, before its union with Kiti proper, the seat of the highest chief was Eleniong, a farmstead in section 7. The capital of Sokehs was anciently section 16, though some later rulers lived in section 20 as well as in a number of other places. In Net it was section 21. In Uh six farmsteads, all in section 7, comprised the capital: Nanpei, Lukoapoas peiei, Lukoapoas peilong, Nandeke, Tipwenkepwei, and Pohnweinpwel. The first five of these are now privately owned, but the sixth is the site of the modern-day tribal government offices in Uh; it is thus still the seat of government, although the Nahnmwarki no longer lives there. In Madolenihmw, however, a portion of the ancient capital in section 23 is still the residence of the Nahnmwarki. Most Nahnmwarki of Madolenihmw originate in sections 4 or 8, where, until German times, the land of their sub-clan was inherited matrilineally and where they still live until they reach the title of A2; but even today when they become A1 they move to section 23.

The Nahnmwarki and Nahnken are said to ride or sit astride (*dakedake*) the sections where they live. Nowadays they hold land under deeds, like other people; formerly they might have farmsteads of their own before they took office, but upon accession of the titles of A1 or B1 they would give their land in tenancy to near relatives since the first fruits they received would be enough to support them.

Inheritance of the capital does not seem clear. Most informants say that it always went from one Nahnmwarki to the next. Some assert that it proceeded from father to son, but it is difficult to see how the Nahnmwarki could have continued to live on it generation after generation if it passed to another line, as it would with patrilineal inheritance combined with matrilineal clan exogamy. Possibly a part of it was inherited by sons; but it appears that the actual dwelling site of the Nahnmwarki itself (the *pos*) went always to the next Nahnmwarki.

# Promotion and Succession

## THEORY AND PRACTICE

In native theory, as repeatedly expounded by informants, when a title becomes vacant through death or other cause, all men of lower title move up one place in the line of titles affected. In theory, again, all of the higher titles in the two lines are held by members of the two ruling sub-clans, and position in the order of titles follows precisely seniority within the sub-clans. The proper succession to a vacant title is thus supposedly a matter of common knowledge; the Nahnmwarki is the senior man of the royal sub-clan, the successor to a deceased Nahnmwarki should be the man of the same sub-clan of next highest seniority, and this man should previously have held the next lower title, A2. Likewise with the Nahnken and the noble sub-clan and his successor the B2.

The actual state of affairs is, however, quite different. We find that instead of automatic succession there is often much deliberation as to who will actually succeed. For all tribal titles except their own the Nahnmwarki and Nahnken make the decision when vacancies arise; in practice the Nahnken often has the decisive voice, but he usually seeks advice.[21] If the office of Nahnmwarki itself becomes vacant, the first two or three titleholders in the B-line, and sometimes also A2, meet and choose a successor; similarly, if the title of Nahnken is to be disposed of, A1, A2, and perhaps A3 and B2 decide on the new occupant of the office.

The criterion of seniority within the sub-clan is one affected by several modifying considerations. Thus it is not Joseph, the present Nahnken of Net, who is the senior man in his sub-clan, but the present Lepen Net. This title was once the highest in Net, being the equivalent of A1, but when Net adopted the title system of the other four tribes, as previously described, it and the other titles in the older series continued in use but sank to a lower position. It has been given to its present holder, even though he belongs to the B-clan, in a kind of sentimental gesture of harking back to older days. Though the senior man of the noble sub-clan, he was ineligible to become Nahnken because his father was not a member of clan 7. In Net the titles in the A-line are supposed to be held by the men of the senior sub-clan, which bears no name, of clan 7, and those of the B-line by the men of the senior sub-clan, Lukelapalap, of clan 6. Supposedly, in each tribe the royal and noble sub-clans formerly intermarried exclusively, so that because of matrilineal descent all the holders of the titles in the A-line were either fathers or sons of those of the B-line, and vice versa. The present Lepen Net's mother failed to contract such a marriage, whereas the present Nahnken of Net is of proper descent on both sides. Hence, though the Lepen Net is considered as chief of the noble sub-clan, Joseph outranks him in the title series and is B1.

A sub-clan chief is called *meseni en keinek,* a contraction of *mese,* face; *en,* of; *ngi,* tooth; *en,* of; *keinek,* sub-clan. This refers to the smiling, benevolent countenance of the chief, according to some; to his fearsome, wrathful expression, according to others. *Ngi* also can mean a certain hard, refractory wood. All of these alternative translations are suggestive of the attitude of the members of the sub-clan toward their chief and of their expectations of him. But *meseni* is also translatable as first-born. In cases where the Nahnmwarki or Nahnken (or other high-titled man) is not the senior member of his sub-clan he is not usually called *meseni.* It is the above-mentioned Lepen

[21] In Uh the exclusive right of the B1 to choose a new A1 has now become a matter of law, the modern-day council of that tribe having passed an ordinance to that effect following a dispute over succession that is recounted elsewhere. (Information from Father Costigan in 1966.)

Net who is regarded as the *meseni* of the Lukelapalap of clan 6, not the B1 of Net, who is also a member; it was to the Lepen Net that the A6 of Net went in 1947 to ask permission for his daughter (who is also of that sub-clan) to marry, as is the custom, not to the B1. Again, the *meseni* of the sub-clan to which the present A1 of Madolenihmw belongs is not the A1 but the Kulap, a title that always adheres to that *meseni,* whatever other title he may hold.

Relative age is also a modifying factor in matters of seniority. Johannes, the present B4 of Net, also belongs to the same sub-clan as Joseph, and unlike the Lepen Net both of his parents belong to the proper sub-clans. Moreover, he too is senior to Joseph, for his mother's mother was the elder sister of Joseph's mother; in the Ponapean kinship system Johannes is "great maternal nephew" (*wahwahlap*), Joseph is "little maternal uncle" (*uhlaptik*).[22] However, Johannes was allegedly too young at the time of the occurrence of the last vacancy in the title of B1 to be considered eligible. The present B1 was already B5 when Johannes, at the age of 20, got his first title, B12. Supposedly he is next in line for B1.[23]

Although it is generally clear who is most eligible for the two highest offices, occasionally a promotion comes as a surprise to the populace and to the new titleholder himself. In one case the A10 of Sokehs was made Nahnmwarki in a single jump; he had thought he was going to become A2. The reason for this promotion has been forgotten, but usually when promotions come unexpectedly it is because the person actually entitled to the vacancy is considered too young, as Johannes, the B4 of Net, was alleged to be. When Paul, a Nahnmwarki of Kiti, was about 12 years old, he was A2. The old Nahnmwarki died and Paul was scheduled to take the vacant place. A boy may succeed to a title at any age, but Paul's mother refused to allow it, considering that he was too young and would therefore be too vulnerable to sorcery directed against him by jealous persons; instead she advised the Nahnken to appoint another man, Mikel, the father of the present Nahnken, Benito. This man belonged to the proper sub-clan but was well down the seniority list, only A14, and had never expected to become Nahnmwarki. In the community house, where the promotion ceremonies are held, the Nahnken raised the traditional bowl of kava and called the A14 to come up to the main platform from the central area where he was sitting. The latter was greatly surprised and demurred on the ground that he was unworthy. The Nahnken grew angry, came and seized him by the hair of his head, and dragged him up to the main platform, where he presented him with the bowl of kava, put the royal wreath on his head, and proclaimed him Nahnmwarki. Paul remained A2 but received first fruits from Kiti proper; the new Nahnmwarki got first fruits only from Wene. This was the second time Paul had passed up the title, the first opportunity having come when he was only a baby. He was past 30 when the third opportunity came and was accepted.

Sturges, the missionary, describes the making of a new A1 of Kiti in 1852, the old one having died on September 30 of that year. On the third day of a feast prepared for the occasion, in the presence of the assembled people, the Nahnken, holding a cup of kava in his hand, put the question to the A2 and the A3, "Which of you will be the Nahnmwarki?" The question was put three times, without reply; whereupon the Nahnken rose up and threw them both bodily out of the community house. After a few moments of thought he then sent the cup to the A3, thus constituting him the new Nahnmwarki. According to Sturges he did not promote the A2 in order to silence the talk of certain busybodies who were saying, "Of course he will make the A2 the new king, for he is his uncle."

(This description by Sturges raises some questions that are not answerable after this lapse of time. But I would guess that the Nahnken's question was purely a rhetorical one; it is almost impossible for a Ponapean, in public, to be so immodest as to put himself forward or to state an ambition openly. The Nahnken had evidently already made up his mind anyway. The display of temper is entirely in accord with Ponapean expectations of chiefly behavior; the Nahnken here concerned was Nahnku, also called Solomon, a man of unusually strong personality and qualities, to whom we have occasion to refer several times elsewhere. The reference to an uncle-nephew relationship must have to do with a patrilineal one, for mother's brother and sister's son would have been in the same clan and the same line.)

Additional factors are to be considered in choosing a new titleholder, some of them due to foreign influence. The current A2 of Madolenihmw is debarred from becoming Nahnmwarki because he is blind. (Hambruch mentions also ringworm as sufficient cause to prevent accession to the highest offices, but modern informants deny this.) Also, he belongs to the third-ranking sub-clan of the A-clan (clan 13) of Madolenihmw. Moses, the A1, belongs to a branch of the highest sub-clan, the Upwutenmei, as did his predecessor Alexander, his mother's brother, who called Moses back from Kiti, where he had been living, to become A2 and then to succeed to A1. The A3 belongs to the senior branch of the Upwutenmei, which should theoretically rule Madolenihmw, but nearly every-

[22] Actually, though it was Joseph himself who told me that Johannes was his senior, many Ponapeans would dispute this formulation that a man is senior to his mother's mother's younger sister's son.

[23] The source of this information was the B1, whose own ambitions must have been involved. Since there are a number of holders of high titles even younger than 20 years, other factors possibly entered into the decision not to promote Johannes to B1.

one says neither A2 nor A3 will succeed the present A1, but A4, Samuel, the A1's brother, will.[24]

In Uh, the A5 is sister's son to the present Nahnmwarki and next in line, if strict seniority were considered, since there are no younger brothers. His clansmate, the A2, is senior to him in title but junior in blood, being mother's sister's daughter's son to the Nahnmwarki. The A5 should therefore go ahead of the A2 in the succession to the title of Nahnmwarki. But the people believe that the A2 knows more about modern government practices and the A5 may defer to him on this account.[25]

Occasionally a Nahnmwarki will express his wishes regarding his successor on his deathbed, though this is regarded as unusual. In Net, when the last A1, Saturlino, was an old man, the A2 was Benito of his own sub-clan. Actually Benito was senior to Saturlino, his mother having been Saturlino's mother's older sister, but Benito had deferred to his cousin because of his relative youth at the time the previous A1, Eduardo, died and the office became vacant. Benito expected to succeed Saturlino as A1. When Saturlino approached death he took the title of A2 away from Benito and gave it to Max who was A4. Informants' accounts differ as to why he did this; some say he was angry at Benito (and also at the A3) for not helping him during the hard times of World War II; others say Benito agreed to this arrangement amicably, while waiting to become A1, and that Saturlino had dictated a written statement that specified Benito was to follow him. As Saturlino in his dotage lay dying, in 1946, there was much maneuvering for position, with Joseph, the B1, intriguing on behalf of his son Max, who belonged only to the eighth-ranking sub-clan of the royal clan. The Net people were rent in two by the struggle. The A6, Arnold (now the A4), actually went to Benito and anointed him as A1, a highly irregular and improper maneuver. The U.S. Navy had just taken over from the Japanese, and Joseph put Max forward to a naive American administrator as the best candidate and induced him to go to Saturlino and ask him to designate his successor. Although the B1 normally selects the new A1, Joseph evidently felt that he could not bring off such a coup by himself. There was much badgering of the old man, particularly by his sister's daughter, until Saturlino finally acceded and named Max, in the presence of the American. Benito took the usual measure that Ponapeans employ in such a situation; he went into self-exile to Madolenihmw.

Foreign influence has sometimes affected succession in other ways; the present B1 of Uh passed by his mother's brother, the former B2, because of interference by the local Japanese policeman. In Madolenihmw there was even more direct foreign interference with the succession in consequence of the incident of the *Falcon* in 1836. This vessel, a whaleship, was burned, its contents looted, and its captain and some of the crew killed by the A5 of Madolenihmw and his adherents. In revenge, a party of white men in league with the A2 and four or five hundred of his men made war on the A5 and finally captured and hanged him. The A1, whose burial name was Luhkenkasik, was the A5's brother; though less directly implicated in the affair he was shot. The two brothers belonged to the senior sub-clan of clan 13, called Upwutenmei. The man who then became A1 was apparently the A2 who had fought alongside the whites, and he was placed in power with the help of those whites. This man, known as Luhkenkidu (see p. 16), seems to have belonged to a more junior branch of the Upwutenmei, to which all succeeding Nahnmwarkis of Madolenihmw have belonged. (Some people refer to this junior branch as Pahnmei and regard it as a separate sub-clan; as with the other ramifying unilinear groups on Ponape, different people have different opinions as to whether their groups are subdivisions of others or have become independent.) At that time it was also decided by the chiefs that no one of Luhkenkasik's branch could ever rise again above the position of A5.[26]

---

[24] Information from Father Hugh Costigan in 1966 is that when the A2 died in 1960 Samuel, the A4, received the A2 title, and that when Moses in turn died, Samuel became A1.

[25] According to Father Costigan, the A2 did succeed when the A1 died, and the A5 is now the A2. As in the case previously mentioned in Net, the A1 of Uh, Edmund, decreed on his deathbed that he would be succeeded by the A3, Bruno. There had been a dispute over the title of B2, described elsewhere. The A2, Johnny, had not joined the dissident faction but was known to be sympathetic toward it, his own sister was married to the B6, who was a member of the faction; and Edmund continued to retain some resentment against the dissidents after the matter was settled. This was in spite of the fact that both Edmund and Johnny were members of the same sub-clan of clan 2, the Sounpasedo, while Bruno belonged to a different sub-clan, the Sounpeinkon, which once ruled Uh but was long ago deposed. When Edmund died Bruno immediately assumed the role of A1, but after the funeral the B1 formally awarded Johnny the title. A stalemate developed, and both factions went around Ponape visiting the Nahnmwarkis of the other tribes to get their support. It was finally decided to employ the modern-day institution of a popular vote, and Johnny won the election. It was after this that the Uh council passed the ordinance previously referred to giving the B1 sole right to choose a new A1 in Uh.

[26] Moses, who was A1 in 1947, however, had broken this tradition by elevating a member of Luhkenkasik's branch to the position of A3. Father Costigan says (1966) that when Moses was dying the chiefs agreed that all titles would move up one place; Samuel, the brother of Moses, was then A2, so he became A1, and the A3 became A2. The Madolenihmw chiefs have agreed that in the future there will be no skipping of places in the hierarchy, so it is possible for the new A2 some day to become A1 and for his branch of Upwutenmei to be restored to the power they held before 1836. But since both A2 and A3 are older than Samuel, the present A1, and will probably predecease him, it is likely that the A4, who is of the same sub-clan as Samuel and his predecessor Moses, will succeed and that the second branch will remain in power.

In Kiti the B4 should succeed to Nahnken; Kiti is unique among the five tribes in that the B2 never belongs to the noble clan but is always a member of clan 9 and hence is not eligible to become B1; and the B3 title is held at present by a commoner. The B4 is therefore next in line, being next senior in the B1's sub-clan. But the present B7 also belongs to the proper sub-clan, is the Secretary of the tribe under the civil administration, and is familiar with office procedure, and many people think he will succeed.

In Madolenihmw there are several possible contenders for the position of Nahnken. The present B2 belongs to one of the proper clans (clan 2) but not to the proper sub-clan (Sounlehdau). The man considered best versed in office work is the A14, who is "acting Nahnken" under the American administration; though he holds an A title he belongs properly in the B-line, since he is a member of the second clan (clan 9) of the two clans which in this tribe are noble. He belongs to the same sub-clan as the Nahnken, being a son of the Nahnken's sister's daughter, hence is eligible.[27] The Nahnmwarki, it is said, however, will probably choose as next Nahnken his own son, who is a member of clan 18 and is presently B6; the Nahnmwarki has not followed the traditional pattern of marrying a woman only of the opposite line but has married instead a commoner. If the son becomes Nahnken, he will be the first holder of that title in this tribe who was in neither clan 2 or clan 9.[28]

In Uh the situation is more complex. Here the Nahnmwarki traditionally puts his own son up as next in line for Nahnken, whatever his clan may be. Informants elsewhere in Ponape often say that the incumbent Nahnken is actually demoted when a new Nahnmwarki of Uh steps in, being replaced by the latter's son. Study of past successions does not bear this out; [29] it may be that the reference is to an ancient practice that has not been followed in recent years; but it is true that the son of any past or present Nahnmwarki is raised high in the B-line. The last three Nahnkens have successively been members of clans 9, 8, and 5. The present Nahnken obtained his office, according to informants, by currying favor with the Japanese and by false accusations against the previous Nahnken; he is a member of clan 5, which never held the office before, and he is not the son of a Nahnmwarki. His younger brother should follow him if the principle of seniority were followed, since he is next in line in the clan; but informants say that the B2 will probably succeed, since his father was a Nahnmwarki [30] and since the Nahnken's brother holds only a small title of Uh.[31]

Previously (p. 16) I referred to the fact that in Net all but one of the first fifteen titleholders of the A-line belonged to the royal clan, while only nine of the first 15 B-titled men belonged to one of the two clans regarded as noble. In Uh the contrast is even more pronounced; of the first 12 A-titles, 11 are held by clan 2, the royal clan here. The one exception, A6, is held by Oliver Nanpei, a wealthy landholder, who is also A6 of Kiti, and who has influence far beyond what his title suggests. Of these 11 titles, eight are held by members of one sub-clan of clan 2, the other three by men of three other sub-clans. But in the B-line, the first 12 titleholders belong to nine different clans.

It is especially in the foregoing description of affairs in Uh that it becomes clear that statements by natives that such-and-such a sub-clan constitutes the only legitimate royal or noble class are to be discounted as idealizations, based perhaps on knowledge of a limited period of history or a nostalgic harking back to things as they are supposed once to have been, and sometimes on personal interests. This is particularly applicable to the B-line, where shift of power seems to have occurred most often. The earlier remark (on page 18) that a commoner in Kiti can advance only as high as B3 now requires qualification. In Kiti clan 11 has been the B-clan for many generations, having replaced clan 17 more than 100 years ago; the A and B clans having preserved the custom of intermarriage, there was always available to become B1 a clan 11 man with the proper clan 4 (A-clan) father. But the present A1's wife is of clan 7, which in Kiti is a commoner clan; a child born to her now would be Born Upon the Ditch (see page 18) and nearly everyone (except members of clan 11) says that he would by custom become B1 ahead of any brothers, real or classificatory, of clan 11; thus clan 7 would become noble. The A1 and his wife are not likely to have more children, but the A3 who is a potential successor and who is sister's daughter's son to the A1 (hence of the same sub-clan, Lipohnroahlong, as the A1) is young and his wife is still having children; the wife is of clan 17, and any son born after A3 became A1 would be Born Upon the Ditch and hence would outrank other candidates for the title of B1, member of clan 17 though he would be, again displacing clan 11 as the noble clan. Therefore the people of clan 11 are pressing hard for A2, who has a clan 11 wife, to succeed

27 This man, who was A14 in 1947, subsequently fell out of favor, Father Costigan says. He is now B11.

28 The foregoing, given in present tense, is from 1947 notes. In 1963 I learned that this prediction, upon death of the old Nahnken, had become fact. Also the new Nahnmwarki, Samuel, is married to a woman of clan 4, so it is possible that that clan may some day provide the Nahnken.

29 Gulick in his vocabulary does say that the Bl is "usually" the son of the A1.

30 I also have the conflicting information that his father was a younger twin brother of a Nahnmwarki named Eluit and died when he was A12; but the Nahnmwarki would have been regarded and addressed as father.

31 The B2 actually did succeed, about 1955.

A1, even though A2 belongs to a low ranking sub-clan of clan 4, the Sounkiti, which once ruled Kiti proper but has not ranked high since the Kiti-Pehleng war, when the last Sounkiti A1 was killed.

Succession to the title of Nahnmwarki or Nahnken by a member of an "improper" clan is not a new phenomenon, even though it causes grave headshaking by the old men. A number of instances are recorded from pre-Spanish times. The A-line of Net has traditionally belonged to clan 7 for many generations, but the eighth A1 (then bearing the title Lepen Net) before the present one designated his own son, of clan 6, to succeed him.[32] The B-line of Sokehs has traditionally been in hands of clan 6 since the precontact conquest of Net and Sokehs by clan 7, which became the A-line; but the succession of clan 6 members to the title of B1 has been interrupted by pre-Spanish Nahnkens who belong to clans 5 and 13 and who gained office because their fathers were particularly powerful Nahnmwarki.

Martial exploits in the past often would advance a man out of turn. During the wars with the Spanish the Nahnken Alexander of Madolenihmw fled to Kiti to take refuge. Nicholas, a man of an eligible sub-clan but of low station because his father was a member of the commoner clan 8, fought bravely to protect the Nahnmwarki, Paul, and was rewarded with the vacant title of Nahnken. When Alexander returned, he was made B2 and had to wait for Nicholas to die before he could become B1 again.

There are a number of instances of accession to office by violent means and of the overthrowing of a whole line of titleholders by another line. In the semihistorical legend of the conquest of Ponape by invaders from Kusaie, the pre-Nahnmwarki line of kings known as Saudeleur was replaced by the new Nahnmwarki line; but this was essentially the overthrow of the then ruling clan in Madolenihmw, clan 6, by clan 13. In Uh one sub-clan of clan 2, the Sounpeinkon, formerly furnished the chiefs of the A-line. One day all the men of this line went fishing and during their absence another sub-clan of the same clan, the Sounpasedo, held a war feast and laid their strategy. When fishermen return from fishing they carry their catch to the community house to be distributed and receive in exchange land produce from the other people who have assembled to await their coming. When the Sounpeinkon arrived at the community house they found that the Sounpasedo had taken all the places of honor on the main platform and had crowned themselves with royal wreaths. The Sounpeinkon were few in number and retired without a fight, giving up all their titles to their kinsmen, who still constitute the A-line of Uh.[33]

Another coup d'état occurred in Kiti; here the now extinct Inanweies or Liesenpal sub-clan of clan 4 displaced the Liesenpahlap sub-clan of the same clan as the A-line in a bloodless war that found the latter fleeing at the sound of the triton trumpets of the approaching enemy. The aggrandizement of a junior branch of the senior sub-clan of the A clan (clan 13) of Madolenihmw, at the expense of a more senior branch, has already been alluded to. A saying, "The younger stands in front" (*mehtik uhmas*), refers to the fact that junior sub-clans are sometimes in political status superior to that of senior sub-clans of the same clan, and also to cases where a man holds a higher title than his older brother.

War as a means of accession to power is nowadays a thing of the past; it has been replaced by the law courts of the successive foreign administrations and in American times by elections, in certain instances. Other means are sometimes also employed when disputes arise. In 1953 Edmund, the A1 of Uh, attempted to resurrect an old title, Soumaka en Mesentakai, and to award that title to the Oun Souna, X1 of section 6. The title is one of historical significance and power, and it was Edmund's intention to place the Oun Souna in charge of a subdivision of Uh containing about six sections. Various people demurred on the ground that the title Soumaka en Mesentakai was one that belonged to or was the equivalent of Nahnmwarki, and that they would thus be serving two Nahnmwarkis. The B2 in particular objected very strenuously. At a feast he spoke his mind, was told by the A1 to hold his tongue, and stalked out in a temper. On the way to his canoe he told his people to take a particular yam from the pile of yams outside the community house, claiming it as his share, although the food had not yet been divided. The Oun Souna followed indignantly, an altercation arose at the shore, and the Oun Souna was stabbed and died. Whereupon the A1 deposed the B2 and awarded his title to the Oun Souna's sister's son, who had been B5. A number of high-titled men, especially men of sections 10 and 11, immediately resigned their titles; these included the B3, B6, A5, and the X1 of section 11. The dispute reached the law courts. But before a decision was given the people agreed to call in Moses, the A1 of Madolenihmw, the senior tribe. Since the time of Isohkelekel, who was the semilegendary first A1 of Madolenihmw, and of his son, Lepenien, who was the first B1 of Madolenihmw and the later the first A1 of Uh, the Nahnmwarki of Madolenihmw has had a kind of arbitration role in the

[32] The fifth A1 before the present one ruled about 1875, which should place the eighth well into pre-Spanish or even precontact times.

[33] Another version of this affair omits the fishing incident; the Sounpasedo considered the Sounpeinkon too weak to look after state affairs properly, hence seized power.

other tribes, but especially in Uh, and can assume authority when it becomes obvious that the local Nahnmwarki cannot solve his problems. Moses sounded out public opinion in Uh and decided in favor of Edmund and of his appointment of the B2, and the titles of the other dissidents were returned to them.

## IRREGULARITIES IN POLITICAL ADVANCEMENT

Thus, in spite of native theory, methodical progression up the ladder of titles is a principle of great flexibility. Clan seniority principles conflict with it. A boy might skip several places simply because he was the last of his sub-clan, and therefore outranked men of junior sub-clans who had achieved higher titles heretofore because they were older. Industry and obedience to the Nahnmwarki and Nahnken might produce differential rates of promotion, a sluggard being passed over to give preference to a more active man. Military feats formerly were also important factors.

Sometimes a title awarded to a member of a clan that is neither royal nor noble remains in that clan through force of tradition. Thus the B2 of Kiti, as already described, is always a member of clan 9, instead of clan 11 as are the rest of the holders of B titles, because of certain historical reasons; he is succeeded always by a member of his clan. The present B2 of Net, also mentioned earlier, belongs to clan 2, instead of to the noble clans 6 or 9. He holds the position because of his admirable personal qualities, and the B1 says that he will probably be succeeded by his sister's son (who of course is also in clan 2). Another example is that of the title of A7 of Kiti which, until its present incumbent received it, had been held for a number of generations by members of clan 11, the B-line in Kiti. The reason for this state of affairs goes back to the series of wars in Kiti already described, when the ruling lines were overthrown by dissidents from the section of Pehleng, and Wene, hitherto independent of Kiti proper but ruled by the same clans, joined forces with her deposed brethren and reconquered Kiti, installing Wene's priest-king, the Soukise, as the Nahnmwarki of the now combined tribe. A man of Pehleng who had taken the title of A7 was killed during the battle by Mahsohr, a man of clan 11. For this feat Mahsohr was granted this very title of A7, and it remained in the clan for several generations. There is today some resentment against the present Nahnken for having returned the title to the royal clan, which holds the other A titles. A clan in this position of holding a title properly belonging to another clan comes to think it has proprietary rights to it, especially if the first member to achieve it did so through warlike deeds, and strenuously objects if the title is given to someone else.

Analysis of individual careers shows that progress in the hierarchy of titles is far more often a series of skips than a step-by-step rise, the factors previously described being the reasons. Francisco, a former A2 of Sokehs, became A2 in one jump from A5. (In Sokehs in those days the A2 was the ruler, and for legendary reasons there was no Nahnmwarki for several generations until Spanish times.) This was because the A4 belonged to a nonroyal clan, and the A3, though of the proper clan (clan 7), was junior by blood to Francisco. For similar reasons a Nahnken of Sokehs, Oundoleririn,[34] jumped from B7 to B1. The present Nahnmwarki of Kiti first held the Enipeinpah section title of Nahlik en Enipein (X4 of that section), then Souan en Enipein (X2), then successively the tribal titles of A9, A3, and A1. The present Nahnken of Kiti has held only three titles in his lifetime, becoming B12 as a small child, then B4, and finally B1. The present Nahnken of Madolenihmw at the age of ten acquired the title Souwel, then Nahnsahu, and then Nahnkrou, all titles of Mesihsou (section 6 of Madolenihmw); as a young man he acquired his first tribal title, B12 of Madolenihmw, after which he was B2, and now for many years B1.

In succession to the A1 and B1 titles the ideal, if often not actual, order of preference is: first, the brothers of the previous holder of the title in order of birth; second, the oldest sister's sons in order of birth; third, sons of younger sisters in order of the sisters' births; fourth, male parallel cousins of the same sub-clan in order of their mothers' births. The succession thus follows clan seniority. Each candidate should have a father of the proper sub-clan, that sub-clan which furnishes the titleholders of the opposite line. Only after men with proper fathers are exhausted does a member of the sub-clan with a father of commoner clan membership come into consideration, as has been the case of the last four A1's of Madolenihmw. When the sub-clan is exhausted, the next senior sub-clan of the same clan inherits.

If the logical successor lives in another tribe, he may be called back to accept the vacancy. During the last years

[34] This is properly a title but, as is common in Ponape, is used as a given name. Sometimes a man will be referred to by a title he once held in lieu of using his actual but secret name. A title is frequently given as a name when a child acquired the title at birth; for example, in 1947 the B8 of Madolenihmw, a boy, had both name and title of Ouririn.

of Pwas, who was a Nahnken of Sokehs, his sister's son, Soukep, who lived in Net and previously had had no Sokehs title, came to Sokehs to wait for Pwas to die so that he might take his place. Soukep was given the title of B9 in the interim. But when Pwas died, the Nahnmwarki insisted on another man, Soulik en Soledi,[35] taking his turn first. Soukep then accepted the title of A4 and became B1 only after Soulik had died.

Soukep's career illustrates a number of points. In lieu of a brother, Pwas' sister's son was Pwas' logical successor, since in clan seniority he outranked Soulik en Soledi. But Soulik en Soledi was an older man, he was a Nahnmwarki's son, and he had married a Nahnken's daughter. These factors outweighed mere seniority in the opinion of the then Nahnmwarki, and Soukep was willing therefore to defer his promotion. Such factors are still more important when members of more than one sub-clan (or more than one clan, as in the B-line of Madolenihmw) are equally eligible to provide a successor. They are subtle factors, which are weighed one against another and make prediction difficult for an outsider, even though he may have recorded all pertinent genealogies.

Deference to a junior is not infrequent. When a number of brothers are living, the younger ones may sometimes allow their sisters' children to go ahead of them; or when two sisters have sons, some of those of the elder may step aside to give their cousins a chance to advance. In a hypothetical case expounded by a Kiti native, if the senior sister had three sons the first would be A1, the second A3, the third perhaps A7, leaving the intervals to be filled by sons of the second or third sisters; but in the promotion to A1, A3 would normally succeed his brother.

The temporary acceptance of an A-line title by Soukep also reveals how freely future candidates for the position of A1 or B1 migrate from one line to the other during their early careers. Such lack of restriction to one line is ordinarily characteristic only of sons of a Nahnmwarki or Nahnken.

Factors involved in promotion include also judicious choice of a wife. Thus the previous A2 of Kiti owed his position to the fact that he married the sister of the Nahnken, who was his mother's brother's son; he belonged to the A clan (clan 4) and, in fact, to a senior sub-clan thereof, Liesenpahlap, the one that ruled Wene before the conquest of Kiti proper; but this sub-clan was deposed long ago and has sunk in rank, and he would not have risen so high in the hierarchy except for his marriage. The present A2 of Kiti belongs to still another sub-clan (Sounkiti) of clan 4 and advanced this high only because he married the daughter of the earlier A2 and the Nahnken's sister. (See also the section "Feminine Titles," p. 47.)

Promotion through martial exploits and through service for and tribute to the chiefs is discussed elsewhere.

## PROMOTION CEREMONIAL

The duty of making promotions belongs to the Nahnken, who, however, is supposed to consult with the Nahnmwarki. The Nahnken also does the actual conferring of a tribal title (*ta mwar* or *pwuk mwar,* to raise up to a title). First he makes a short speech recounting the good qualities of the man about to be promoted. Then he performs the Kava Holding ritual (*sapwsakau*), that is, he takes a cup of kava in both hands and raises it high before him, and he says loudly, "This is the coconut shell vessel of ———" (*Met ngarangar en* ———). The title represented by the dash in this formula is conceived to be in the vessel. Then the man being promoted comes up to the main platform of the community house where the Nahnken is standing; if he is a member of the A-line, he will have been in the central ground level area of the community house, as most members of this line should be. With him comes as his sponsor the senior member of his line, next below the Nahnmwarki or Nahnken, that is, the A2 or B2; but if these are not present, the next in seniority takes his place; or it may be his sub-clan chief or his mother's eldest brother. The sponsor, if the man to be promoted is not a member of the royal or noble clans, is most likely to be his sub-clan chief. Sometimes he comes up alone and takes the cup, then he calls the sub-clan chief to come and drink it. The function of the sponsor is to make a *lapweiepwei;*[36] that is, he takes the vessel of kava from the Nahnken, turns toward the assembled people so that the Nahnmwarki and Nahnken are behind him, says "This is our cup," and takes a draught; then the newly promoted man and his sponsor return to their proper places. Frequently, before he drinks, he will call out the names of all the distinguished members of the sub-clan who are present. Occasionally the candidate for the title himself drinks. Rarely the Nahnmwarki functions instead of the Nahnken, on a special occasion such as when he is elevating his own son.

[35] This again is a title used as a name.

[36] Apparently some religious ceremonial was once connected with this performance, since the term *lapweiepwei* is also applied to a prayer made to a spirit by a soothsayer.

At the coronation of a Nahnmwarki, the Nahnken places a wreath of *Ixora carolinensis* (an *elin katieu*) on the new ruler's head. (This royal wreath is also called *nihn* or *ninnin*. A wreath worn by a commoner is called *mware.*) Similarly, the Nahnmwarki crowns the Nahnken when the latter assumes office. The A2 is supposed to crown the B2 and vice versa; but their crown is *elin seir,* made of the blossoms of the tree of this name (*Fagraea sair;* called *pwur* in Kiti). The crowning is followed by the drinking of the vessel of kava. Men promoted to titles lower than A2 and B2 are not supposed to be crowned but only to drink the kava, but nowadays it is done for men of much lower title. No one except the A1 and B1 is supposed to wear a wreath of *Ixora,* unless the blossoms are mixed with other flowers.[37]

The Nahnmwarki of Madolenihmw was formerly crowned in secret at night at a place called Peipwel, in section 26 of Madolenihmw. Lepen Wapar, the X1, was custodian of the place. The crowning followed immediately upon the death of the old Nahnmwarki, which was likewise kept secret for fear of anarchy and civil war. Peipwel was a stone structure where the Nahnken and seven other men of title awaited the Nahnmwarki-to-be, who was led thither by the Nahntu in a torchlight procession. (By another account the Nahnken and his party, who came by canoe, were met at the shore of section 26 by Nahntu, who with the Kirounaip led the procession to Peipwel. The Kirounaip ["Steward of the drum"] had particular duties connected with the drums that were part of the arrangements.) After the wreath of flowers was placed on the Nahnmwarki's head (or after he was struck by the Nahnken with a turmeric plant, according to Luelen) the Nahnken took in his hands a stone (a short basalt prism, says Luelen) upon which two *sedei* had been laid. (A *sedei* is a coconut pinna whose ends are folded together in a peculiar manner to form a crown and which is worn on the head for various ritual purposes. See Plate 5.) He then thrust the stone toward the Nahnmwarki's face, as though he were about to strike him, while he uttered a phrase meaning roughly, "Useful and long reign." If the Nahnmwarki flinched, it was a sign that he would soon die. Then all went to a place where a certain stone stands; all the people were called to assemble and prepare a feast in the community house there, and when the new Nahnmwarki took his place on the main platform, they would know for the first time that the old Nahnmwarki was dead and see who had been chosen to be their new ruler. The secrecy involved and the drum beating (at least two sizes of drums in Kiti) applied to all the tribes.

The foregoing description was obtained largely from modern informants. The missionary L. H. Gulick, writing in 1855, describes similar ceremonies that, however, are different in some details. The Nahnmwarki of Madolenihmw, Luhkenkidu, who in 1836 succeeded Luhkenkasik of *Falcon* fame, died in September 1854 during a smallpox epidemic and was in turn succeeded by Luhkenmweiu. Then on June 5, 1855, Luhkenmweiu died. He was buried immediately, as was the custom, enveloped in mats and together with all his belongings. Then guns were fired to announce the death to the people. The A2 now became A1, but for some reason the usual immediate installation did not take place. On June 7 the new A1 with six of the highest chiefs and four priests went in canoes to a place in the artificial islands of Nan Madol (which, from the description given, is evidently Pahnkedira). Here a shed had been erected and in it two priests pounded kava and brought out cups to the chiefs who sat in a line in order of rank. Prayers were said over the chiefs, sips of kava were drunk, miniature cups were stuck on reeds before a certain stone, and circles and lines were drawn on the A1's hand. Gulick terms this the religious inauguration. Then the whole party returned to the community house at the capital and all the chiefs were confirmed in their new offices by further cups of kava over which the different titles had been pronounced. In referring to this last as the political inauguration, Gulick says that more often it came ahead of the religious one. Then on June 9 the party visited another place that is evidently the aforementioned Peipwel. Here the new A1 sat before an altar consisting of a pile of stones, with peculiarly folded coconut leaves around his neck and arms and in his ear lobes, and the other chiefs sat some distance from him. The B1, serving as both chief and priest, said incantations over a cup of kava, gave it to the A1, who drank, then threw the cup under a stone of the altar.

Nowadays, the ceremonial is much simplified, and the ritual frequently consists only of handing the recipient of the new title a bowl of kava or a piece of sugar cane. On one occasion that the writer witnessed, which was at a funeral feast, the Nahnmwarki of Kiti only delegated a man, apparently arbitrarily chosen for this one occasion, to stand, announce the successor to the dead man's title, and counsel everyone to respect him as such; the new appointee, though present, made no acknowledgment.

All tribal titles except those of Nahnmwarki and Nahnken must be confirmed by a title-payment feast (*iraramwar* or *kapasmwar*) held in the community house and given for the Nahnmwarki. At 1947 values this was estimated by natives to cost, for nearly all titles, something like $200 worth of pigs, yams, kava, etc. Not all the cost is borne by the man who is being promoted, since his family contributes a large part to it.

Vacancies in section titles are filled by the X1 of the section, but the X1 himself, though often chosen by the people of the section, must be confirmed in office by the

---

[37] Hambruch speaks of the Nahnmwarki giving his crown to someone else as a method of conferring honor upon him, but my informants had never heard of this practice.

Nahnmwarki or Nahnken, depending on which is overlord of the section. Succession is not automatic; the Nahnmwarki or Nahnken usually agrees with the wishes of the people, but sometimes he may consider that the candidate is unsuitable and reject him, then a second choice is necessary. He might then choose another member of the same sub-clan, or the dead man's son, or someone else. The title-payment feast is then made by the chosen man to the Nahnmwarki or Nahnken. After the feast is made, the title cannot be taken away without cause, but if the promotion is not confirmed by a feast, the title is revoked.

Lower titleholders of the section make their title-payment feast to the X1, who alone makes the appointments, and the tribal chiefs do not attend. Similarly the X1 performs the office of installation for the head of a farmstead; this practice continues today, even though the actual inheritance is according to the terms of the German deeds and the confirmation by the X1 has therefore become purely formal.

Elsewhere than Net each man who is being promoted makes a separate feast, and there are no standards for his lavishness. In Net the present Nahnmwarki and Nahnken, with their customary acumen, have systematized promotion feasts by having them all held in December and January of each year, so that a number of titles are simultaneously paid for; the payments also have been standardized, so that each man is required to pay a pig, a large kava plant, and one or two 2-man yams. The same pair of chiefs has similarly consolidated the honor feasts (q.v.) given by the various sections into a single feast.

On the same day that an X1 dies the appropriate chief, Nahnmwarki or Nahnken, is supposed to come and bury him and award the title and, until German times, the land to his successor. The section, which was held in fief under the Nahnmwarki or Nahnken or indirectly under them through intermediary chiefs, theoretically reverted upon the death of the X1 to be reissued to his successor. Informants almost always say it reverted to the Nahnmwarki; when pressed for details they usually give, instead, the title of some chief who held the land under the Nahnmwarki or Nahnken. The chief of any area is still expected to attend the burial of his tenants; on one occasion the writer was forced to postpone a trip with A6 of Kiti because one of the A6's tenants had died and, as he put it, his people would have become "discouraged" had he not gone to the funeral and funeral feast.

In former days all work would cease as soon as it was known that a section chief or a Nahnmwarki had died, and a state of lawlessness would prevail. To avoid anarchy and outbreaks of violence the dead chief was immediately buried in secret and, ordinarily, the people would not learn of what had happened until his successor was inducted. When the A1 of Madolenihmw died in 1854, Gulick reports his immediate train continued to talk as though he yet lived. Gulick, in describing the funeral of another high chief in 1853, states that from the moment of death until the grave was closed—during which time the corpse was rubbed with oil, wrapped in mats, dressed in his finery, the grave dug, and the chief's woven belts, bead ornaments, adzes and other belongings placed in the grave with him—a total of 25 minutes elapsed. Hundreds of people joined for several hours in the howling, shrieking, and contortions that followed, and formal wailing in set phrases by relatives continued for weeks, the mourners all with shaved heads. (The standardized mourning phrases are still heard nowadays, but most of the other customs have vanished, including the hastiness of burial, which has been superseded by Christian practices.) The missionary Sturges, in 1856, describes in similar terms the funeral of a high-ranking woman, the aunt of the B1 of Kiti, and states that feasting all day and dancing all night followed for a week at Ronkiti, where the B1 lived, and then for another week at Wene, where the A1 lived. All of these early reports, including others by the missionary Doane, refer to lawlessness and to general destruction of coconut trees, yams, and dogs at the place where the dead chief lived and to a lesser degree elsewhere. His lands and other property would be taken and divided up among the other chiefs, sometimes in an orderly way, but often a rush was made by all to seize what they could. This was true after a commoner died too; all his accumulated balls of twine, his mats, sometimes even his house, would be appropriated, and the widow turned out. My own informants give similar descriptions and add that for a time afterward many people would feign madness, run about wildly besmearing themselves with mud and throwing dung at each other, lose their normal inhibitions in dress and speech, and sometimes engage in sexual license. It was to avoid these excesses that the attempt at secrecy was made and that the new A1 was immediately installed in office; ideally the general populace was not to know anything until they were summoned to the feast in the community house and saw the new incumbent in the place of honor on the main platform.

# Other Titles

## PRIESTLY TITLES

Although Hambruch states that the now extinct priests (*samworou*) were Royal Children, this seems to have been true only of the higher ones. The principal priest was the Nahlaimw who today is the B2 chief. In Madolenihmw he could be a member of either clan 2 or clan 9, the two clans that constitute the Royal Children in that tribe; but whichever of these two clans the Nahnken belonged to, the Nahlaimw had to belong to the other, as is also true today. The second highest priest, the Nahnapas (B4 chief today), however, had to be of the same clan as the Nahnken. The third priest, Soulik en Madolenihmw, could likewise belong to either of the two clans, but the lesser priests might belong to any clan; in Madolenihmw they were Oaron Maka, Serihnei en Patele, Seioar en Wilek, Ninakap en Temwen, Sihpwil Lihken, Kroun en Mwalok, Lepen Souleng. One additional lesser priest, Soused en Roti, a title that plays a significant role in the Isohkelekel story and which persists today, however, has always been a member of clan 2.

There are two similar lists of priests, presumably applicable to Kiti, from natively written manuscripts. One by Luelen gives the Nahlaimw (the present-day B2) and the Nahnapas (B4) as the first two priests, as in Madolenihmw. Soulik en Kiti is given as the fourth priest, whereas in the previous paragraph I have given Soulik en Madolenihmw as third. Soulik in the various columns of Table 4 is today B8 to B14. The third priest was Nahnkei (B6–B11 in Table 4). Then followed Nahnsaumw (B10–12), Soulikin Sapawas (B15), Nahnawa Iso (A18), and Nahnsou Wehi (A20). The other manuscript, by a man named Silten, probably written about 1935, lists Ounsona third, Nahnkei fourth, then follow Soulik, Oun (possibly my Ou, B8–13), Nahnsaumw, and Soulikin Sapawas.

The history of these priestly titles is not clear. Several informants say they formed a separate line in former times, a statement the two native manuscripts would support, though also known as Royal Children; they say the priestly titles were fitted into the present-day B-line by Paul, Nahnmwarki of Madolenihmw in Spanish times. According to these informants the other tribes then copied Paul's scheme. Presumably this was because priestly duties had become defunct after Christianization. Whether or not this is true, it is certain that the Nahlaimw succeeded the Nahnken in office, so whether there was one line or two lines of Royal Children, they functioned much as the B-line does today.

A number of titles apparently antedate the titles of the present-day A and B series. Most of these do not bear the prefix "nahn," in contrast with the majority of modern titles. The native explanation most commonly encountered is that the Nahnmwarki-Nahnken series began only with the semihistorical conquest of the island by Isohkelekel; before that, Ponape was unified under a single, tyrannical ruler whose title was Saudeleur. If a ranked order of titles existed under the Saudeleur it is no longer recalled, but many of the titles of that era persist outside the present ranked A and B series and are accorded high honors. Such chiefs as Lepen Moar, Lepen Deleur, Lepen Palikir, Soulik en Awak, and Nahmadau en Pehleng, for example, receive the third or fourth share of food at a feast. Some of them nowadays are only section chiefs, such as Lepen Palikir and Soulik en Awak, but it is apparent that their influence was once much greater; Palikir, for example, was always a semiautonomous area, only nominally part of the tribe of Sokehs, and its ruler, the Lepen Palikir, frequently acted entirely independently. The Soulik en Awak was likewise largely independent of the rest of Uh, once joining with his Catholic co-religionists in

Net and Sokehs in a war against the Protestant area of the remainder of Uh, Madolenihmw, and Kiti. This event was in Spanish times but is indicative of a pre-Spanish cleavage. The Nahmadau en Pehleng, now only a section head, formerly had under him two sections besides his own; the story of how a holder of that title overthrew the Nahnmwarki of Kiti and for a period ruled in his stead, until Wene reconquered Kiti, has already been related.

Some of these earlier titles seem to have combined many priestly offices with their chiefly duties; some of them until relatively recently seem to have been held by priests who had temporal powers as well. Such was the Saum en Long, a high priestly title in Kiti, who ruled section 21. The ruler of Wene was Soukise, who was similarly a priest-king. These priests were apparently of a different category from those in the later "nahn" series such as B2 and B4, who seem to have had no temporal functions until quite recently.

Several religious cults devoted to worship of different gods seem to have existed in various parts of Ponape, and Wene was apparently the center of this development. Hambruch (1932 II, pp. 130 f.) discusses these cults and their priests rather briefly; already in his time memory of them was fragmentary. Each cult seems to have had its separate body of priests, with their own sets of titles, apart from those already discussed. Also a major division into two levels of priesthood cut across the cults, the upper level known by the general term for priest, *samworou,* the lesser priests called *laiap* or *leiap.* But native information about them is today so scanty as to make it unprofitable to discuss further their connection with the political organization.

## TITLES OF ADDRESS AND TITLES OF REFERENCE

The holders of most of the older titles, i.e., the ones antedating the "nahn" series, have a special title of address, *pwoud* or *pwoudo.* These include Lepen Net, Lepen Palikir, Lepen Enimwahn, Lepen Moar, Saum en Long, Kroun en Lehdau, Soulik en Awak, Lepen Wenik, Nahmadau en Pehleng, Kirou Meir, Lepen Deleur en Kiti, and Kelahk en Takaiu. Gulick (1872, p. 39) gives the term *pwoudo* (which he spells *pauto*) as another title of the Nahnken, but it is not used as such today. It is the same word as the word for spouse, in reference to the close bond between chief and commoner.

The Nahnmwarki also has special titles used in address. The Nahnmwarki of Madolenihmw is addressed as Isipau [38] and has the additional titles of reference Soumaka en Ololap, Lepen Seipel, an a third, secret one. The Nahnmwarki of Kiti has Rohsa, Soukise, and Soumaka en Long as additional titles; the Rohsa title has been awarded to the present A6, and Soumaka en Long to the former A12, but they are properly the Nahnmwarki's; Soukise was the ruler of Wene, and when one of the holders of this title ousted the Nahmadau en Pehleng from his brief occupation of Kiti proper and united all of modern Kiti under his rule, he retained his old title while assuming that of Nahnmwarki as well.

In Uh, the Nahnmwarki bears the additional title of address of Sangiro.[39] In Net, the present Nahnmwarki (who has replaced the former ruler Lepen Net) has three additional titles.[40] The highest chief of Sokehs was for a long period the Wasai, who is chief A2 in the other tribes, and his title of address was Nahnpwutak, "Lord Boy," which is that of every Wasai.[41] He also seems to have been addressed as Isoeni, "Sir Ghost," but a particular ruler of Sokehs who lived about 1870 is usually meant when that term is used. All Nahnmwarki are likewise known as Wasa Lapalap,[42] "Important Place," though Luelen and some informants apply the term only to the Nahnmwarki of Madolenihmw; each Nahnmwarki is also known as Mwohnsapwaka, a form of "First of the Land," an expression already discussed.

Each of these terms has its special use. In Madolenihmw, Wasa Lapalap is held by some to be preferable to Isipau as a form of address for the Nahnmwarki. In Uh, Sangiro is preferred. Isoeni was used in place of Nahnpwutak during a period of mourning for the dead A2 of Sokehs. In direct address to a Nahnmwarki, Wasa Lapalap is used to attract his attention, Mwohnsapwaka

[38] In Gulick's vocabulary this title seems to be applied to the Nahnmwarkis of all tribes, not just Madolenihmw; he defines it as "the highest *monjap* title in a tribe (equivalent to *nanamaraki* . . .)," not making a distinction between address and reference. It is sometimes used nowadays for the A1 of Uh too. It may be derived from the name of the god Isopau.

[39] The word may be related to the name of the god Sahngoro.

[40] One of these titles, Soulik en Daun, listed on p. 19 as having been that of the A2 of Net until German times when the Nahnmwarki-Nahnken series of titles was adopted, has more recently been given by Max, the A1, to Benito, who was Max's rival for the title of A1 and who had lost a lawsuit that he brought in the American courts in an attempt to gain it. In 1947 the title Soulik en Daun belonged to the B1.

[41] The story goes that Sokehs once had a Nahnmwarki, like every other tribe, but a series of misfortunes to these rulers occurred and finally the Wasai refused to accept the final promotion due him but ruled in the name of the second highest A title.

[42] Gulick gives it as *Oj lapalap*, which would mean great or important "growth," not "place."

during speech with him. Soukise is used in referring to the Nahnmwarki of Kiti during the distribution of food at a feast, but in the part of Kiti known as Wene where the Soukise title had its origin, it is used on other occasions as well. In referring to the belongings of the Nahnmwarki of Kiti, as when one observes his canoes passing by or asks where his house is or refers to his wife, the proper term is Rohsa; this is also used in address when his B-line relatives are present.

Corresponding to the honorific title of address Nahnpwutak for A2, the address forms for A3 and A4 are Nahniau and Nahnno respectively. In Net, the form Iso is used in addressing A5 and A6, according to one informant; A5–A10, according to another. Madolenihmw informants apply this term to A5–A14.[43] The A11 and the Soumadau (a low A-title) are according to different informants addressed as Sahu in Net, as is the Souruko in Madolenihmw. B1–B4 in most tribes are called Iso, but one Net informant gives B3 as Sahu and B5 as Luhk. There are apparently no such special forms of address for women.

The titles of address are supposed to be courteous and deferential forms, the proper titles (Tables 3 and 4) are theoretically reserved for reference only. But whatever may have been the practice in the past, nowadays they are frequently used interchangeably in direct address.

## HONORIFIC FORMS

A large vocabulary of honorific forms serves to emphasize the differences in rank between the various classes on Ponape. Most of the forms are used to distinguish between commoners on the one hand and the royalty and nobility on the other, or between the two classes of chiefs, or between the higher and lower chiefs in the two lines. The subject of honorifics requires a linguistic treatment for which this is not the place.[44] A number of terms and usages connected with ceremony, however, deserve some description here.

When the Nahnmwarki is concerned food and all appurtenances connected with food are spoken of as *koanoat.* In the food distribution at feasts the Nahnmwarki's share is formally announced as *koanoat.* The equivalent term for the Nahnken is *sahk.* These two terms are applied to the persons themselves as well as to the objects involved; that is to say, the Nahnmwarki himself is said to be *koanoat,* the Nahnken *sahk.* Everything else belonging or pertaining to both Nahnmwarki and Nahnken—clothes, houses, canoes, etc.—is *sapwellem.*

When the Nahnmwarki is present at a feast in the community house, the food of all other chiefs is formally announced as *kepin koanoat,* except that of the Nahnken, which remains *sahk.* (An equivalent term to *kepin koanoat* is *tungoal,* and the titled men who receive *kepin koanoat* shares are referred to as being *tungoal,* although not announced as such.) But if the Nahnmwarki is absent and the A2 has taken his place, the latter is no longer *kepin koanoat* but instead becomes *sahk,* like the Nahnken.[45] Similarly, if the A4 is the senior chief of the A-line present at the feast, he likewise becomes *sahk* instead of *kepin koanoat.* But if the A3 is the senior chief present, he is *koanoat,* like the Nahnmwarki. No satisfactory explanation could be obtained as to why only A1 and A3 in the two ranked series of titles should be *koanoat.*

A5 and holders of lower titles in the A-line remain *kepin koanoat* and do not become *sahk* like A2 and A4, regardless of whether they are the senior A-line chiefs present.

If the Nahnmwarki is absent but the Nahnken is present, all other men of title become *kepin sahk,* except for the A3, who is *kepin koanoat.* If the Nahnken is absent, the B2 takes his place and is *sahk* and lower titles in both lines are *kepin sahk;* but if the B3 or the holder of a lower B-title is the senior B chief, he remains *kepin sahk.*

A few informants, however, extend the use of the term *sahk* as far as A12 and B12. Wives of men who are *koanoat* are called *pweniu,* but wives of men who are *sahk* are themselves *sahk.*

When titleholders below A4 and B2 are at home and no titleholders senior to them are present, or at a section meeting under the same conditions, they may be called *sahk.* Between commoners, in the absence of chiefs and ceremony, the term *kahng* is used for food.

Besides the Nahnmwarki and the A3, certain titleholders outside of the two series are also *koanoat.* Most of these titles are ancient priestly ones, though other ancient titles are *sahk.* In Net these include, among others, Souruko, Soulik en Daun, Sou Kiti, Soulik en Popat, Souedi, and Lepen Net;[46] in Sokehs they are the Lepen Palikir, Soulik en Palikir,[47] Soulik en Soledi, and Sapadan; in Uh,

[43] Father Costigan tells me he has heard the term *Iso* applied only to A5, A7, and A8 in Madolenihmw.

[44] For a fuller treatment see Garvin and Riesenberg, 1952.

[45] Hambruch, following Hahl, is in error in making the A2 *koanoat;* he is *sahk.*

[46] A Kiti informant says Lepen Net is *sahk.*

[47] A Kiti informant and a Sokehs informant state that Lepen Palikir (X1 of Palikir) is *koanoat* only because he simultaneously holds the title Soulik en Palikir, otherwise he is *sahk.*

Souruko, Souedi, and Soulik en Awak; in Madolenihmw, Lepen Moar, Souedi, and Kroun en Ledau;[48] in Kiti, Aulik, Saum, Soumaka, Souruko, Sau Wene, Nahmadau en Pehleng,[49] Soukise, Sou Kiti, and Lepen Deleur. Unlike the A3, many of these are *koanoat* regardless of the presence or absence of the Nahnmwarki. Many of them are entitled to places of honor in the community house and to other manifestations of deference. Some of them, as Soulik en Daun and Lepen Moar, have the privilege of sitting between the A1 and the B1 on the main platform, facing the people, in contrast to others who must sit to the left of the B1; they are third in food distribution, after the A1 and B1, and they are entitled to be addressed in the highest forms of honorific language. The Lepen Moar, who for certain legendary reasons is "the crown of the Nahnmwarki," may lean his back against the Those Who Face Downwards post (the rearmost central post of the main platform of the community house), he may leave the feast without making his excuses as ordinary men must do, the kava pounding rhythm called *sokemwahu* (see the section on kava ritual) is different when done for him, and he has the privilege of conferring certain titles that pertain to the old area of Senipehn without reference to the A1 or B1, and the further privilege of receiving the title-payment feasts for them.

The Nahnmwarki is in all five tribes considered *koanoat* in food distribution, but some informants say this is only because of the additional, older titles he possesses; thus the Nahnmwarki title in Kiti is said to be *sahk* in itself, but its holder is *koanoat* because of the additional titles of Soukise and Rohsa that belong to him; and since the present chief A6 of Kiti has been given the title Rohsa, he too is considered to be *koanoat* and is third in food distribution at feasts, following A1 and B1. Similarly, in Madolenihmw the Nahnmwarki is said by some to be *koanoat* only because of his older title of Isipau; in Uh because of his title of Sangiro.

Men entitled to *koanoat* used to receive large shares in the food distribution at feasts. As an indication of the position to which some of the old titles not in the two ranked series have sunk, the present Soukoahng of Net, whose title gives him the right of *koanoat,* refused, at the time the title was offered him, to accept it unless he was considered as only *sahk;* he felt that he would be subject to ridicule if, when his small share of food was announced in public assemblage, the presentation was accompanied by the pretentious term *koanoat* prefixed to his title.

The titles are similarly ranged according to the honorifics used for the verb "to come." In Net, the titles A1 to A7 and B1 to B5 are *katido;* chiefs from A8 and from B6 down to an indeterminate level are *apehdo;* the commoners are *kohdo.* In Madolenihmw, A1 to A8 and B1 to B8 are said to be *katido* and lower titles are *apehdo.* The references do not change when the higher chiefs are absent, as do the words for food.[50]

The ancient priestly titles just mentioned, which are *koanoat* and which do not become *kepin koanoat* or *sahk* under the circumstances described, are also *katido.* A recent practice that began in the early 1960s in Madolenihmw and is being taken up in the other tribes is to give the senior man of each clan and of some sub-clans a *koanoat* title. Sometimes these are ancient titles that have been regarded as belonging to those clans and now are dignified by being referred to as *koanoat* at feasts. These titles often do not include the word Madolenihmw in them but rather the ancient name of that tribe, Sounahleng. The rationale is that the clan has given much service to the tribe over the years and the Nahnmwarki wants to demonstrate his pleasure and gratitude by this means. These men are also regarded as First of the Land (see p. 17). If they are older men they are sometimes led up to sit on the main platform facing the people. But they are *koanoat* only if the Nahnmwarki is not present, otherwise they are *kepin koanoat;* and they are not *katido,* nor is the highest honorific speech used with them.

---

[48] According to the B1 of Madolenihmw, the Kroun en Ledau is only *sahk.* Also, the same informant said that Moses, the then A1, had only recently elevated two more titles to *koanoat,* Lepen Sehd and Soueda, and that in Madolenihmw only A1, A3, and Lepen Moar are properly *koanoat.* Hahl (1901, p. 7) gives also Saun and Aulik as *koanoat* in Madolenihmw.

[49] The Nahmadau en Pehleng, who is X1 of section 35 of Kiti, is simultaneously B2 of Kiti. This is always true, whoever is the occupant of these offices, and is traceable to an event in the time of the Kiti wars described elsewhere. The B2 title is *sahk* everywhere, but in Kiti the X1 title of Nahmadau en Pehleng that the B2 holds makes him *koanoat.* Similarly with the wife of this man; as wife of the Nahmadau en Pehleng her title is Nahnkedin en Pehleng and she is *pwenieu,* as are wives of all men who are *koanoat,* although as wife of the B2 her title is simultaneously Nahnkulei and she would ordinarily be *sahk,* as the wife of the B2 is elsewhere than in Kiti.

[50] Hahl (1901, pp. 6–7), in discussing Madolenihmw, shows A1–A3 and B1–B2 as *katido,* A4–A11 and B3–B14 as *apehdo.* (My reference to titles by letter and number in this instance follows Hahl's list, as given in Tables 3 and 4, column Hah). Also Saun and Aulik are shown as *katido,* and a whole group of other titles as *apehdo,* some of them belonging in the A and B series as given by my informants. Hahl adds: "Den Königsgeschlechtern gegenüber heisst 'kommen' kotito, dem Adel gegenüber apeto, beim gemeinen Volke koto. Die Mitglieder der königlichen Familie werden in der Mehrzahl und mit 'Hoheit' (koten) angeredet. Die Eintheilung der Würden geschieht geradezu nach diesen Sprachregeln, indem man von einem Manne sagt, er is koten, kotito, apeto u.s.f."

## FEMININE TITLES

Each title in the chiefly series has a feminine counterpart, which the wife of a titleholder automatically assumes. When her husband is promoted to a new title, she abandons her old title and takes the title appropriate to her husband's new position, though without the ceremony or promotion feast incumbent upon him. In the days of polygamy a man held a title for each wife he took and each wife had the feminine counterpart of it; indeed, a few informants questioned whether new titles were taken for new wives or whether a man took as many wives as he already held titles for.

The feminine series in Net that parallels the masculine series of Table 3, column B2NI and Table 4, column B1N is as follows:

| | |
|---|---|
| 1. Nahnalek | 1. Nahnkeniei |
| 2. Nahnnep | 2. Nahnkulei |
| 3. Nahnte | 3. Nahlisau |
| 4. Nahnado | 4. Nahnapasepei |
| 5. Nahleo | 5. Nahnkedin Idehd |
| 6. Nahnpweipei | 6. Eminalau Lapalap |
| 7. Nahlikirou | 7. Lempein Ririn |
| 8. Nahlikiei | 8. Li ou Ririn |
| 9. Nahnihdpei | 9. Kanep |
| 10. Pweipei Lapalap | 10. Kadipwan |
| 11. Kedindel | 11. Li Ounpei |
| 12. Nahntupei | 12. Li Oundol |
| 13. Likendlap | 13. Li Ou |
| 14. Kedinkapw | 14. Kedpwan |
| 15. Nahnkar | 15. Nahnkupei |

Titles elsewhere vary slightly, apart from dialect difference: in Kiti, for example, B11 becomes Li Oun Pohnpei and B9 is Kanepein Ririn. In Uh and Madolenihmw, A1 is Likend.

In addition to the title a woman receives because of her marriage, there are in three tribes two titles outside the foregoing series that are reserved for daughters and sisters of a Nahnmwarki or Nahnken. These are Nahnkakas and Idingel in Kiti and Uh, Isohlap and Idingel in Madolenihmw. The last Nahnmwarki of Madolenihmw, Alexander, was brother to an Isohlap and son of an Idingel; the same Isohlap [51] is mother of the present Nahnmwarki and her daughter is now Idingel; another daughter will take the Isohlap title when the mother dies. In Madolenihmw the rule as stated by informants is that only sisters, not daughters, of a Nahnmwarki can have these titles, and that a sister or daughter of a Nahnken can have one only after marriage. But in Uh it is said that only one daughter of the Nahnmwarki and no sister may have one of these titles, and only the eldest daughter or eldest sister of the Nahnken may have the other. Actually, the Nahnkakas of Uh today is the eldest daughter of the Nahnken, but the Idingel title belongs to the daughter of the B2, himself a son of a former Nahnmwarki. The previous Nahnmwarki issued the Nahnkakas title to his adopted daughter.

These titles are given to women of proper descent, not because of marriage. In addition, a number of women have masculine titles of the A and B series. This is said to be irregular and is looked upon with disfavor, but it does not seem to be a practice very recent in origin. Daughters of a Nahnmwarki or Nahnken may acquire such titles in infancy. In Madolenihmw these titles may be, among others, B9, B10, and Ou. (Column B1MI of Table 4, which we have chosen to use for purposes of reference for Madolenihmw titles, does not list the title Ou, but Column B1MII lists all three titles immediately adjacent to one another.) Another example is provided by the present A5 of Kiti, who is daughter to the present B1. If the female holder of such a title marries a man of lower title, he takes her title and she takes the feminine counterpart thereof; if she dies, he reverts to his former title, unless it has been reissued, when he receives another of about the same level. If she marries a man of higher title, she gives up her old title and takes the female counterpart of his; then if he dies the next man in line gets his title and she goes back to her old title.

When, in this manner, the husband takes his wife's title, or when she has not held any title but he is awarded a high title upon marriage, he is said to hold the title "for" her. Thus, the present A13 of Net belongs to neither of the clans that form the A or B lines but is a member of clan 12, and his proper title is a section one; but he is married to the daughter of a former Nahnmwarki, and he holds his tribal title because of her. If she died he would lose his title.[52] The wife herself did not hold the title before her marriage. The "sister" of the Nahnken of Uh is married to the B5, who is a member of clan 15 (a commoner clan); in this case she held the title before she married him. (In Uh this title B5 is subject to a peculiar provision: it is said to "go back" on the death of its holder to the Nahnmwarki and Nahnken to be reissued as they please without reference to seniority or clan membership, in contrast to the other titles.) The present B8 of Uh is the unmarried young daughter of the Nahnmwarki; when she grows up she must have a higher title (informants emphasize the word "must"), which her husband will hold for her, because of her father's rank. A previous Nahn-

[51] According to Father Costigan, this woman was given the title Kedindeleur when she approached death. This title was buried with her and may not be used again. The reason was that the Madolenihmw people did not want to bury so important a title as Isohlap, which was given to one of her daughters.

[52] Uh informants deny that such loss of title is customary.

mwarki's daughter's husband was first B11 of Uh, later A8; he got the first title from his wife upon marriage to her; the second he earned, but by native theory it was she who really got the promotion, giving it then to her husband.

A man who elevates himself in this way by marriage to a high-ranking woman is called a "Big Bones" (*tihlap*), because he must work harder than other men and make a better showing at feasts; formerly he had to be in the forefront in battle.

Other influences are sometimes involved in achievement of titles by women. The B10 of Net today is a woman and is said to have been given the title because her former paramour, the B1, wanted her to be in a position to have a good share in the distribution of food at feasts.

# Machinery of Government

## THE POSITION OF THE NAHNMWARKI AND NAHNKEN

The existence of two supreme chiefs in each tribe provides a mechanism of government that is always in a rather delicate state of balance. The Nahnmwarki, in virtue of his semisacred person, was formerly considerably removed from the general populace, who came more closely in contact with the Nahnken. The Nahnken made most of the practical decisions and the promotions, though theoretically in consultation with the Nahnmwarki. In many respects, as Bascom points out, his position compares with that of the talking chief in Samoa. He was looked upon as a sort of champion of the people and intervened for them in the face of the capricious temper of the Nahnmwarki. Consequently, he was in a position to become the real master, and some incumbents of the office seem actually to have done so; thus Nahnku, the Nahnken of Kiti from about 1850 to 1864, was the real ruler of Kiti and completely eclipsed the Nahnmwarki. But Nahnku was an exceptionally powerful individual, as many anecdotes about his career show; the missionary Gulick writes in admiring terms about his impressive figure and strong personality. In theory, at least, the Nahnmwarki had and in practice nowadays has more power, and in any difference of opinion the decision was supposed always to go his way. Sometimes the two chiefs reverse their traditional roles and it is the Nahnmwarki who approaches the Nahnken to intercede with him on behalf of the people.

That open discord seldom arose attests to the stability of the state of balance between the two chiefs. Occasional quarrels might arise; at one time a dispute between Paulino, B1 of Net, and the then Nahnmwarki nearly split the tribe asunder. But Paulino after 3 days made a feast of apology. He was considered extremely rash to have waited so long, for after 3 days without an apology a war between the A and B clans is supposed to ensue. Another time a ruler of Sokehs, who is remembered only by the honorific form Isoeni, in a coup d'état seized power in Net and became head of the A-line in both tribes; the Nahnsoused (at that time the title of the B1 of Net) sulked for a period, but his ultimate reconciliation to Isoeni attests to the pressures exerted against a falling out between the two lines. The present A1's of both Kiti and Madolenihmw have had violent quarrels with their B1's but these were quickly made up. Although numerous instances were recorded of clan wars and of wars between sub-clans of the same clan, no wars were reported between the A-line and B-line clans of any tribe. If a quarrel arose between the A1 and B1, a reconciliation by means of a feast of propitiation must soon be effected, otherwise the tribe would be considered to be falling apart. The devices used to force such reconciliation, particularly the power ascribed to kava to bring about a change in attitude, are arbitrarily recognized mechanisms in which all concerned concur.

The social pressures for political stability are numerous. The A and B lines are supposed to intermarry, and the members of the B-line stand in the fictitious relationship of children to the A-line, as their designations Royal Men and Royal Children respectively show. Sometimes a Nahnmwarki and Nahnken will be actual father and son or son and father, as is true in Net today. The mutual respect or affection immanent in this relationship, real or ascribed, is indicated by the failure of overt jealousy to develop when a section switches allegiance from one to the other. Each of the two leading chiefs finds himself surrounded by attendants of the opposite line, since members of one's own line may not take the familiarities that necessarily develop in that situation. A variety of attachments may thus spring up. An extremely strong bond in the kinship organization is that between a man and his sister's husband or between a man and his wife's brother; brothers-in-law (*mwah*) are bound to go to one another's assistance in any difficulties, to respect and honor one another, if need be die for each other; the saying goes, "My *mwah* is my Nahnmwarki." Since the two lines intermarry, every man of A-title must have a number of men in the B-line in the actual or classificatory brother-in-law relationship, and vice versa; thus the kinship bond serves to reinforce the political bond.

Formerly when the Nahnmwarki and Nahnken could not come to an understanding the priests might intervene. The B2 as principal priest was particularly charged with this duty and, though he is no longer a priest, assumes the same function nowadays. Certain other powerful chiefs might likewise mediate; in Madolenihmw the Lepen Moar is one of these. In addition the personal attendants of the Nahmwarki and Nahnken, particularly the Oun Mwarki and Lepen Kin, who were simultaneously priests, might come between the two rulers.

## PRIVILEGED BEHAVIOR OF THE B-LINE

The Royal Children or B-line titleholders in their position of fictitious children of the A titleholders have a number of privileges peculiar to them. When the Nahnken, the highest member of the B-line, is not present in the community house during feasts, the Royal Children may stand or sit anywhere, in contrast to the commoners and the members of the A-line. High Royal Children need not bow when they pass before the Nahnmwarki. Traditionally, they may violate all sorts of standards of behavior to which others must conform. A Royal Child can often be recognized by his loud talking and his free demeanor, particularly in the community house but also outside it; "they go about yelling and respect nobody." The head of the B-line, the Nahnken, who is considered to be the eldest son of the Nahnmwarki, can take familiarities with his ascribed father that are permitted to no one else; at a feast of propitiation (*tohmw*), if the Nahnmwarki proves too obdurate in forgiving those who are seeking to atone for some offense, the Nahnken might go so far as to violate the sacredness of the Nahnmwarki's head by seizing him and forcing him to drink the proffered cup of kava, which is the sign of forgiveness. He may take an impertinent tone in conversation with the Nahnmwarki, and there have been incidents when the Nahnken on being struck by the Nahnmwarki has replied in kind.

Traditionally such privileged behavior dates back to the time of Isohkelekel, the conqueror of Ponape and the first Nahnmwarki, whose son, Lepenien, became the first Nahnken. In the Isohkelekel legend the son does all manner of forbidden things: he climbs up on his father's canoe from the outrigger side, he hands his father fish on the end of his spear instead of strung together, he stands in the canoe in his father's presence as it nears the bank, he alights from the middle of the canoe, he enters the community house from the front end of a side platform instead of through the central area, he walks down the inside edge of the side platform instead of down its center, and he steps to the main platform inside the corner post where the platforms join instead of going around behind it. From these legendary times on, unconventional and indecorous behavior was to be expected of members of the B-line. The Isohkelekel legend referred to several times in this work is in a sense a kind of political charter for Ponape.

The theory behind these ascribed behavior patterns is that the Nahnmwarki is an indulgent "father" and permits his "sons" to take liberties that no one else dares. Not so with members of the A-line; such men, though potential heirs to the Nahnmwarki's position, must be meek and humble in demeanor, for they have no fiction of being favored children to support any untoward behavior. Whether the fiction has any fact behind it other than the legend of Isohkelekel is problematical. Some informants state that formerly, when a Nahnmwarki whose son was Nahnken died, the A2 would take his place, depose the Nahnken, and install his own son instead; Kiti informants charge other tribes with still following this practice, and everywhere Uh is held up as the horrible example. It is true that upon accession of a new Nahnmwarki to office his children, who are of course in the B-line, are in a favorable position to receive promotions and often are soon elevated. A saying that the five tribes apply to each other goes "Tribe of alighting, embarking" (*Wehi en keredi, kerada*); it refers disparagingly to this shuffling of position to benefit Royal Children who are literally such. But examination of the history of promotions of titleholders in Uh and elsewhere does not corroborate the charge insofar as the Nahnken himself is concerned. A number of cases in various tribes in which the A1 had been father to the B1 were revealed, but only rarely did the son assume office while the father still lived; and the converse situation, when the B1 was father to the A1, also occurred. A possible explanation for the conventionalized behavior pattern, other than the legendary one, is that such deposition actually occurred formerly. If this is so, the Nahnmwarki must have played a more active political role in earlier days than he seems to have done in early postcontact times, and the parallel between the position of the Nahnken and that of the talking chiefs of Samoa loses some of its force.

There may be some connection also between the fictitious parent-child relationship and the Crow system of cross-cousin terminology which exists in Ponape, but only if we assume that the institution of exclusive intermarriage between A and B clans of each tribe that prevailed until recently was in more ancient times asymmetrical. With symmetrical marriage, an A-clan man marries a woman of the B-clan, and vice versa, so that in this matrilineal society a man of either clan should always find his father and sons in the opposite line of titles to his (except for those few cases where a man takes a title in the wrong line, as discussed elsewhere; that is, in the case where A-clan is not equivalent to A-line of titles, and B-clan to B-line). In the Crow system, maternal cross-cousins are called by filial terms, paternal cross-cousins by parental terms, and these terms are extended downward several generations.[53] Thus, if A and B clans intermarry symmetrically and exclusively, a man of one line will find not only his father and sons in the other line, but also his mother's brother's son, called "son" by him, and his father's sister's son, called "father" by him. But if only men, not women, of the A-clan married into the B-clan, there would be "sons," actual and classificatory, but no "fathers" in the B-line, and the fiction that Royal Men are "fathers" but not "sons" of Royal Children would become reality; and conversely, men in the B-line would have "fathers" but no "sons" in the A-line. Presumably women of the A-line and men of the B-line would have to marry commoners. However, we have no evidence to support a hypothesis that such a state of affairs did once exist.

We might also speculate that there was once no B-clan, and that there was one ruling clan which took marriage partners from any of the other clans. The children of the royal women would still belong to the royal clan, but the children of the men would be commoners. They might receive special titles and deference would be paid to them by virtue of their fathers' positions, but then their children, if they in turn married commoners, would sink to lower position. The temptation would become strong to require the children of the men of the ruling clan to marry back into their fathers' clan, so that the grandchildren would become royal again. This practice might then become institutionalized and the titles of the Royal Children would become a formal series, like that of the existing A-line. The behavioral expectations and the kinship terminology involved would then be extended from the actual to the classificatory relationships, and the B-line that thus came into being would consist of fictitious as well as real Royal Children, as it does today.

## POLITICAL COUNCILS, COURTS, AND TRIALS

None of the Nahnmwarkis ever approached the absolute, despotic authority of their semihistorical predecessors, the Saudeleur line of kings, which ended with the conquest by Isohkelekel. These kings, it is said, made such continual and arbitrary demands upon their subjects that, informants report only in half-jest, a man could not so much as find a louse on his head without having to deliver it to the Saudeleur. But different Nahnmwarkis varied considerably according to their individual characters and those of their opposite numbers, the Nahnkens; some were tyrannical, some were permissive or weak; and from time to time a section chief or a strong warrior might challenge their authority.

That the chiefs, at different levels, did not have everything their own way is evident from the occasional calling together of the people in an assembly to discuss various projects, such as the building of a big community house. This might be a meeting of a sub-clan, of the people of a section, or of all the people of a tribe, under their respective heads. They were apparently called when the majority of the people seemed to be opposed to a course of action by the chief, in order to persuade them to come around to his point of view. A chief who acted too unilaterally might come to grief. A Nahnmwarki in Madolenihmw in precontact times is said to have made numerous decisions without consulting his subjects, who rose and marched against him. He called upon his own clansmates to help, but he had alienated them too and they did not respond to his plea; finally, he was killed.

[53] It might be noted at this point that with exclusive intermarriage between A and B clans all cross-cousins would be in the opposite line. In spite of the use of filial and parental terms for cross-cousins in the kinship terminology, cross-cousin marriage is preferred and is urged on children by A and B clan parents.

Nowadays, of course, political councils are things of the foreign administrations and have a markedly western complexion.

Meetings of the highest chiefs of a tribe, of a clan, or of any political or social grouping are known as *kopwung*. Hambruch describes them as much more formal affairs than they actually appear to have been. He refers to them as lawsuits, whereas actually they seem to have been meetings of chiefs for consultations concerning war, work projects, or the awarding of titles, and only occasionally involved law. In its legal aspects the *kopwung* resembled a criminal trial more than a lawsuit. In addition to the tribal chiefs the head of the section where the accused lived would attend. Generally the Nahnken would preside, less often the Nahnmwarki, who was usually considered to be above such mundane affairs and would not know his subjects well enough to function effectively in such matters. Today, however, the Nahnmwarki is occasionally the judge under the civil administration. The section head would previously have investigated and have brought the accused to trial, and the only testimony taken was from him. The Nahnken would pronounce judgment on any commoner and on members of his own clan; if a member of the royal clan was on trial, the Nahnmwarki or A2 would give judgment.

For seduction of the wife or widow of a Nahnmwarki or Nahnken, and sometimes wives or widows of other men of high rank, the penalty was death. Gazing upon a married woman of high rank at her bath was the equivalent of seduction in native eyes, and the same punishment was required. Sometimes, however, banishment was employed instead. These crimes might be forgiven if the whole clan of the guilty man quickly made a feast of atonement, but even then the culprit was restricted for a time to his section. The woman was not ordinarily punished. Rape was considered the same as seduction. But if the woman was unmarried rape was no different from any sexual adventure, to which no penalty was attached, except that there was some element of disgrace when force was involved; but, in any case, rape seems to have been very rare. Sexual perversion was similarly regarded, and ridicule was the only social sanction employed; that it was effective is attested by a number of suicides that resulted. Murder of a member of the royal or noble clans was punished by execution; similarly with incest involving members of these clans. Stealing from a chief resulted in a beating, but most thieves were punished only by ridicule as lazy fellows.

It seems obvious that for the most part the tribal court dealt with crimes against the ruling clans; similar crimes against commoners were most often directly avenged. It is difficult to draw the line between personal vengeance and legal punishment. When a commoner exercised blood revenge for the murder of his clansmate, there was little difference, essentially, between his act and that of a judge, the Nahnken, in delegating someone to execute the murderer of one of his own clansmates. An offense against a commoner seldom was brought before the tribal court; instead there might be a meeting of the clansmen of the injured person and his relatives in other clans, and from among them were chosen the instruments of revenge. In the court the assembled judges would belong to one or both of the two chiefly clans, and the crime being tried would have ordinarily been committed against one of their clansmates; since the members of these two clans were considered to be in the actual or fictitious relationship of parent and child, and since they were further bound by ties of marriage, the circumstances were not very different from a meeting of a group of related commoners, and the crime involved virtually the same factors as did a crime which among commoners was punished by blood revenge. Informants in speaking of these matters make little distinction between clan and tribe. For example, they say that in Net the punishment for incest was not death, as it was elsewhere in Ponape; but it develops that they are speaking of clan 7, the A-line in Net, whose members were different from members of other clans in that they are supposed once to have intermarried among themselves. Some informants refer to the court as a clan, not a tribal, meeting. Here, as in other respects, the state has the aspect of a clan, but a clan paramount among other clans and able, because of its coercive powers, to lend some show of formality and legal trappings to an institution it otherwise shared with the clans it ruled.

Under such circumstances, then, the legal code could not be a very formal one. Descriptions of various trials are vague and inconsistent, as one might expect with such a loosely organized institution. For the same crime a trial might be held on one occasion and direct vengeance taken on another. There was also inconsistent treatment of quarrels between commoner clans. Individual chiefs varied greatly in this respect; usually they tried to settle matters by arranging a trial court, but often they did not interfere with blood revenge; at other times they might become angry when a clan war started and send messengers to stop the fighting or kill the man who began it.

Usually a crime was expiated when one act of retribution had taken place, and the quarrel was not pursued further unless the first act led to a war. If the actual culprit was not caught, anyone else in his clan would do as a substitute. If a clan war began and one clan was driven away by the victorious side, or by a Nahnmwarki who had decided to punish one side, the exiled party would sometimes seek to take vengeance on clansmates of their enemy in their new home.

When personal property was damaged or destroyed, the usual thing, if the victim felt strong enough, was to reimburse himself directly from the culprit's property or to destroy it. When an injured man did not feel capable of taking up the quarrel himself, he could lodge a complaint with the Nahnmwarki or Nahnken, and the chief would try to redress the harm. He could beat the wrongdoer, or drive him from his land, or assess him a fine in such valuables as sennit, mats, and canoes, which he would pay over to the wronged party. But such complaints seem to have begun only in later times; people were usually ashamed of them, for they constituted a confession of weakness, and to some extent this feeling of shame persists in the modern courts.

Informants find it difficult to understand Hambruch's statement that the Nahnmwarki punished "Schuldigen oder Streitenden" (1932 II, p. 150). Such matters were largely up to the clans concerned. It was considered most reprehensible for a clan not to attempt to take revenge for an insult or injury to one of its members, and such craven conduct earned the ridicule of all. Nevertheless, sometimes an unfaithful woman and her lover might be taken before a chief to be scolded or beaten, or in German times to be given manual labor to do. Possibly such action was taken when blood vengeance was deemed likely to array relatives on opposite sides, since in a war brothers-in-law were expected to help, yet being necessarily in different clans because of clan exogamy they would be subject to opposing pressures.

If capital punishment was imposed, certain men were delegated to carry out the sentence. About the time of first white contact the Nahnmwarki himself or his brother seems occasionally to have been the executioner, but in earlier times certain titled men were appointed to this duty. Torture, it seems, was rarely practiced. The doomed man had his hands tied behind his back and he was then clubbed or speared; a brave man would sit with his hands unbound. In Spanish times there was a case of burning alive.

For first offenses within a sub-clan there was ordinarily no punishment, even for murder. But if a man made a reputation as a troublemaker, he would be disposed of by his fellows under the direction of the head of the sub-clan. A man of clan 2, Reisip by name, living in section 3 in Madolenihmw, was an obstreperous person, always bullying and striking his clansmates and acting proud and independent. Finally three men of the same sub-clan (Soun Tamworohi), after consultation with their sub-clan chief, knifed him to death. The sole survivor of the trio, Simrait, reports that the Spanish jailed him for 4 months and the Nahmwarki, Paul, who had been converted to Christianity, gave him 4 months of labor on the canals; probably a non-Christian ruler would not have concerned himself.

Incest within a kinship group was always punished by death. But nowadays a number of incestuous unions, though matters of common gossip, are tolerated.

## DIRECT PUNISHMENT BY CHIEFS

The causes of offense to a high chief were many, the consequence of which was condign retribution. Among them were failure to pay suitable deference, to observe proper etiquette, to respond to a call to give service, and especially to offer the customary tribute and first fruits. Chiefly retaliation took several forms, but stripping a culprit of his land and title and banishment were perhaps the most common. Tenure by a commoner of a piece of land was always precarious, the concept being that all land belonged to the Nahnmwarki and was issued and revoked at his pleasure; however, since the institution of private ownership by the Germans the chiefs have in this regard lost their coercive power. But taking a man's title from him is still practiced, and in fact some say more frequently than in pre-German times, perhaps in compensation for the loss of power by the chiefs in other respects.

A chief might formerly have the house of someone at whom he was angry burned down; this act is *isimw*. Only the Nahmwarki, Nahnken, and a few other high chiefs possessed this privilege. Henry Nanpei, who was chief A6 of Kiti, is said to have exercised it several times, but his position was far greater than his title would indicate, owing to his father having been a Nahnken when Henry was born and especially because of his great wealth. On one occasion a relative of his, married to a man of clan 2, eloped with a man of clan 17; Henry went and brought her to his own home, but the man came that night and carried her off again; whereupon Henry grew very wroth, gathered his people together, and went and burned a number of houses of people of clan 17 in sections 25 and 29 of Kiti.

Usually the A1 or B1 did not need to go and do the burning himself, or even order it to be done. The A2 would know that the A1 was angry at someone and would take it upon himself to inflict the punishment; similarly the B2 might do it for the B1. If houseburning was the punishment imposed no banishment ordinarily followed.

Besides his house, a man's canoes, fishing nets, and other belongings might be burned; or his canoes might be broken with stones and the outrigger lashings cut. Other punishments included shooting of pigs and digging up of bananas, yams, young breadfruit, young coconut trees, etc. Such destruction at the order of a Nahnmwarki or Nahnken is known as *oudek,* the same term that is applied when a Nahnmwarki or Nahnken lies ill and the people of all the sections must bring him quantities of food to eat; it is of interest that the people view these heavy obligations, at least so far as vocabulary goes, in the same light as punishment for an offense.

Giving of blows was common enough in a moment of pique, but when the Germans first used flogging as punishment the natives were, to use their own words, "greatly astonished." Worse than blows by a Nahnmwarki or Nahnken are considered his scolding and curses.

Stone-throwing was a common practice of chiefs. It is mentioned in the early 1830s by O'Connell. It was done not only out of anger, however; often it was intended simply to impress upon the people their low status. Or it might be done simply because it was expected of a chief. As soon as a man was promoted to Nahnmwarki he would often throw stones at the assembled people, and they would flee and return bearing kava in supplication. At a feast of atonement it was considered proper conduct for the person being appeased to throw stones. A Nahnken of Kiti, Nahnawa en Mwudok by name, is described as carrying a stone in each hand every time he entered the community house and flinging them at random among the people; he considered this as a species of elegance, incumbent upon a man in his position. This was about 1870, but the custom persisted until very recently; Sigismundo, Nahnmwarki of Kiti in Japanese times, is said to have practiced it frequently. The Nahnken even more often than the Nahnmwarki followed the practice, and occassionally would throw stones for the Nahnmwarki if the latter was vexed for some reason.

## Banishment

The Nahnmwarki, the Nahnken, and the head of a section had the power to banish. A lesser tribal chief could banish someone only if he were simultaneously a section head (but one informant states that chiefs A2 and B2 also had this power in their own right). The Nahnmwarki and Nahnken seldom carried out an act of banishment or destruction by themselves, but usually delegated chiefs A2 or B2 to do it. (Actually, cases of banishment as recorded often show men of much lower rank carrying out the execution of the order.) The section chief derived his power to banish from the fact that he was, in many instances, of the same clan as the Nahnken or the Nahnmwarki, depending on which of them owned the section.

Banishment of an offender is known as *kalipehda.* The term is sometimes extended to cover all acts of destruction by a high chief, including destruction of a man's crops, *oudek.* Banishment of a whole sub-clan or clan (*pokousala*) also occurred.

Persons banished had to leave at once. Usually they took refuge with their sub-clan chief, even if the latter lived in the same tribe; one man, banished by the Nahnmwarki from his home in section 23 of Net, went to live in section 2 of the same tribe, at the home of the chief of his sub-clan. But the Nahnmwarki might order the sub-clan chief not to shelter him, in which case he would go to live with clansmates in another tribe or, if these were lacking, with members of his father's clan. As a last resort he could go to a friend who was an outstanding chief and become his servant.

Banishment was seldom imposed for a first offense. Most often an apology feast sufficed to atone in such a case. Usually banishment was for life, though when the chief who had banished a man died the offending party might sometimes return. Sometimes he chose to remain in his new home if circumstances were better there.

Reasons for banishment included not presenting first fruits and other food offerings, eating foods forbidden to commoners, adultery with the wife of a high chief, or failure to obey any order. For example, in building a community house or a chief's house each section would be assigned as its share of the construction the width between two upright studs in the wall (a *dinak,* one armspan in width); if one section failed to complete its share its chief might be banished.

About 1840 a man of clan 2 named Tulal, living in section 16 of Kiti, was caught gazing upon the wife of the chief of that section when she was at her bath. He could have been executed for this offense, known as *mwoanipil,* for it is equivalent to adultery. But the chief, since he was a member of clan 4, hence clansmate to the Nahnmwarki, had the power to banish him. Tulal took his family and went to Uh to live.

The last banishment in Net occurred about 1900. The Soumadau (X6) of section 1 went fishing and caught a merer fish, a species reserved for the highest chiefs. In section 1 the senior tribal chief was the Nahnsoused (the title which then was B1 in Net, corresponding to Nahnken in the four other tribes) and the fish should have been presented to him. The misdeed came to the ears of this chief, who summoned the culprit and gave him orders to go fishing again and bring him the whole catch. The Soumadau did not obey. Then the Nahnsoused instructed the Soulik (X8) to go and burn the house of Soumadau, kill all his pigs, dig up his yams, and drive him and his family away. With all the food the Soulik then made a feast for the Nahnsoused. The refugees went to Uh and lived there until the Nahnsoused died, when the section head called them back.

The land vacated by a banished man was awarded to someone else or taken by the chief who banished him. In a number of cases the high chief of Sokehs called upon the Lepen Net (the then A1 of Net) to carry out the banishment for him and the two chiefs would then make a feast together, using the exiled man's belongings. The confiscated land, though in Sokehs, would then belong to the Lepen Net. This was possible only between Sokehs and Net, not between any other two tribes, because their respective rulers were clansmates.

Occasionally a man was in a strong enough position to defy the Nahnmwarki or Nahnken. Such was the case of a member of clan 5, the head of section 18, Madolenihmw, in Spanish times; this man repeatedly refused to obey the Nahnmwarki of the tribe but suffered no penalties in consequence. His independence stemmed from his fame as a brave warrior against the Spanish.

A man may also seek to be banished. He may become convinced that there is no chance in his present residence of getting a higher title because elder clansmates and brothers precede him in seniority. But there is no way for him to state his ambitions frankly, since under the Ponapean pattern of personal modesty it is a shameful thing openly to seek advancement, and he cannot move elsewhere without his brothers questioning him or insisting that he remain. Therefore he will provoke banishment by his behavior. For example, the present A4 of Net formerly lived in section 23 and despaired of ever becoming the section chief, since his elder brother took precedence over him. He therefore began to flout Kalisto, the then Nahnmwarki. He killed pigs to sell and offered none to Kalisto; he stopped offering first fruits; he pretended to be sick when called upon to join a work group. Since this was in Japanese times the Nahnmwarki no longer had the power of banishment, but Kalisto acted as nearly in the old pattern as possible; he and the elder brother advised the younger brother to move to section 10, where his relatives gave him a piece of land. The head of this section was an old man and the present A4 ingratiated himself into his favor, taking over his work and ultimately becoming head when the old man died. Now he was able to offer first fruits direct to the Nahnmwarki (at this time Eduardo) instead of indirectly through the section head. He also insinuated himself into the good graces of Joseph, the present B1 (then the B2), and his wife, without directly asserting his ambitions, although it was obvious what he wished. Joseph helped him become Soukeperoa, next A7, then A4. The elder brother was only A12; he became ashamed and left Net to live in self-exile in Madolenihmw.

For a similar reason the present A7 of Sokehs, who was formerly a Madolenihmw man, moved to Sokehs. Ostensibly this was in order to marry a girl who lived there, but really it was because he had little hope of promotion at home. He knew it was easier to get a title in Sokehs; Sokehs is populated largely by out-islanders who have not been thoroughly assimilated to Ponapean title-seeking ways, and competition is therefore less severe.

Self-exile because of humiliation, usually caused by being passed over for a high title, is not uncommon. The case of Benito, who failed to become A1 of Net and went to live in Madolenihmw, has already been related. A similar case is that of Leon, who was B2 of Sokehs and expected to succeed Tionis, the B1, when the latter died a few years ago. Kalio, the A1, however, promoted the B3, Johannes, instead and Leon in anger went to live in Kiti. Again, when the B2 of Net, Vicente, was dying, the B4, Mainrat, fully expecting to succeed him, brought pigs and prepared lavishly for his anticipated title-payment feast. But Vicente was offended at Mainrat because he had failed to visit him while on his sickbed or to come and welcome the high chiefs who did come (both Vicente and Mainrat lived on Param Island, and Mainrat was chief of that section, being the Lepen Param as well as B4 of Net; he was therefore remiss in his duties). So Vicente advised the B1, who was then Augustine, to appoint Joseph (the present B1) to follow him, which Augustine did, and the present B2, Johannes (a different Johannes from the man mentioned previously), became B3. Mainrat in shame and frustration exiled himself to Uh, where he is presently Souruko.

## ATONEMENT FOR OFFENSES

A feast given to beg forgiveness of an offended person is known as *tohmw*. It is rather similar to the feast called *aluh*, which is given when an illness afflicting a person is diagnosed as being supernatural punishment for an affront to a chief or other person of authority; but with *tohmw* there is no propitiation of a god or ghost, as there is with *aluh*.[54] An intermediary is involved. To beg pardon of a man of the A-line a man of the B-line should ordinarily serve as the intermediary, and vice versa. If the

[54] For a fuller account see Riesenberg, 1948.

298-818—68——5

A1 is the person whose forgiveness is to be sought, the go-between should be the B1, B2, or the A1's mother's brother's son or daughter. These persons are in the B-line, but sometimes the A1's mother's brother serves as go-between. If the B1 is the person offended, the A1, A2, A3, or the B1's equivalent relatives should come. If the A1 is angry at the B1 or the B2, or the B1 at the A1 or the A2, the offending parties must present themselves without intermediary.

Kava is indispensable at any atonement. For a light offense the kava alone will suffice, although usually sugar cane and coconuts are also offered. For a serious transgression, a regular feast with a stone oven and all the customary trappings is usual. If the affair is between Nahnmwarki and Nahnken, the stone oven with baked pig or dog and yams is mandatory; such a feast is called Burning Unhappiness (*isikala insensued*).

The foregoing is native theory as informants expound it. In practice, details vary considerably. In one observed case the Lepenkin, whose title is a low one in Net, had slandered the Nahnken, and the fact had come to the Nahnken's ears. The Lepenkin requested the senior tribal chief in his section, the A6, to go and beg pardon of the Nahnken. But the Nahnken felt too aggrieved to accept a man of such comparatively low title as mediator; he scolded and railed at the A6 and refused to accept the proffered apology, insisting that a man of higher A-title be sent. The Lepenkin hovered about the door of the house where this scene took place, but the Nahnken ignored his presence. I did not witness the further development of this episode but was told that a higher chief was later employed as intermediary, and that the apology was accepted and reconciliation effected.

The intermediary usually brings with him as a token of supplication kava, sugar cane, a basket containing five young coconuts with the bottoms opened for drinking, or nowadays cigarettes. (This information is largely from Net people; a Kiti man says one or two drinking coconuts are brought.) Only the kava and sugar cane are ordinarily brought to a Nahnmwarki or Nahnken; the other objects are suitable for presentation to lower chiefs or between commoners who are becoming reconciled after a quarrel. In other circumstances, if sugar cane is brought in whole stalks and laid on the floor before a chief, it always signifies an invitation to a feast or other affair; but if the sugar cane is prepared for eating, it can mean only pardon-begging. In the episode involving the Lepenkin the intermediary presented a length of sugar cane of five sections, with the terminal section peeled back so that eight strips hung from the node; the peeled section he ringed with three shallow grooves to facilitate the breaking off of pieces for chewing. Then he knelt on the floor, holding the sugar cane stalk upright with the lower end on the floor. The Nahnken expressed his displeasure by refusing to accept the stalk; in the course of his scolding he suddenly lashed out and knocked off the uppermost section.

Another apology I observed again involved the Nahnken of Net. The Nahnken and I, sitting in the Nahnken's house, saw the A2 approaching with a kava plant on his shoulder. The Nahnken immediately ceased talk, sat upright, and assumed an air of calm repose. The A2 entered bearing the kava with root foremost, as is the usual practice, but instead of laying the plant down with the root toward the Nahnken, as is always done with an ordinary offering, he flipped it over so that the branches and leaves lay on the head and shoulders of the Nahnken, who continued to sit unmoving. This act at once showed that it was neither an offering nor an invitation to a feast, but an apology. The A2 proceeded to hack off the roots and then, speaking for the first time, gave a greeting; this again was a clue that it was an apology. Then he took the roots away to the nearby community house to pound them. On an occasion like this the kava must be pounded with as rapid a beat as possible. The A2 said nothing until he brought back a cup of kava, then he offered it to the Nahnken and explained his mission. The daughter of the Nahnken had left her husband the week before, and the husband, who has only a small title, was now asking pardon of the Nahnken for offending the woman, using the A2 as intermediary. The Nahnken accepted the apology. Had he shown anger or cut at the kava plant with a knife, the A2 would have had to leave without saying anything more and would have returned with more kava; this he would do up to three times, then the Nahnken would have had to accept, for as natives say it is inconceivable that he could have continued to refuse atonement involving kava.

On still another occasion witnessed by me, the offended party was a man whose younger brother had not helped him to make the feast known as the honor feast due the Nahnmwarki of Uh, but instead had joined with other people to make a separate feast. When the younger man heard of his brother's displeasure, he made an apology feast to him. Again, an apology feast was given by a chief of low position who had been summoned by the Nahnmwarki of Net to record songs for an American linguist. He refused to come because he believed that the Nahnmwarki was being paid and that he himself would get nothing; whereupon the Nahnmwarki called him to account before a large assembly of people, rated him severely, and required him to make the apology, with his section head acting as intermediary.

The missionary Doane, writing in 1870, describes a rather different kind of formal atonement which he witnessed. A man had indirectly caused another's death. The culprit assembled a large number of articles (mats, twine, pigs, dogs) and brought them to the community house, where he gave a feast; he led a procession of his people into the building, each carrying some of the goods. All were presented to the offended party, a high chief. Then he came, trembling, to that chief and gave him a lighted pipe, which was accepted. The chief in turn gave him a piece of sugar cane, and other members of his clan did likewise. There followed discussion, after which the Nahnmwarki announced that the sin was absolved. This peaceful settlement Doane ascribes to the effect of the visit of the U.S.S. *Jamestown* to Ponape in 1870. But in 1871 a chief of the offended side gathered his forces and attacked a house where the offending man and his party were sleeping. We are not told why the settlement was not enduring.

Occasionally the procedure for atonement is more complicated. This usually is followed when it is the Nahnmwarki who is the offended party and a commoner who is the culprit. If the commoner feels that his own status is too low to approach a high B-line chief, he may go to the senior member (*meseni en keinek*) of his sub-clan to secure his services as go-between. The sub-clan head, if he is also a commoner, may not approach the Nahnmwarki directly but first makes the apology to the B1 or B2. Then the two go together to the Nahnmwarki and repeat the feast to him. If it is the Nahnken who has been offended, the A1 or A2 may be asked to intercede.

If a member of one commoner sub-clan has insulted or injured a member of another and a war threatens, the procedure is similar; the head of the first sub-clan approaches the Nahnken, who intercedes with the Nahnmwarki, who then summons the head of the second sub-clan. If this sub-clan head and his party are very angry there is little talk at first; a simple apology is made with a kava plant. The Nahnken gives the head of the second sub-clan a cup of kava and begs him to be appeased, and when he has drunk, the Nahnken hands the first sub-clan head another cup, which he in turn hands to the second sub-clan head; then the Nahnken gives the head of the offended sub-clan a third cup, which is passed on to the offending sub-clan head, who drinks and passes it back for the other to drink. Thereupon the offense is erased.

Apologies between sub-clans should be made as soon as possible; formerly the offended party would wait at most three days before beginning hostilities. A war of this sort occurred in German times in Kiti in a quarrel over a seduced woman.

It is the Nahnken who in such cases is most often approached to act as go-between because he is considered the protector of the people against the wrath of the Nahnmwarki, who is traditionally remote from the commoners. When the Nahnken intercedes with the Nahnmwarki, he takes the cup of kava and offers it to him; if he refuses to drink, the Nahnken will argue and scold, and has been known even to seize the Nahnmwarki about the head with his left arm and pour the draught down his throat. A Nahnmwarki who sees the Nahnken coming with a kava bush will sometimes flee from his house. If the intermediary meets the Nahnmwarki on the path, he may take two small pieces of kava root, roll them in a kava leaf, and offer them as a symbolic cup of kava. Lesser chiefs than a Nahnken, acting as intermediary with a Nahnmwarki, may not rail or force the drinking of the kava; but the Nahnmwarki's father or father's brother, who of course would be in the B-line, may scold. Sometimes the argument lasts for hours, the Nahnken speaking for the people, until the Nahnmwarki at last accedes. Less often the two high chiefs reverse their roles; the Nahnmwarki then acts as intermediary and may force the other to drink.

At such times the supplicating chief quotes old sayings, e.g., "chiefs make naught of things" (*menin kasohr soupeidi*) and "commoners destroy things" (*menin kau aramas*); the purport of this being that though commoners, being base in nature, do not overlook an offense, it should be disregarded by a high chief. A chief is supposed to have the attitude that all difficulties and unpleasant events are things that pass and should be ignored; a Nahnmwarki should not scold or lose his calm but should remain dignified under any stress. Therefore he must allow himself to be placated. If the Nahnmwarki in anger begins to throw stones (the patterned outlet for chiefly spleen), the Nahnken might immediately come with a kava bush and flip it over on the Nahnmwarki's head; his anger would supposedly be immediately stilled.

A high chief is ideally responsive to the needs and requests of his subjects. The proverb "a chief is a hibiscus in the wind" (*keleunieng soupeidi*) expresses this chiefly attribute; just as the wild hibiscus tree bends readily before the wind, so should a Nahnmwarki accede to his people's wants.

Kava plays an extraordinary role in these circumstances or, for that matter, in any emotion-charged situation. To kava is ascribed the greatest inducement in making atonement. A Nahnmwarki or Nahnken is not supposed to be able to scorn an offer of kava; if he did, he would be held in contempt by the people. The Nahnken of Net regards Hambruch's remarks about severity of punishments and the use of the death penalty as exaggerated, for a high chief ought sooner or later to be mollified by repeated offers of kava. Often he only plays a role expected of him, his reluctance to forgive is feigned, and should the intermediary leave without a settlement being made, "he would feel bad." On one occasion, previously referred to, Paulino, a Nahnken of Net, quarreled with Eduardo, his contemporary Nahnmwarki; Paulino went to his home and sulked for three days, but when he returned and made two apology feasts to Eduardo, one in his home and one in the community house. Paulino was very rash to wait this long, for it might have led to a war between his clan and that of the Nahnmwarki. If either a Nahnmwarki or a Nahnken failed to accept a proffered cup of kava, it would be a sign that the tribe was falling apart.

Moreover, only two refusals of kava are permissible. The same Paulino was once angry at some people who failed to appear when he summoned them to help build a house. The offenders brought him a kava bush but he slashed it in two with a knife. They went away and returned with more kava, pounded the root, and gave him a cup, but he dashed it from him. But the third time they came to make the apology he felt it necessary to accept the cup and they were reconciled. (Some informants say that more than two refusals may occur, but when a cup is finally presented as *"sakau en peidi,"* literally "kava facing down," its refusal would mean war.)

We have until now been discussing the kind of apology and apology feast called *tohmw*. In spite of native theory to the contrary, there have been instances when the apology was not accepted and severe punishment was meted out or war followed. But there is another kind of propitiation and atonement more drastic than *tohmw*. It is called *sekenpwoud* (*sak,* to eat; or possibly from *sakara,* to petition; *pwoud,* spouse; referring to a woman's giving herself to a man to use as he wishes); in this case no go-between is used, but the culprit delivers himself completely into the hands of the chief, body and life and possessions, throwing himself abjectly upon the chief's mercy. Supposedly a plea of this nature is impossible to reject. About 1898 two men of section 1, Net, went to section 23 to fetch a *parem* tree to make a canoe. It was the custom for the canoe makers, after the hull was shaped, to lay their adzes before the highest chief of the section and beg permission to finish the job. But the two men here concerned failed to do this. The section head heard that they were making a canoe; he took an axe and came to the place where they were working; as he approached they took to their heels, but he pelted them with stones and laid them both senseless; then he chopped up their canoe. The two men, when they had recovered, made a *sekenpwoud* feast to the chief; one of them brought a large boar with long tusks (a *ngihpwar,* "teeth emerged"), the other a large sow past productive age (a *iepwou,* "barren"), both of these being exceedingly valuable offerings; each also brought five 10-man yams and one 10-man kava plant; and they put themselves completely at his mercy. Thereupon they received forgiveness.

## SUPERNATURAL SANCTION OF CHIEFLY AUTHORITY

The authority of a chief is supported by his protective spirit (*ani* or *eni*). Each chief has one or more such spirits, who may be an ancestral ghost (*eni mel* or *eni aramas*) or his clan deity (*enihwos*). When a Nahnmwarki or other chief is angry at a man who has neglected to perform proper acts of fealty, the ghost also becomes angry, because the chief and his protective ghost are always in the same, harmonious mood; or even if the chief is not aware of the affront, the ghost will know about it and become irked; in either case, the result is a sickness of a special kind (*riahla*) that befalls the offender or, more often, his child. Such a disease comes if the Nahnmwarki or Nahnken is not invited to a new-house ceremony to dedicate the building or to any other feast where his presence is required; if the owner sleeps in the new house only one night, he will fall sick and die. Likewise, if a man fails to present first fruits or any of the fishes and turtles which are the due of a chief, the disease will come.

What is required when the *riahla* disease strikes is the giving of an apology feast of the kind called *aluh,* which is intended to propitiate a spiritual being and which differs from the hitherto discussed temporal apology feast called *tohmw* in certain details described below. It is not possible to make a clear distinction between the kinds of offenses that result in the disease and those that do not, nor is it easy to distinguish between the symptoms of the *riahla* disease, which vary widely, and those of ordinary diseases. The distinction is made by having recourse to a diviner, and it is thus determined which kind of apology feast is necessary.

The imminence of supernatural punishment was in former times enough to ensure complete control by a high chief over his subjects. Nahnku, who was an exceptionally strong B1 of Kiti in the middle of the last century, had only to intimate that the spirit of his father, who had been A1, required a certain feast to be made, and the people would drive themselves day and night to execute his wishes.

Some recorded accounts of ghostly punishment shed light on the ideas surrounding these beliefs. A sick child was brought by its parents to a female shaman to have the cause of the disease diagnosed. The shaman entered a trance and the god Sahngoro spoke through her lips; he was angry because the father of the child had pounded a large kava root and drunk with his friends in private, not offering any to the local high chief, the Lepen Palikir. Sahngoro is the deity of the Dipwinwai clan, to which the local high chief belongs, hence it was he who had avenged the affront to his human partner. The father of the child now made a spiritual apology feast to the chief and the child recovered at once.

Another child died from supernaturally induced disease because its parents had caught and eaten royal fish and had not brought any to the Nahnmwarki of Madolenihmw, whose subjects they were; that this was the cause of the illness was seen from the fishlike actions of the child on its deathbed. In a third case a little girl was sick and a female doctor, in preparing the medicine, saw signs that the disease was caused by a ghost, the chief of the section where the parents lived being angry over their neglect to bring him first fruits, fish, and kava and their failure to bring pigs to feasts. The parents performed a spiritual apology feast and the child immediately recovered. Again, a woman who had adopted the child of the A6 of Net refused, when ordered to do so, to contribute a pig to a feast the A6 was making to some visitors to section 1, where he is the senior tribal chief; the A6 was vexed and the ghost of his dead father, as determined later by divination, caused the child to become ill; it recovered only when the woman made a spiritual apology feast to the A6. The woman herself did not become sick because the A6's father's ghost had no power over her, even though they were of the same clan; but the child, though of a different clan, was his lineal descendant. An ancestral ghost can cause only his own descendants to fall ill.

The concept of supernatural punishment for an affront to a chief is identical with ideas about the effects of disrespect shown to the head of a sub-clan or the head of a family; the ancestral ghost or deity associated with a kin group helps to enforce the authority of the senior member of that group over its junior members in exactly the same way that the authority of a chief over his subjects is supported. Ghostly retribution is exacted even from younger siblings when they fail to grant the eldest his prerogatives. Thus, a woman's newly purchased chickens died and her largest pig disappeared; the pig was found only when she came to beg forgiveness of her elder brother for not having given him any of the fowl. Somewhat similar is the experience of the sons of the A6 of Net, who had new canoes made but failed to invite their father to the dedication feast when they were completed; as a result, the protective spirit caused the canoe hulls to split. Taking things without permission from an older relative, speaking disrespectfully to him, or failure to make presents cause the anger of the offended relative to be transmitted somehow to the god or spirit of the clan, sub-clan, or family, who then exacts supernatural punishment. The family ghost acts even to enforce domestic authority; in one instance an unruly boy's mother's dead brother visited him at night and caused a recent wound to throb unceasingly, then explained why he had done so; the informant could hear him plainly, he insists.

The spiritual apology feast, held in consequence of spiritually induced disease and requiring propitiation of a ghost, differs in some respects from the feast offered to someone as an apology and in appeasement of anger for a temporal offense or, as in the incident of the canoes previously related, when supernatural punishment not involving disease is concerned. Three objects must be brought by the parents or other relatives of the sick person; kava, a dog or pig, and yams to be baked. The kava bush is laid before the Nahnmwarki or other offended person and the already slaughtered animal is placed among its branches. (This resembles a first fruits presentation except that in the latter the animal, presented alive, is never laid on the kava branches.) After the stone oven is started, the Nahnmwarki makes a special prayer (*sakarkihda*) to his protective spirit for the offerers; nowadays many chiefs pray instead to the Christian God. If the offended ghost is a family spirit, as determined by a diviner, it is sometimes propitiated directly, with an old man or woman familiar with the proper procedure making the prayer and the whole family assembled by the sick person before whom they lay the food being offered. Formerly a shaman might function in the community house in place of a chief.

The foregoing descriptions throw some light on the relationships between political units, kinship units, deities, and ghosts. Most gods (*enihwos*) are said to have existed always, and on this ground are distinguished from ghosts, which are the disembodied spirits of dead persons. But gods are also linked genealogically to clans. Thus Isohkaniki is a clan 11 god, Likendkahnpein is a clan 13 goddess, Luhkensed is a clan 17 god. In the tribe of Net the gods of the Nahnmwarki are Liesenkomwmwad, who is the god of clan 7, to which the Nahnmwarki (and of course his mother) belong, and Lumwohdeleng, the god of clan 6, to which the Nahnmwarki's father belongs; at the same time the Nahnmwarki has, as an additional spirit protector, the ghost of one of his more immediate ancestors, who is likely to have been a high chief. Legendarily, the deities are in the position of mother (*ihn*) or mother's brother (*uhlap*) to members of the clan. It therefore appears that the supernatural being which becomes angered at disregard of political prerogatives and dues of men senior in title and the being who likewise is vexed at neglect of kinship obligations owing senior men of kin groups are always the actual or legendary ancestors, direct or collateral, of the persons they protect. A commoner's protective spirit, who is ordinarily a recently dead ancestor, is called a human ghost (*eni aramas*), but the equivalent ancestral spirit of a Nahnmwarki or other high chief is a great ghost (*eni lapalap*) and serves as a bridge in the probable apotheosis of gods (*enihwos*) from ghosts; the various types of supernatural beings are prayed to indiscriminately at the feast of spirit propitiation, with no difference in attitude or objective. A principal difference between these beings, however, is that a god can make a man who is not his descendant fall ill, whereas a ghost can visit disease only upon his own descendants. A Nahnmwarki, who is both head of his clan and chief over all the clans of his tribe, is thus supported in his position by supernatural sanctions applying to all his subjects, while an ordinary senior man of a kinship unit is supported in his authority over only the members of that unit. We may therefore speculate that an evolution of gods from ghosts on Ponape was paralleled and accompanied by the development of state from clan and paramount ruler from clan head.

### Taboos

A taboo (*inepwi*) may be imposed by a Nahnmwarki during times of scarcity of any product. Yams, kava, pigs may be placed under a ban and during the period involved no one may make a feast and all must eat sparingly. Yams particularly were tabooed formerly, since they were fewer in number and variety than nowadays. Breadfruit was never tabooed, since it grows without cultivation and is plentiful. The eating of some types of fish is also prohibited periodically; *kioak,* which are scarce in February, are often tabooed for the month and sometimes, if the scarcity continues, during March as well. The eating of some species is prohibited during their spawning period.

Such prohibitions have no spiritual concepts attached to them and merely serve practical purposes. Nowadays a similar edict by the Trust Territory administration is called by the same term, *inepwi.* No supernatural sanction is involved in support of them. The same word, however, is also used for the act of a man who protects a valuable tree or other object by tying a coconut leaf around it, at the same time saying a charm; or when he wishes to prevent trespass on his land and lashes a coconut leaf between two posts. In such a case spiritual punishment would come to the transgressor in the form of affliction with ulcers, whether the taboo were violated wittingly or not.

## WARS

Fights between two tribes consisted of single raiding expeditions of short duration, unless a formal invitation to battle was involved. Usually the victors returned home the same day. No one caught, regardless of age or sex, would be spared. The invaders would destroy banana, kava, and yam plantations, as well as the smaller breadfruit trees; the large trees were too difficult a job to tackle in a short time with shell adzes and knives. The houses would be burned after being looted. Such prisoners as might be taken would be killed, either on the way back or after arrival home. A return raid by the surprised party usually followed, and sometimes intermittent hostilities of this nature might continue for years.

Formal battles often involved an invasion with a fleet of canoes that would be met by the opposing fleet some distance off shore. First slingstones were used, then at closer quarters spears and clubs came into play. O'Connell describes also bows and arrows, but all informants insist that they were never weapons of war. If the defending fleet was forced back to shore, the battle continued on land. O'Connell gives an account of one such encounter in which he took part, when some 300 lost their lives, but living informants who participated in wars after the introduction of rifles recall at most twenty deaths in a single engagement except against the Spanish.

The missionaries, writing in the 1850s, after the introduction of guns, speak deprecatingly of these engagements. They describe them as exchanges of volleys at safe distances until one side exhausted its ammunition, then the other side would attack and carry away or destroy property. A surprise attack or an ambush might perhaps accomplish the death of one old woman. But by Spanish times war had become considerably bloodier, and the numbers of Spaniards who fell in single engagements against the Ponapeans occasionally numbered in the hundreds; Finsch (1893, p. 235) mentions one battle alone in 1890 when over 300 casualties occurred.

The history of the earliest documented wars between Kiti and Madolenihmw, though fragmentary and largely compiled from missionary letters, is revealing as to the character of aboriginal warfare, even though it was carried on with guns. In 1850, 2 years before the Protestant missionaries arrived, there was a culminating battle between the two tribes, won by Kiti. For 15 years previously, according to Gulick, the high chiefs of the two tribes had not met except in battle, and Madolenihmw had consistently dominated Kiti. This 1850 warfare is apparently the same as that described in a native text in Hambruch (1932 II, pp. 356–357). According to the latter, the B1 of Kiti invaded section 18 of Madolenihmw and killed a man. In return Madolenihmw sent a party to section 3 of Kiti and killed three people. Whereupon Kiti forces descended on Madolenihmw sections 27–28 and left several people dead, then climbed the mountains across to section 14 and killed one more. Section 14 now sent its men to Kiti section 20 and took a life, and Madolenihmw laid waste several small Kiti islands. The B1 of Kiti was now wrought up and sent a message to the A1 of Madolenihmw, appointing a formal battle ground off Madolenihmw sections 27–28. He assembled an army from among his own followers of Kiti sections 9–11, 17–20, 22, and 25. Many were slain, and the battle ended in a decisive defeat for Madolenihmw, and "since then no more fighting has occurred" between the two tribes. A kind of treaty was effected, and the B1 of Kiti became overlord of section 18 of Madolenihmw, placing the head of Kiti section 9 in charge of it.

Nevertheless, in September to November of 1852, according to the missionary letters, eleven people were killed in three skirmishes between the two tribes. Because of a series of thefts, war resumed in October 1854, and continued until May 1855, with little parties robbing and murdering almost nightly. A typical report is one of December 1854 when a Kiti fleet of 28 canoes and 160 men attacked, joining an equal number of Kiti men who had gone by land; the net accomplishment was the death of two Madolenihmw women. In the same period there was civil war in Uh, fighting between Sokehs and Uh, and some skirmishing between Uh and Madolenihmw, with three "bloody battles" in 1853. Through 1856–59 Uh, or at least that part of Uh known as Awak, was at war with both Sokehs and the northern part of Madolenihmw; the reports typically mention "a woman and a girl killed," "five people killed," "two boys killed," "six men killed," etc. "Truly wonderful" breastworks of stone and watchtowers are described. The outbreaks of fighting in both 1856 and 1858 are attributed to elopement or theft of women married to high chiefs. In 1868 the Lepen Palikir (Palikir being part of Sokehs), the B1 of Sokehs, and the B1 of Uh formed an alliance with the A1 of Madolenihmw and fighting occurred all year against the A2 of Madolenihmw and his party, with what results we are not told.

It is of interest that in 1855, 5 years after Kiti had overthrown Madolenihmw, under whose domination it had previously been, it was still rendering tribute to the latter tribe even in the midst of hostilities; and at the annual major religious ceremonies, held in the fourth month, when new canoes that had been built during the year were launched, the two A1's exchanged new canoes, suspending warfare when necessary to do so.

O'Connell records that in battle there was strict segregation by class, chiefs fighting only against chiefs, commoners against commoners. Modern informants know nothing of this but do remember that the life of the enemy Nahnmwarki or Nahnken would always be spared; nevertheless, in the conquest of Kiti proper by Pehleng (described elsewhere), before Wene intervened and united all Kiti, it is related that the Soukiti, whose position corresponded to that of Nahnmwarki, was killed.

The usual plan of formal battle was to send a challenge to the opposing side, appointing a time and place for the engagement. But military strategems were not wanting. There were numerous cases of spying and of ambush. The clan 7 conquerors of Net and Sokehs, according to legend, spied upon the enemy by hiding under taro leaves. In the Kiti wars the Pehleng people were defeated when they massed against an apparent attack by a fleet of canoes only to discover that the sea attack was a feint and the canoes were filled with dummy warriors made of coconut leaves, the main Wene forces having come from behind them by land. The legendary account of the overthrow of the Saudeleur dynasty by the hero Isohkelekel, who became the first Nahnmwarki, describes an order of attack involving groups of men called literally "living water," which informants interpret as reserve units. In Spanish times a clan 13 man killed the brother of the Nahnmwarki of Madolenihmw, also of clan 13 but of a different sub-clan. He took refuge in a mountain fort. The Nahnmwarki and the Lepen Moar, after planning their strategy, pretended to have a falling-out with one another and staged a mock battle, during which a few men on each side received light wounds. The Lepen Moar then retired with his people to the area he governed and called upon the murderer to come and help him. When he arrived with his forces, they set out together, ostensibly to attack the Nahnmwarki, but en route through the woods the men of the Lepen Moar seized the murderer, bound him and delivered him to the Nahnmwarki, who had him burned alive.[55]

Land was seldom taken by a winning army. When the object of a war was to replace one ruling clan by another there would be a wholesale shift in the holders of titles, but the only immediate economic effect was that the new Nahnmwarki or Nahnken and such section chiefs as were replaced received offerings instead of the old ones; the greater number of families remained on their farmsteads. Occasional shifts of a section from one tribe to another

---

[55] Another version I recorded attributes the fight to a quarrel between two sisters; the son of one, Oun Sapawas, in revenge killed the A5, son of the other, and it was the A5's brother, the A2, who concerted with the Lepen Moar to take vengeance in this manner. Christian (1899, p. 116) gives an account of what seems to be the same incident but apparently puts it in an earlier period.

are recorded, but these were more often through peaceful means than by conquest; thus section 32 of Kiti was for a period transferred to Net because of the gratitude of the A1 of Wene to the B1 of Net for his help in the war against Pehleng. The similar transfer for a time of section 18 of Madolenihmw to Kiti in consequence of the war between those two tribes in the 1850s has already been described.

Wars between tribes, according to native theory, resulted not from economic causes but from vainglory and pride. A Nahnmwarki "would feel proud when he saw how many people he had and that they were ready to go to war"; he might himself pick a quarrel on slight pretext. Net and Uh frequently warred for no apparent immediate cause; the members of clan 2, the A-line of Uh, remained bitter after they were ousted by clan 7 from their similar position in Net and would seize every opportunity to take revenge. The wars between the two tribes are referred to as games of Uh (*kousor en Wenik; kousor* being a certain violent game; *Wenik,* the ancient name for Uh, but by some definitions also including Sokehs, Net, and the part of Madolenihmw called Enimwahn); they were thought of only as manly sport. After such a war each side was supposed to be satisfied for the time being; the members of the two tribes would visit one another with large fleets of canoes to exchange the formal apology feast expected after cessation of hostilities, at which times they would behave like good friends.

Sometimes, when a man was given a title, instead of making the usual title-payment feast he would prefer to gather his kinsmen and wage war for his overlord in token of his fealty. Paying for a title in this fashion was considered to be of higher merit than giving a feast. The Nahnmwarki might order the would-be warrior not to set forth, but usually he consented to the war; if so, he might choose the enemy against whom the man would exhibit his valor.

Occasionally a clan war resulted from a quarrel over titles. It might happen that a title was given to a great warrior in return for his deeds in battle, after which his clan might come to think of the title as belonging to it. In Spanish times a clan 7 man of Madolenihmw distinguished himself in fighting against the Spanish; in return he received the title of Kaniki of Madolenihmw. When he died, however, the Nahnmwarki Solomon gave the title to his own adopted son, a man of clan 6. The members of clan 7 were incensed. They raided the property of the head of clan 6 at Temwen and destroyed his houses, canoes, and yams; then they fortified themselves under their principal chief, the Lepen Moar, in their own sections. The clan 6 people ranged themselves around the Nahnmwarki at Temwen, and the Nahnken and all the men of high title came to stay with them. Neither side could approach the other. Finally a number of chiefs, friendly or related to both sides, mediated and some of the leading men of clan 7 were induced to come and make an apology feast to the Nahnmwarki. Though all was forgiven, Ponape was by this time under German rule and each side had to send a number of its partisans to penal servitude in Rabaul for a year. The title of Kaniki was given back to clan 7.

Wars between sub-clans of the same clan were not uncommon. One such occurred in Madolenihmw, at some time after first contact but before 1860, between two sub-clans (the Pahnmei and the Inanpaileng) of clan 13. A woman of clan 9 was married to a man of the second sub-clan but had a lover who belonged to the first; they were surprised together at a place of assignation. He was speared as he fled, but she escaped without punishment. A war then broke out between the two sub-clans and the people of the first sub-clan were driven away to Uh and Net.

# Prerogatives of Chiefs

## CONFISCATORY POWERS

Aggrandizement and avarice of chiefs seem to have had few checks. A chief who possessed one section but wanted another as well might simply go to the second section, command the people to prepare a stone oven for him, and proclaim that henceforth the section belonged to him. Such an act was known as Knotted Basket (*kiam pwuk;* translatable also as Pleading Basket). This term seems to be applicable primarily to cases of dispute in land inheritance, when each applicant sent a basket of coconuts to the Nahnmwarki in token of his claim. The term is also applied when a section voluntarily, or even against the will of its chief, transfers its allegiance to another chief. But here it is applied to a case of outright confiscation. The chief of the section supposedly could do nothing to prevent it if the interloper had a title higher in rank than his.

A confiscation of this kind might also be made by the head of a section immediately after he learned that the head of another section had died; haste was necessary, because there might be competition in the seizure. The expression Knotted Basket as used here applied only to a change in ownership between clans, since members of the same clan were not supposed to aggrandize at one another's expense. Usually the change was between the royal and noble clans, and might involve even the Nahnmwarki and Nahnken themselves. Thus, in Kiti, sections 2 and 13 at one time belonged to the Nahnmwarki but were taken from him by the Nahnken (see p. 27). Some of the sections that form the part of Kiti known as Lukoap were similarly taken from their independent heads by the Nahnken. Sections 23, 28, 29, and 32 were once under the Nahnken of Kiti, but while (about 1870) a man named Nahnawa en Mwudok was Nahnken he built a community home that required a large amount of cordage, then built a chief's canoe (*warasapw*) whose outrigger also took much of this material. The people of these four sections despaired, since they were called upon to deliver the required fiber which is arduous and tedious to make. They decided to switch their allegiance to the Nahnmwarki. In this transfer, referred to as a case of Knotted Basket, as in those of sections 2 and 13, there were no difficulties; it is reported that the two chiefs concerned merely laughed the matter off, since a Nahnken is always in the position, actual or fictional, of son to the Nahnmwarki, and there is supposed to be generosity and harmony between them.

In Net and Sokehs, which were ruled by the same clan, the A1 of one tribe might ask the A1 of the other for a piece of land, and when he went to take up the claim the second A1 would give him a feast, which was also called Knotted Basket. But such a thing was possible only between these two tribes, since the others were under different clans. Or if a high chief drove someone from a piece of land in order to possess it himself, the tenants of the land involved would make a feast called by this name to him.

Knotted Basket is a term also applied to confiscations of land in punishment for a misdeed. The banishment of the X6 of section 1 of Net, referred to previously, was an act of Knotted Basket insofar as it involved reversion of his land to the B1 of Net.

A high chief might confiscate any article he wished, simply out of greed, not necessarily as an act of punish-



298-818—68——6

ment. Such an act was known as *kuhl.* (In Kiti the term is also used for acts of destruction by a chief.) A chief or his messenger would go into a house and point out things he wanted or go to the community house in a section and demand that various things be brought him. People with fine objects would hide them in the bush or surrender a poor substitute, if they could get away with it, when they heard that such demands were being made. A Nahnmwarki or Nahnken (but no lesser chief) might send a messenger from house to house with a tiny sponge hanging from a strip of hibiscus bast or a small shuttle wound with a piece of twine; the messenger would show these symbolic articles to the householder, saying only "command," and the people would have to deliver to the messenger whatever sponges or balls of twine they had. Such a demand for twine is *pohn kepei mwahu* (*pohn,* upon; *kepei,* thigh; *mwahu,* good; referring to manufacture of twine by rolling coir on the thigh).

The Nahnmwarki might also demand other articles, for example, he might require that all the women make sleeping mats. He would notify the section heads, who would pass the word on to the women in their sections; the women would begin to gather pandanus leaves in January or February, the period of less rain, and present the finished mats to the Nahnmwarki at the end of the year; he would keep the best specimens, distribute others to his higher chiefs, and return the poorest ones.

The insatiability of the chiefs in their demands on the people in former times is well expressed by the Ponapean proverbs "The chiefs are hollows of no return" (*Peden seupwur soupeidi*) and "In the bottom of the channel there is water of the chiefs" (*Kepindau pilen soupeidi;* meaning, no matter how low the tide, even if the channels through which canoes must pass be dry, tribute in food and goods must nonetheless constantly flow to the chiefs).

Not only the highest chiefs felt free to call on their subjects to deliver up their possessions to them. The Soukoahng of Net (A3 in the old Net series) of three generations ago used to call fishermen ashore from where they were fishing in the lagoon and pick out the best canoes, which he would keep for himself.

These forms of confiscation were practiced frequently, though the form called *kuhl* was somewhat rarer and was considered more drastic. They are said to have been commoner in Kiti than elsewhere and persisted into late Spanish or early German times. More recently the term *kuhl* has been used to mean legal permission given by a Japanese judge to a creditor to seize property in satisfaction of a debt.

But the arrogance described above was not always tamely brooked. About 60 years ago the B1 of Net, who lived in section 21, came to sections 8 and 9. In each section he went to the community house, seated himself, and demanded that kava be prepared. He drank, then called for various objects to be brought him and took them away with him, the form of confiscation called *kuhl.* He returned a second time and repeated his performance. The third time he came to section 9 he seized the whole section. This strained the patience of the people beyond the limits of sufferance; despite the high status of the B1, a number of them, led by two men of clan 6, seized his canoe as he sat in it at the water's edge, capsized it, and held him under water until he was nearly drowned. Though the B1 had four men with him, they were outnumbered and stood helplessly by. He was allowed to leave and never returned to these sections nor exacted any vengeance.

The function of the political council as a check on chiefly arrogance has also been mentioned in previous pages. Another view of the power of the chiefs is provided by the Protestant missionaries, writing in 1855–60, after smallpox had decimated the population, reducing it to perhaps one-half or one-third of its former size. The chiefs had become disproportionately numerous, since it had been necessary to elevate commoners to the vacated titles. Sturges states that the commoners, hitherto always subject to a chief's call, never certain of retaining their few possessions and greatly oppressed, had now become insolent and the high chiefs were finding it hard to get men to do any work. Mere boys gave their opinions in public with as much authority as the highest chief. Chiefs became careful not to give commands or even to make requests not in conformity with ancient customs or with the active desires of the people. A commoner, if piqued, would escape to another master, where he was made welcome; this losing of men was regarded as disgraceful and kept the rulers almost in bondage to their subjects. Young men, who had been given titles and were anxious to prove themselves, would in lieu of a title-payment feast issue a challenge to battle to neighbor tribes, independently of the wishes of the high chiefs. Subtribes and sections had become virtually independent of the tribe.

This was of course an unusual and temporary state of affairs brought about by the epidemic, but Sturges says that the process had been in operation on a more limited scale over many years before—presumably since European contact. And the chiefs never again regained their erstwhile position of near-absolute power.

## ATTENDANTS AND SERVITORS

Chiefs A1 to A5, A7, B1 and B2 have a number of personal attendants (*erir*) who receive special titles. These are as follows:[56]

| | *Madolenihmw* | *Net* | *Kiti* |
|---|---|---|---|
| A1 | 1. Lempwei en Isipau | 1. Mwarekehtik | 1. Lempwei en Isipau |
| | 2. Souwel en Isipau | 2. Oaron Mwar | 2. Mwarekehtik |
| | 3. Oaron Mwar | 3. Oun Mwarki | 3. Oaron Mwarki |
| | 4. Luhen Mwar | 4. Luhen Mwar | |
| | 5. Oun Mwarki | | |
| A2 | 1. Souwel en Wasai | 1. Lempwei en Wasai | 1. Lempwei en Wasai |
| | 2. Lempwei en Wasai | 2. Souwel en Wasai | 2. Oaron Pwutak |
| | 3. Oaron Pwutak | 3. Oaron Wasai | 3. Oaron Wasai |
| | | 4. Oaron Pwutak | |
| A3 | Oaron Ahu | Oaron Ahu | Oaron Ahu |
| A4 | Oaron No | Oaron No | Oaron No |
| A5 | Oaron Awa | Oaron Awa | |
| A7 | Oaron Kirou | | |
| B1 | 1. Oaron Kin | 1. Oun Kin | 1. Oaron Kin |
| | 2. Oun Kin | 2. Lepen Kin | 2. Oun Kin |
| | 3. Lepen Kin | 3. Oaron Kin | 3. Lepen Kin |
| B2 | 1. Oaron Laimw | 1. Oaron Laimw | 1. Oaron Laimw |
| | | 2. Wahlaimw | 2. Wahlaimw |

In the other two tribes, Uh and Sokehs, the titles and number of attendants are said to be similar.

Some of these titles are of fairly high rank, sufficiently high to have been listed in Tables 3 and 4, in the A and B lines. In former days the successor to one of the titles which carried with it the right to attendants would inherit the same attendants his predecessor had. The main duties of these titled attendants are to function as bodyguard, messenger, and police. (A Kiti informant refers to them also as cooks.) As a member of the guard, an attendant, if he sees someone standing on the main platform of the community house with his head higher than the heads of the highest chiefs, tells him to desist; formerly he would have thrust him through with a spear, which he always had by him. (But attendants were not the official executioners; these officers were junior clansmates of the Nahnmwarki, whereas his attendants belong to any clan but his.[57]) If one of the workers walks about or idles in the central area of the community house or drinks kava without permission (a kava worker is supposed to drink only at the call of "*dipenkeleu*" by the master of the kava ritual), he is seized by the attendants and forced to perform an apology ceremony (*tohmw*) immediately; the kava already pounded on his stone is thrown away and he is made to supply another kava plant and pound it. This is true whether it is the Nahnmwarki or the Nahnken to whom disrespect has been shown, but offenses of such nature are looked upon with more severity by the Nahnmwarki's attendants. The attendants also see to it that no one uses commoner speech before the highest chiefs. Their function as mediators in a quarrel between A1 and B1 has already been described.

The attendants formerly did no work beyond their various specified duties. Some of them were part of the domestic ménage of the chiefs they served. They always accompanied their master when he traveled. Today, some of the titles listed above are purely honorific titles and are given to men who do not perform any of the functions theoretically associated with them; all of their holders nowadays maintain independent households.

The attendants cannot belong to the clan of the man they serve, since clansmates of a chief are prohibited from undertaking the various familiarities with him that attendants must perform in the course of their duties.[58] For example, a clansmate of the Nahnmwarki is not supposed to enter his house (although today this prohibition is no longer stringently observed), an act an attendant was often required to do. In Madolenihmw, where the Nahnken may be of either clan 2 or clan 9, an attendant of the Nahnken can belong to neither clan, regardless of the clan affiliation of any particular Nahnken.

The word used for attendant, *erir*, is often extended to those persons who sit before the high chiefs on the main platform of the community house and serve them kava or pass them other objects. Although the titled attendants sometimes function in this fashion, far more commonly

[56] The three lists here given are from informants; the Kiti informant admits that his list is incomplete. The manuscript by Luelen, who was a native of Kiti, lists six attendants for the A1, presumably the A1 of Kiti. The first four are the same as those I have listed above under Net (with numbers three and four in reversed order and number three spelled Aun Mwar); the fifth is the same as my first as given above under Madolenihmw and Kiti; the sixth is my second under Madolenihmw. The manuscript gives as attendants of the A2 the same four titles I have listed under Net, but in the order 3, 1, 2, 4. For A3 and A4 it gives the same titles as mine.

[57] In Madolenihmw the royal executioners were three of the Nahnmwarki's clansmates: The Kroun en Lehdau, the Kulap, and the X1 of section 26.

[58] The Mwarekehtik, who is A14 or 15, is an apparent exception, but though in the same line as the A1 he is considered as the latter's son and has a number of peculiar privileges, such as sole right to remove the kava plant placed in the beams above the A1's head in the community house. His title means literally "little Nahnmwarki." His position in the A-line is probably connected with the privilege, previously discussed, of sons of the A1 and B1 taking a title in either line during their early political careers.

they do not, and to distinguish the attendants from the kava servers I shall call the latter servitors. The servitor who waits on the Nahnmwarki is very often the head of the section where the feast is being held, though he might also be someone else, picked just for the occasion. Lesser chiefs, when they are the highest men of title present, may sit in the place of honor on the main platform and have servitors to sit before them and pass them kava; likewise with a visitor and whoever else is entitled to sit facing forward on the main platform.

When a servitor functions on ceremonial occasions, he sits not in the usual crosslegged manner of men but sideways, in front of the chief, in the position normally taken by women, that is, with both legs bent at the knees and to one side, and leaning with one shoulder toward the chief, the elbow on the leaning side resting on the knee on that side; the head is averted from the chief and bowed. If a chief has two servitors, they sit facing each other in front of him, one leaning toward him with the right shoulder, the other with the left.

The servitors are the only persons not of the highest rank who may hand things directly to the Nahnmwarki or Nahnken. Among the chiefs, B1 to B4 and the sons of men of the Nahnmwarki's sub-clan may hand objects to the Nahnmwarki; and similarly chiefs A1 to A4 and sons of men of the Nahnken's sub-clan may serve the Nahnken. In Uh the master of the kava ritual may pass a cup of kava directly to the Nahnmwarki or Nahnken instead of to a servitor first.

The servitor hands the kava or other object to the chief whom he attends with either hand, depending upon which of his shoulders is leaning in the chief's direction. If his left side inclines toward the chief, as is commonest when there is only one servitor, he takes the cup with his left hand from the kava pounder or master of the kava ritual; then with his right hand he wipes it clean and passes it on to the chief, who also takes it with his right hand. The chief passes back the drained cup with the same hand with which he received it, and the servitor receives it likewise with the same hand. If the servitor leans with his right side forward, he and the chief use their left hands in giving and receiving. In giving, the servitor supports the hand holding the object with the outer side of the crooked elbow of the other arm; this gesture is characteristic and striking, though often performed in a careless and perfunctory manner. When the chief has drunk, he thrusts the cup back, without looking at the servitor and paying no heed to whether the servitor is prepared to receive it, for the latter is supposed always to be ready. The chief's wrist is caught on the crooked elbow of the servitor as he thrusts the cup or other object back, then the object is taken with the opposite hand. (See Plates 7a, 11a, and 11b for serving position.)

Besides attendants and servitors others formed a kind of retinue to the Nahnmwarki and other high chiefs; they were servants and retainers of all kinds, some of them landless exiles, others tenants or hangers-on. There were enough of these so that the Nahnmwarki and Nahnken constituted a true leisure class, doing no work of any kind; some of the lesser chiefs, depending on personal power, likewise had their retainers to do all the necessary work. Life in ancient days, by informants' accounts, was easier and more leisurely for all. Such work as there was to do was mostly gardening and fishing for the men, household tasks for the women; people today look back on the old days as a time of much feasting and little work. So many people were idle that, it is said, the chiefs would put them to work cleaning the forests and there was not a leaf on the ground. Many, for lack of occupation, went to live with their relatives of higher rank as retainers and servants. Titled men would also attract unrelated retainers from among those who had been banished from other tribes for various crimes. Thus, many lesser chiefs could afford to refuse to collect breadfruit or care for yams; many would not build canoes; no chief would ever paddle a canoe or make a stone oven, and some even today refuse to undertake such menial tasks. The wives of a Nahnmwarki or Nahnken likewise had little to do; they occupied themselves chiefly with the making of valuable articles, such as sleeping mats or woven belts; the servants prepared the food, carried water, fetched wood, and cleaned the house, and the section chiefs brought in first fruits and other offerings daily, so that all the necessities were provided. But a man of lesser title often had only the workers of the section where he lived, and his wives might have more to do.

## INSIGNIA, DEFERENCE, AND ETIQUETTE

Chiefs and rich men formerly wore necklaces (*el en pwur*, or *el en pwul*) made of discoid beads of a yellowish or pinkish oyster (*pwahke*) strung on banana fiber. Fiber kilts (*koal*) are made nowadays of a variety of materials, but aboriginally they were of coconut leaves; these are first baked in a stone oven, then left overnight in water to bleach, then dried and shredded with a special tool consisting of a slab of wood, the end of one face of which is set with needles (formerly shark's teeth) and suspended from a waist cord. This is the dress of commoner men,[59] but the special chiefs' kilts (*koalihkos*) were more elaborate; each strip of coconut leaf was finely crimped with a certain sea shell (*kommol* or *kopol*). The crimping required the laborious efforts of several women over a period of about a week. Such crimped kilts are not seen today. Above the kilt was worn a belt of loom-woven banana fiber called *dohr* (Plates 7b, 11a, 11b); from it hung a number of pendants of the pink oyster shell, shaped into isosceles trapezoids. Headbands (*nihn*) were frequently loom-woven of banana fiber or made of tapa. Neither of these articles is made any longer. (Royal head and neck ornaments, reconstructed from archeological materials, are shown in Plates 11a and 11b; their reconstruction was done by and according to the ideas of the B6 of Madolenihmw.)

These ornaments were probably only indirectly a badge of rank, more directly reflecting the wealth accrued through the offerings that came to a man of title and the retainers he gathered about him; it is stated that commoners could wear them "if they had enough relatives," that is, became head of an extended family large enough so that there would be ample surplus time for women to spend making the articles. Priests also were eligible to wear them, and in the community house the attendants of the chiefs wore the woven belt.

At a tribal assembly the Nahnmwarki was privileged to wear a headband with four red "spurs," two pointing back and two forward; the chief priest (the B2) also wore one of these, but all others, including the Nahnken, could have only two such "spurs." A Kiti informant speaks of bamboo combs worn by chiefs and priests, who wore their hair piled on top of the head; the chief's comb was red, the priest's comb yellowish; commoners let their hair hang loose. But combs are denied by several Net informants as having existed in Ponape; they say that people wore their hair loose or in "bundles," meaning, no doubt, the typical Carolines chignon.[60] Drawings of Ponapeans in the Peabody Museum at Salem, made about 1850 or 1860, show both men and women with long hair loose down their backs, but other men with short hair; in this connection Gulick's remark that those with whom the spirits are supposed to hold intercourse wore long hair is perhaps explanatory.

Apparently no special distinctions in dress according to rank were made by women.

The chief's house was called *ihmw en nei*. It was constructed like a dwelling house, the *ihmwalap*, but instead of being built of mangrove wood it was made of hibiscus wood, with the lower beams of breadfruit wood, and lavishly covered with coconut-twine lashings. In the house of the Nahnmwarki was a special sleeping-room for his use (*nanweip*). For visiting chiefs a special house was built, called *ihmw en kinte*. Only the *ihmwalap* persists, but much westernized in form. The houses of high nobles often receive special names. That of Nahnku, who was Nahnken of Kiti until 1864, was called "Ponape fears." Those not named are referred to as *tehnpas*, an honorific used in place of the common name for house (*ihmw*); e.g., *tehnpas en wasa lapalap* for a Nahnmwarki's house (from his title of address) or *tehnpas en nihleng*, the house of the present A4 of Kiti in the farmstead of Nihleng.

Certain relatives of the Nahnmwarki and clansmates with low title could not enter his house. The holders of the three highest titles below his in the same line (A2, A3, and A4) could enter his house but not his sleeping chamber. But the Nahnken and other titleholders in the B line could enter both house and bedroom. And conversely, titleholders in the Nahnken's line, except for B2-B4, could not enter the Nahnken's house but those in the Nahnmwarki's line might. These restrictions today are defunct.

Near the community house and between it and the Nahnmwarki's dwelling house was built a little chief's house (*ihmw en patok*); this was similar in construction to an ordinary house of four spans length (*ihmwalap pahkis*). Here the servants of the Nahnmwarki slept; sometimes it served as a cookhouse for the Nahnmwarki, and old women and widows who were relatives of the Nahnmwarki or his retainers kept his provisions here and prepared his meals. But its main purpose seems to have been a place of concealment for the Nahnmwarki during preparations for meetings or feasts in the community house. When all was made ready he would take his place on the main, front platform of the community house. Apparently there was no prohibition against the populace seeing the Nahnmwarki;[61] his waiting in the small house seems simply to have been a means of enhancing his dignity by his abstention from vulgar activities, and his appearance at the appropriate time was a kind of theatrical demonstration. If the communal activities were in progress at night, the Nahnmwarki would sleep in the

[59] However, Kubary (1874, p. 267) reports that in his day commoners wore hibiscus-bast kilts, while chiefs had kilts made of young leaves of the coconut palm.

[60] Hambruch does not mention any comb, but Gulick lists the term *koko* for it. Bamboo was introduced only in postcontact times, so the comb, if it existed, must have been of other material.

[61] Yet this was not always strictly true. Father Costigan points out that in Madolenihmw, at least, the community house is usually built so that the open front faces east, whence the prevailing wind comes. The reason is said to be so that the smoke from the stone ovens will blow toward the main platform at the rear, where the Nahnmwarki sits, and will envelop him so that he will not be easily visible; damp wood is sometimes placed in the fire to enhance the effect. See also the remarks later concerning the Nahnmwarki's concealment in the special cabin on the royal canoe.

little house afterwards, since commoners slept in the community house. The Nahnken and a visiting Nahnmwarki could also make use of this house, but the Nahnken felt no need to hide himself. Men with titles below A2 and B2 could not enter the house at all; A2 could enter if the Nahnken was there alone and B2 if the Nahnmwarki was alone, but neither could enter if both of the ranking chiefs were present. Men of lower titles (only as far down as A4 and B2 according to one informant) could remain outside and talk to the Nahnmwarki, but commoners might not. The house served also as a place for discussion between Nahnmwarki and Nahnken. Nowadays, the Nahnmwarki has been assigned various governmental functions by successive foreign administrations and his aloofness from the people has perforce been considerably diminished.

The community house of a section (the *nahs en kousapw*), which is constructed by the head of the section and his people, and that of a tribe (the *nahs en wehi*), built at the command of a Nahnmwarki, are actually the same type of structure and are considered to be for the use of the whole tribe, despite their names. A tribal community house, however, was not built in a section but in the tribal capital. Today community houses are usually on privately owned land and men will often speak of owning this or that community house even though it may be called by one or another of the names appropriate for the public structures and is used for public purposes for the most part. Under present conditions, with private ownership of land and a money economy, a not always clear distinction between private and public community houses has come into being. In 1947 the Nahnmwarki of Net was building a private community house, with the aid of kinsmen, on the land of another man with whom he had made appropriate arrangements; suddenly he decided to convert the building into a tribal structure and summoned community labor from the whole tribe to do the job. There was some resentment until the people learned what the building was to be.

In the front center of the main platform of the community house was built a little structure with a wall 2 or 3 feet high; this was called *kelepap isoh*. Behind this the Nahnmwarki and Nahnken sat. The structure is not seen nowadays. Formerly the front right corner of the main platform was fenced about with a similar wall, made of cloth, within memory of informants, probably of a kind of cane, *Saccharum spontaneum* (*ahlek*), anciently. Into the privacy of this room (*kepinpwalek*) the principal wife of the Nahnmwarki and of the Nahnken (wives of A1–A4 and B1–B4 according to another informant), accompanied each by a female attendant, retired in order to be shielded from the gaze of commoners during menstrual periods. The seclusion hut for menstruants, widely distributed in the Caroline Islands, is, apart from this weak manifestation, absent in Ponape. The cane flooring of the building's platforms continued over this corner too, but underneath it was a pit built into the stone foundation, just large enough for a woman to sit over, which was used for disposal of the menstrual tampon of cloth or, more anciently, sponge. Informants differ as to whether the woman remained in the room during meetings and feasts or only used it to change the tampon privately. No such provision was made for commoners. The little room continued in nearly every community house until German times, when boards began to be used for flooring in place of cane and stone foundations were often replaced by piling.

The Nahnmwarki's principal wife was not supposed to be seen by anyone but her husband, though this custom was subject to modification; in the community house, for example, she sat in her rightful place in full public view. To some extent the practice applied also to the secondary wives, depending on such individual matters as uxorial jealousy and affection; sometimes one secondary wife would be regarded as highly and treated in the same manner by her husband as the principal wife. It was the clanbrethren of the Nahnmwarki who particularly were not supposed to enter her presence; the death penalty might be inflicted for a violation of this custom. When all the people were assembled in the community house and word came that the Nahnmwarki's wife was approaching the call went out, "All Sore Eyes (*lekerwait* [62]) go and hide." This term indicated the male members of the clan of the Nahnmwarki and was used only in these particular circumstances. At once they left (one informant says they were chased out) and hid themselves. After she took her seat they might return. All of this is conceived of as a form of honor towards her. The missionary Doane, in commenting on these customs, ascribes them to the fact that the Nahnmwarki's clansmates were in some sense his equal and so might be tempted to take liberties with her.

Similarly, no member of the Nahnmwarki's clan was supposed ever to see the Nahnmwarki's wife in her house. But none of this applied to the wife of a Nahnken or of any other high chief.

Sometimes, on a visit by a Nahnmwarki to a community house in his tribe, he would send his principal wife directly to a dwelling house nearby and let a secondary wife sit in

[62] Gulick (1872, p. 25) gives a spelling close to this as a term of abuse. Modern informants describe it as a condition in which the lower eyelids droop, exposing the red membrane, and Hahl (1904, p. 27) defines it as an ectropion of the eyelid. Madolenihmw informants say that the expression was used in Kiti, and that in Madolenihmw, when the messenger came to the community house to announce the coming of the Nahnmwarki's wife, he called instead, "Are there any ghosts here? If so, get out," and this was a warning to men not only of the Nahnmwarki's clan but to those of his wife's too.

the public building in her place. But usually the principal wife did not travel with her husband.

The chief's canoe (*warasapw*) and the ordinary canoe (*pahnta*) differ principally in the ornamental lashings and painted and carved decorations used on the former. Both of these might have a platform (*poang*) of *Saccharum spontaneum* built out on the leeward side as an extension of the board (*dinapw*) that covers the central part of the hull from gunwale to gunwale. If this platform was added, the canoe would lack the vertical sheer strake (*pedilik*) that ordinarily extends above the central portion of the leeward gunwale. Such canoes were called *warapoang*. On this lee platform was built a little cabin (*katauk*) where high chiefs hid from the vulgar gaze when traveling. The structure was shaped like a half-cylinder, open at each end; the framework consisted of *Ixora carolinensis* (*ketieu*) withes bent into shape and thatched over with ivory nut (*oahs*) or *parem* palm leaves. When not in use it was stored in the community house, to which it was carried by two men by means of a pole thrust through a loop of fiber fastened to the top of the structure. The chief's canoe, the leeward platform, and the cabin are no longer seen, but middle-aged informants remember them from their childhood.

When the canoe in which a Nahnmwarki or Nahnken is traveling reaches the bank he alone may step ashore from the middle of the vessel; all others must leave from positions closer to either end. When a canoe approaches the shore close to where a high chief is waiting it must not be under sail and all persons aboard must remain seated until it touches land. A man who is fishing when a Nahnmwarki approaches in a canoe must desist from his occupation and leave. Boatmen in a canoe meeting a chief's canoe make a wide detour and salute by slackening sail to allow it to flutter, or, if he is a very high chief, they lower the sail entirely; if the canoe is not under sail but being poled, the boatmen sit down. The chief then tells one of his men to wave the other canoe on. From my own experience such deference is paid to chiefs as low as A8. A canoe passing a chief's house must likewise wait to be waved on. It is especially the members of the clan of the Nahnmwarki who have to show respect to him; formerly, in passing his canoe or house, they had to jump out into the water, hold on to the gunwales of the canoe, and bow their heads; they still bow their heads but since about Spanish times they only pull in the sail and sit down. Clansmates of the Nahnken show similar deference to him.

The character of the respect shown to the Nahnmwarki is indicated by the fact that in his canoe in former times one attendant had the sole duty of sitting, facing him, in the same stylized attitude of respect that in the fishing canoe one of the fishermen is supposed to exhibit while sitting and facing the empty seat reserved for Nahnullap, the fishing deity.[63]

On a canoe trip, when the usual methods of concealment were not possible, the wives of a high chief had to cover their faces and heads with leaves of a variety of *Alocasia macrorrhiza* (*sepwikin*). The reason was not only so that they might maintain their isolation and aloofness from commoners, but also so that young men might not take a fancy to them and seek to come to them by night.

Canoes of Madolenihmw are supposed to turn their "small ends" (*imwitik*) foremost, canoes of Uh their "large ends" (*imwalap*), when passing a chief. The "small end" is considered to be that from the upper part of the tree from which the hull of the canoe was fashioned, the "large end" from the lower part. This custom, according to legend, dates from the time when the first Nahnken of Madolenihmw departed for Uh to become the first Nahnmwarki of that tribe; his son, who later became Nahnmwarki of Madolenihmw, followed to persuade him to return, and they took counsel at Pohn Nintok, the reef opposite section 4 of Madolenihmw; then, as they parted again and the father turned his canoe toward Uh, the son toward Madolenihmw, their canoes were oriented according to the custom which thereupon became established.

Belief in the sacredness of the head persists today. Formerly it was taboo, on pain of death at the hands of the executioners, to touch the Nahnmwarki, especially to touch his head or face or even his kilt. Though the penalty is nowadays void, the respect attitudes continue. (But at ceremonies in the community house a woman might smear oil over the Nahnmwarki's back and chest, as is the custom.) It was a form of respect not to awaken a high chief except by pulling the tuft of hair on his great toe, the part of his body farthest from his head. Few persons may stand so that their heads are higher than that of the Nahnmwarki; among those who may do so are the men whose duty involves calling out the stages in kava preparation and in division of food; but these officials must belong to the opposite (B) line of titles. His personal attendants, who are usually of the opposite line, and the highest chiefs in that line also have this privilege. The missionaries, in the 1850s, write complaints that though they would like the people to stand in church during certain prayers, they could not do so if a high chief was present. If a man wishes to climb a tall tree near the house of a man of high title, he must first obtain his permission; if a man is in a tree when a high chief comes near, he must climb down. In the

[63] Gulick lists in his vocabulary the word *keor*, defined as "the respect paid the ijipau (*isipau*, a title of the A1) when he is on a canoe, by one person who does not paddle and who sits facing him; only the ijipau and the chief ani (ghost or god) are thus honored." The custom was thus evidently still followed in the 1850s.

community house, if it is necessary to fetch some object suspended in the rafters, when the Nahnmwarki is present, one of the highest B-line chiefs (B1 to B4) or a son of a member of the sub-clan to which the Nahnmwarki belongs or the Mwarekehtik, who is considered as the Nahnmwarki's son, must climb up to get it; no one else may raise his head high enough. A man cannot pass the house of a Nahnmwarki or of a Nahnken but must sit outside in the path, some forty or fifty yards distant, and wait for permission from an attendant to go on, or else take a detour through the woods; then, when he walks on, he must do so in a stooped posture. This behavior, *sakarahl* (*sakara,* to beg of a chief; *ahl,* path), is sometimes exhibited toward men of lower title but it is not considered obligatory toward them. In passing a seated chief, a commoner must bend low, and in his presence he is expected to squat with his head at a lower level and in a bowed attitude. When leaving, he must crawl away backwards for some distance before rising. This crawling and stooping behavior is exhibited also before Europeans.

When a man met a chief's wife on the path, he was formerly obliged to sit down until she passed (but informants deny that he hid himself, as Hambruch asserts).

As recently as 1925 commoners could not even talk to a Nahnmwarki, and to this day many of them do not initiate conversation with a man of high title. Commoners take a special tone in talking to chiefs, the principal characteristic of which is a prolongation of vowel sounds. They should talk only in answer to questions and should make the answers as short as possible. This applies also to men of high title when they are talking to someone in the same line with a still higher title; only members of the B-line may speak at length to the Nahnmwarki and only members of the A-line to the Nahnken. If a titled man begins a conversation with the usual greeting, the commoner averts his gaze and answers with a prolonged "ehi," instead of responding with the same greeting as to an equal. When the chief comes to a pause in what he is saying, the commoner interjects an "ah" in agreement. Children of four or five even today already know enough to snatch off their hats, stoop, and give a prolonged greeting when they meet a high chief on the path. It is said of Nahnku, a Nahnken of Kiti, that he was so powerful that he could go about invisibly; hence people, when they were in section 19 of Kiti, where he lived, would bow continually, thinking he might be somewhere near by.

A leaflet of "red" coconut whose rib had been removed was often inserted by a commoner under his kilt and when a Nahnmwarki or Nahnken was met or was about to begin a conversation the leaf was taken out, the end torn off, and the rest folded into a *sedei* (a leaf folded in a peculiar fashion; the length of the terminal fold foretells the future). At the same time a prayer would be mumbled. This was less a form of respect than a method of divining, for so strong was the fear of the rulers that a simple encounter was sufficient to cause a commoner to seek what his fortune would be. But not all people knew how to do this.

A commoner may not eat with a Nahnmwarki or Nahnken; if he eats with any other man of superior rank, he must eat slowly, so as not to be sated first. Nor may he finish his drinking coconut first. Any water left in a Nahnmwarki's coconut may not be drunk by commoners or by the Nahnmwarki's clansmates, but only by men of high title in the opposite line down to Leperirin (B7 to B9 in different tribes); the same rule applies to eating remnants of his meals. Similarly, no one may finish the Nahnken's leavings except men of the Nahnmwarki's line as far down as Nahnid lapalap (A8 or A9). A commoner could not touch a high chief's gourd or coconut-shell water bottle; today the prohibition applies to glass bottles.

If a man of high rank stops at an inferior's house, he must be given a full bottle to drink from; more recently, glasses or cups, once proscribed, have been allowed but they must still be full. In the house of a host or in a community house coconut twine must be tied around the neck of the bottle offered to a Nahnmwarki and twelve leaves of a sort of citrus (*peren*) or of *Campnosperma brevipetiolata* (*dohng*) are lashed to the side; four leaves are used as a stopper. For a Nahnken ten instead of twelve leaves are used. Commoners use all sorts of other leaves as stoppers.

The Nahnmwarki and Nahnken were carried on litters when sick, lame, or numbed by overindulgence in kava. Holders of smaller titles, section heads, and high-titled women were also sometimes carried,[64] but this was not an institutionalized practice and varied according to individual prestige. The two litter-bearers had to be sons of men of the same clan as the man they were carrying but themselves of the opposite chiefly line. Chiefs were sometimes carried to feasts even when in good health. They were also carried astride the back of a servant.

Not only prestige and power affected the degree to which a chief's subjects acquiesced in his demands for the observation of the external signs of his authority. A former head of section 1 of Net lived on a high hill but insisted that his people carry him and his family, seated in a canoe, from his community house on the hill to the water's edge and back again whenever he traveled somewhere by water. The men are said to have been so eager to act as porters that they would surround the canoe in throngs and many could barely lay a hand to it. But at least part of the reason for this enthusiastic fealty was that the chief had several fair and unmarried daughters whose favors were bestowed upon his most obedient subjects.

[64] But informants deny Hambruch's remark concerning the carrying of the Nahnmwarki's wife to her bath.

People could not go to a high titleholder who was a medical practitioner and ask him to come to minister to a sick commoner but had to resort to someone of the commoner class. But a high chief might summon a commoner to cure him if he wished. Such distinctions are no longer maintained.

When a Nahnmwarki or Nahnken lies gravely ill, people of the tribe come in great numbers to pay their respects or simply "to eat," as informants put it, and the commoners in the vicinity must furnish food for all of them.

A Nahnmwarki who visits another Nahnmwarki is accompanied by a large fleet of canoes. Keimw Sapwasap, who ruled over the combined tribes of Net and Sokehs about 1875, used to get followers for such expeditions not only from these two tribes but from Uh and all of Enimwahn in Madolenihmw. When the B1 of Kiti, called Nahnawa en Mwudok, in 1870, went out to a man-of-war that was calling him to account for the burning of a church, some forty canoes followed him as a gesture of loyalty. In theory each section of a tribe sends three or four men to go along with the Nahnmwarki on a visit to another tribe, in the canoe which is reserved in each section for tribal business. Even today, when a great chief goes on a visit, his attendants and tenants will shortly follow him to "protect" their lord. On a visit to section 6 in Madolenihmw, made by the A6 of Kiti in company with the writer, by the second day some eight of his tenants had followed. This is nowadays as much a function of land ownership as of title-holding; the Nahnmwarki of Kiti today has no large estate and no tenants, and there are fewer therefore to perform this service for him than is deemed proper, in spite of his superiority over lesser wealthier chiefs.

When all five Nahnmwarkis meet, the proper seating arrangement is with the Nahnmwarki of Madolenihmw in the position of highest honor, in the center of the main platform of the community house, with the Nahnmwarki of Kiti and Uh sitting somewhat forward of him at 45-degree angles and to his left and right respectively. This arrangement is said to have been decreed by the Soulik of Ant atoll at the time of the conquest of Ponape by Isohkelekel, the first Nahnmwarki. The Nahnmwarki of Net and Sokehs, whose positions date from much later, sit to one side.

For commoners, travel between tribes was always dangerous, but if a man wished to settle in another tribe and could get his Nahnmwarki to send word ahead that he had permission to move, the Nahnmwarki in the other tribe might tell his own people to regard the newcomer peacefully.

Some economic specialization between the five tribes existed, and there was trading to some extent. Sokehs had the reputation of making the best mats, Madolenihmw the best canoes, and Kiti the loom-woven belts. But such trade was virtually a monopoly of the highest chiefs because of the constant danger in travel.

A commoner crossing a boundary was safe only if sent by a high chief. He would carry as a sign of his mission a stalk of sugar cane or a kava plant to the Nahnmwarki of the tribe he was visiting. Men holding titles lower than A4 or B2 could trade only with their relatives in other tribes. Despite the risks involved, visits between Nahnmwarkis do not seem to have been rare. Finsch records the mutual avoidance between two Nahnmarkis when both visited his ship about 1880, but this might only have reflected recent hostilities. Royal visits, however, were always made in considerable force, owing to the precarious state of peace that prevailed in the intervals between wars. On such occasions (known as *seiloak*) a number of unmarried girls would be chosen by the Nahnken from both chiefly lines and made available for the large company of chiefs and retainers accompanying the visiting Nahnmwarki, and valuable articles would be presented. On the inevitable reciprocal visit a few days later equivalent gifts were returned. Such articles were sewed pandanus sleeping mats, decoratively wrapped balls and cylinders of twine, canoes, bailers, sponges, loom-woven banana-fiber sashes, chief's kilts, besides the baskets of food always presented at feasts. The assumption of the frequency of visits is in part based on the fact that some balls of twine still in existence are said to have circulated around the island in this way many times.

The legend of the fall of the line of monarchs which preceded the Nahnmwarkis attributes it, in part, to the sorcery of the X1 of section 21 of Kiti, a powerful priest, who had visited the last of these rulers but had been insulted at receiving only some coconuts instead of the royal gifts he felt he had a right to expect.

The majesty of the bearer of a high title could be affected by individual variability in personality traits or by status not derived from descent, as a number of biographical incidents indicate. Solomon, who later became Nahnmwarki of Madolenihmw, was appointed A2 in Spanish times at the age of 13. At a feast given to him in section 6 he played with other lads, got into a fight and was soundly beaten, and returned to his place on the main platform weeping bitterly. The spectacle of this small boy, the third chief of the land and the future supreme ruler, sitting in the place of honor and sniveling because of a thrashing, still tickles the risibilities of informants who describe the incident today. The plight of the B1 of Net, described previously, who was nearly drowned when his arrogance in demanding tribute and in confiscating land exhausted the patience of his subjects, is another case in point.

Nevertheless, deference to a chief was often carried to remarkable lengths. It is told of the renowned Nahnawa en Mwudok, who became Nahnken of Kiti in 1864, that his runaway wife, who had eloped with a lover, was brought back to him while he lay in a drunken stupor; when he was awakened, he plunged a knife into her breast. Her parents were his servants and were among the witnesses of the murder, yet did not dare to interefere.[65]

A high chief was formerly referred to after his death by a special burial name (*edenpwel*). Ponapean personal names, which are often derived from legend, are regarded as secret; it is considered as an insult for a man to be addressed by it, and the proper form of address is by use of his title, or by his special title of address, if he has one, even by his wife. Even a woman should be addressed by the feminine form of her husband's title. (Nowadays the personal name of legendary origin is supplemented or often supplanted by baptismal names of nonnative origin, which are not held to be secret.) In the case of a high chief, the secrecy involved amounted to a taboo. During his lifetime his name was not to be spoken; in those cases when it was also the name of a common object or, later, the introduced name of a foreign object, a new term had to be devised to refer to the article, for use in his tribe; the older term continued in the other tribes, which accounts for some of the dialectal variations that exist in Ponape. Names of many long-departed chiefs are not remembered, but these chiefs are spoken of today by their burial names or sometimes by a title they held at some time. A Nahnken of Kiti who died in 1864 is not recalled by his native name even by his own grandson (though Luelen's manuscript refers to him as Solomon), but he is known as Nahnku, a title he held in his youth. His successor is also recalled by a title he once held, Nahnawa en Mwudok. Usually, however, the burial name is used. This consists of the prefix Luhken (Luhk, the name of a god) followed by a descriptive suffix; for example:

Luhkenlengsihr (*leng*, heaven; *sihr*, the dart-game known in Polynesia as *teka*, similar to North American snowsnake)
Luhkensohpur (*soh*, negative; *pur*, return; i.e., died a hero's death in war)
Luhkenmelmel (*melmel*, typhoon)
Luhkensakau (*sakau*, kava; i.e., drank much kava)

The name of a chief's widow takes the same suffix as that of her husband, but the prefix is Luhmo. A commoner's burial name is prefixed by Nalang.

The dead child of a Nahnmwarki or Nahnken, but of no other chief, is given a title before burial and the title is considered buried with him and may not be given out again until the father has died. This applies even to a still birth. In November 1947 a dead child was born to the wife of Max, Nahnmwarki of Net; it was given the title of Nahnsahu of Net, which may not be reissued until Max is dead.

To announce the death of a Nahnmwarki tritons were blown in quick, short blasts, similar to those made by a war party; in contrast to this the death of a lesser man was signaled by long blasts, like those sounded by fishermen returning from fishing with a new net. A similar class distinction was made with the playing of the drum, though its exact nature has been forgotten.

Scattered over the island are a large number of stone burial chambers (*lolong*) of variable construction; this is quite apart from the spectacular structures on the artificial islands off Madolenihmw and elsewhere. A number of alternate mortuary usages seem to have prevailed simultaneously; thus suspension in canoes, earth burial wrapped in mats, and placing in stone family vaults are all described. But it may be generalized that the stone structures were used primarily for chiefs, whereas commoners were buried in earth graves. In Wene, at least, low, cairn-like structures (Plate 1b) were in use for the priest-king, Soukise, in combination with secondary burial; burial was done at night in secrecy at Ninlepwel in Section 7; later the stone structure, regarded as sacred, was built and the bones placed therein.

## MARRIAGE AND SEXUAL PRIVILEGES

In contrast to the prevailing rule of matrilocal residence the sons of men of highest rank, perhaps as far down as A4 and B4, brought their wives home with them. If such a man married a woman whose father had a title higher than that of his father, however, residence remained matrilocal; and if the two fathers were of approximately equal rank, the married children lived for indefinite periods in either household, staying longest with the more prosperous one. If marriage was outside of the tribe it was usually patrilocal, regardless of the relative rank of the spouses. Hambruch states (1932 II, p. 148) that around the dwelling house stood the houses of a man's sons, but this would ordinarily be true only for the house of a high chief.

While a Nahnmwarki or Nahnken would often have 10 or more wives, fewer lesser tribal or section chiefs had

[65] Hambruch (1932 II, pp. 74–75), in giving a somewhat different version of this, makes it appear that two similar incidents involving two different wronged husbands occurred.

more than two. An informant past 90 years of age could not remember any polygynous commoners, and some informants deny that a commoner could have plural wives. Keimw Sapwasap, a Nahnmwarki of Sokehs, is said to have had some 30 women in his harem. The first wife married, the *inenmwohd,* was the principal wife; all the others were called *pekehi.* In addition, a chief would have sexual access to the female servants, the *lidu.*[66]

Each wife of a chief received a title. (See p. 47.) The first wife of a Nahnmwarki was Nahnalek; the second Ked; the third Nahnte. The wives of a Nahnken were similarly Nahnkeniei, Karekin, and Emekin. For any additional wives other titles were employed. Under present monogamous conditions the titles Nahnalek and Nahnkeniei persist as forms of address for the wives of a Nahnmwarki and a Nahnken respectively. The Lepen Net, who was A1 of Net until German times, when he was granted the title of Nahnmwarki in order to conform to the practice in the other tribes, gave his principal wife the title of Lempein. At least the later of the rulers who had the title Lepen Net had the additional title Soulik en Daun, and to correspond to this title a second wife took the title Kedinlik en Daun; to his third title, Soumadau en Eirike, corresponded that of his third wife, Kedinmadau en Eirike, and for his fourth title, Soulik en Ais, his fourth wife had the title Kedinlik en Ais. These were his four principal titles; if he took more wives, additional titles were taken by him specifically for each marriage, and the wife received the feminine cognate form thereof.

Theoretically, at least, in Net each wife of the Lepen Net belonged to a different clan, the principal wife belonging always to the clan of the B-line. This was in order to reinforce the political authority of the Lepen Net, since several clans were thus linked to him and were bound to support and revere him. He also enhanced his economic position, for members of those clans were expected to bring him goods beyond normal requirements. The Lempein had to be of clan 9; the Kedinlik en Daun was of clan 6; these two clans have been the B-clans of Net. Clan affiliation of the other wives was apparently not fixed.

Elsewhere than Net a chief seems usually to have taken all of his wives from the opposite chiefly line. Luhkenkidu (a burial name), who was a Nahnmwarki of Madolenihmw, had ten wives, all of them in clan 9 and all closely related. A Lepen Palikir had as wives two sisters, belonging to clan 4. Hezekiah, B2 of Madolenihmw in German times, who was one of the last polygynists, had three wives who were sisters; but they were of clan 18 instead of the A-clan.

The husband lived in one house, the secondary wives in another close by. It is not clear where the principal wife lived; most Net informants state that she lived in the house with the husband while the secondary wives lived apart with an old woman to guard them; but Madolenihmw informants agree that all the wives lived together and apart from the husband. In at least one royal family (that of Keimw Sapwasap, a Nahnmwarki of Sokehs), the most recent acquisition in the harem was set up with her servants in a separate house of her own. In any event, the principal wife ruled the harem. Her designation as *inenmwohd,* literally "sitting mother," reveals her status. When her husband was away, she stayed at home and could not go about; but the secondary wives might travel with him. She did little work, whereas the secondary wives, unless there were enough servants, did such tasks as making kilts, sewing sleeping mats, and weaving belts, and sometimes they would cook, fetch wood and water, and clear grass away from the vicinity of the house. Though a high chief had considerable sexual freedom, many informants state that he had to obtain the permission of his principal wife to sleep with one of the other wives or, according to one informant, to summon any woman for an extramarital affair. If the first wife was a commoner, such permission does not seem to have been necessary and his sexual freedom was therefore greater.

A man of high title had the right to demand any woman he desired (although informants in Net say that the right was restricted to the Nahnmwarki and Nahnken). This right is called *klasopa;* commoners, who did not have the right, were referred to reciprocally as *klapata.* It did not matter whether the girl was married or unmarried; her family or husband would be punished if she demurred. The husband could do nothing to prevent the affair; he might receive a present from the chief, but this was not obligatory. A Nahnmwarki would simply send his attendants to fetch the woman. She would be kept at the pleasure of the chief and would be expected to massage and delouse him, pluck gray hairs from his head and otherwise attend him, as well as to sleep with him. She was not anointed as in a regular marriage ceremony, unless he intended to add her to his harem. A Nahnmwarki, up to the time of Paul of Kiti, could even take a woman of his own clan, even a parallel cousin, and none could say him nay, whereas incest meant death to a commoner. Moreover, there could be no joking at or ridicule of such behavior. The saying goes, "See but don't say . . . the chiefs" (*Kilang seupwa—soupeidi*), meaning essentially for a commoner, "No matter what you see or know about the chiefs, keep your mouth shut." Another proverb is "Wickedness of the chiefs" (*Sakanakan soupeidi*); this is explained to mean that regardless of how reprehensible a chief's actions may be his high position excuses him. These royal prerogatives are ancient, for the Saudeleurs who preceded the Nahnmwarkis are said

[66] One informant denies such access unless the chief was unmarried.

to have sent their chief lieutenant, the Soukampwul, to bring them wives of other men.

The perpetrator of a rape would be chided or punished by one of the highest chiefs, because it was a chief's prerogative alone to force a woman to lie with him against her will.

A woman of somewhat higher rank than her legal husband had sexual privileges similar to those of the high chiefs and could summon any man she liked to come and be her lover. The sister of a Nahnmwarki who was married to B3 or lower, and the sister of a Nahnken married to A5 or lower, could avail themselves of this right to take lovers indiscriminately; but faithfulness was required of a woman whose husband was of equal or higher rank. The class or clan or marital status of the lover was of no consequence, and his tenure as paramour of the woman was entirely dependent on her whim. She would usually notify the wife of the man who had taken her fancy to perfume and bedeck him and then to send him along to her. The degree of sexual freedom permitted to a woman thus seems to have varied roughly inversely with the rank of her husband. A man of lower rank than his wife could apparently do little to halt her affairs, but he himself would be "thrown away" if he were unfaithful.

The use of "higher rank" in this connection should not obscure the previously noted fact that a man of lower rank than his wife receives a title "for" her; he is called by the title she had before marriage, or by one that has been held in reserve for her future husband, but his acquisition of the title through marriage does not raise his rank to the level of hers. Her rank is thought of as being on the level of the titles of her brothers.

Bascom states that royal and noble men and women married to commoners did not have to observe the forms of courtesy ordinarily due to high chiefs, but the writer's informants deny this. Only Royal Children and the few exceptions such as the Mwarekehtik already noted have the right to familiar behavior, regardless of the status of their spouses.

The adulterous wife of a Nahnmwarki or Nahnken was, in theory at least, put to death, along with her lover. The story of the B1 of Kiti who put his runaway wife to death has been related; her lover had already been slain by the wronged husband's attendants. Nevertheless, the fact that a chief's secondary wives lived in a house separate from his tempted many a young man to take the risks involved, and it is said that few members of the harem remained chaste.

A man of lower status who was cuckolded could kill his wife only if he thought he could get away with it, for he had to think about revenge by her relatives; most often he had to be satisfied with beating or otherwise punishing her; but he would usually make an attempt to kill her seducer.

Ordinarily it was the Nahnwarki who had the unfaithful wife of a Nahnken killed, and the latter took upon himself the reciprocal duty for the Nahnmwarki; they would delegate the actual execution to a lesser chief of their own lines. Hambruch (1932 II, p. 75) says that it was the clan of the woman who took revenge for a seduction, but present-day informants insist it was the clan of the husband; contrary to Hambruch, the seducer did not escape personal retribution, but suffered along with his brothers and clan chief.

A high chief could forbid a pretty young girl to marry, but might take her into his house to be raised by his principal wife until she was 13 or 14, then he would make a secondary wife of her. There were even cases of kidnaping.

Widows and divorced wives of high chiefs are referred to as *rohng*[67] *en soupeidi* or *karohng en soupeidi,* by which term is understood a prohibition to remarry. A widow of a man of high title is also known as *rohng en* ——— (the dead man's title). Hambruch, Finsch, and Kubary all state that the prohibition was absolute. However, the prohibition seems actually to have applied only to remarriage to someone outside the clan of her dead husband. That the clan of the dead husband retained rights to the widow is seen in the occasional use of the expression *rohng en* ———(the dead man's clan) to designate her. The brother or the sister's son or sometimes a more remote clansmate of a dead Nahnmwarki or other high chief could take such a woman as his wife, the brother having first choice, regardless of his previous marital status; in fact, it was considered better to marry the widow than to require her to remain unmarried, lest she enter into a liaison with a commoner. (A commoner, however, could marry his dead brother's wife only if he did not already have a wife.) Usually only old widows were left to remain unmarried. If a member of a clan other than that of the dead husband took the widow, he was, within the memory of living informants, beaten up or cut with knives, then banished; more anciently, he might be killed. The prohibition was rigidly enforced by the brothers, sister's sons, and successor in office of the dead man, for the widow was considered to be property of their sub-clan.

Some informants limit the term *rohng* to widow of the three highest chiefs of each line, but extend it also to widows of men with lesser titles if they belong to the same sub-clan as the Nahnmwarki or Nahnken.

Sometimes the prohibition was circumvented by a suitor of the widow by giving a feast to the clansmates of the dead man and by payment to them of such property as balls of sennit, sleeping mats, and other valuables.

Some informants state that secondary wives of a dead man, unlike the principal wife, were ordinarily not con-

[67] The primary meaning of this word is "to hear" and apparently is used here figuratively, for no scandal was supposed to be heard about such a woman.

sidered as *rohng;* it was only a secondary wife who was dearly loved by her husband, one who was always taken about with him on voyages and to feasts, who would be held as *rohng* and prohibited from remarrying after his death. This view may be correct, since I recorded genealogies which show several cases, three and four generations ago, of remarriage of a secondary wife to a man of a clan different from that of her first husband.

However, the missionary Doane, writing in 1870, suggests otherwise, at least for divorced women, if not widows, in his time. The "king" of Sokehs had kidnaped a 12-year-old girl and added her to his harem. The captain of the USS *Jamestown*, visiting Ponape in that year, at the behest of the missionaries forced her release and she returned to her family. But when the ship left there were attempts on her life because, as Doane puts it, it was a great sin for her to be free and mingle with the people, having once been claimed by the king. In the same year Doane writes of a high chief who had a principal wife and four concubines; he wanted to become a Christian and to have a church marriage to his principal wife, but Doane insisted that he must first put aside his concubines. To which the chief replied that if a woman once married or mistress to a chief were to be allowed to appear in public or to get remarried the people would not tolerate it; such an offense might be punished by death.

Sexual activity with a *rohng* apart from remarriage had to be carried on very secretly; if it were discovered, the chief of her dead husband's sub-clan would burn down the man's house and chop down his bananas, kava, and other plants.

A commoner's widow was known as *liohdi* instead of *rohng*. She was free to marry as she pleased and was equally free to engage in amorous adventures. It was considered best for a prospective husband to obtain permission to marry her from the members of the sub-clan of the dead man, but it was not always done, and is not done at all today. Occasionally a commoner might let it be known that his brother's widow was to remain unmarried, but his wishes would be respected only if he were generally feared.

The usages associated with *rohng* have to some extent persisted to present times. The widow of the Nahnmwarki Francisco of Sokehs remained unmarried until her death; the widows of Luis, Nahnmwarki of Sokehs, and of Solomon, Nahnmwarki of Madolenihmw, remain unmarried today. The principal widow of the last Lepen Net married his clansmate and classificatory brother, Saturlino, who later became Nahnmwarki. The widow of the last Nahnmwarki of Uh has married the present Nahnmwarki, Edmundo.

Informants say that probably no punishment would be inflicted today on a man who married a *rohng* but that a feast of propitiation would have to be made by the new husband to chiefs A1–A4 and B1 if she were a Nahnmwarki's widow, to B1–B4 and A1 if she were a Nahnken's widow. No actual remarriage of a Nahnmwarki's or Nahnken's widow out of her husband's clan is known, but the divorced wife of the present Nahnmwarki of Madolenihmw, who is *rohng* by definition, has so remarried without any payments or atonement being exacted.

On the death of a chief the widow and children formerly would take their belongings and steal off that same night to her family, for fear that the common people would come and despoil them of everything they owned. Native informants in describing these behaviors appear to accept them as perfectly natural; people, they say, would obviously be jealous of the power of a chief's wife, and as soon as opportunity afforded, they would give vent to their spite. Apparently the dead man's brothers did not feel the same protective interest in her property that they did in her person.

# Prestige Competition

## COMPETITION FOR TITLES

We have until now spoken as though promotions and succession in the title hierarchy were regulated mainly by the principle of clan seniority. We have discussed the exceptions to this principle and described how a man might, through unusual merit, warlike deeds, or advantageous marriage, overcome the handicaps of birth and achieve a high position regardless of commoner origin. But a significant omission in this presentation remains, namely, the acquisition of titles through prestige competition.

The royal and noble clans tend to monopolize the higher tribal titles, so much so that we have used the term A-clan to indicate the royal clan which holds the highest A-titles and the term B-clan for the noble clan which holds the highest B-titles. Only an occasional commoner receives a title in the first 12 of each series. But there are many more than 12 titles. In Net, which has a total male population of some 450, a list of 210 issued tribal titles was collected, and there are undoubtedly more. If we do not count boys and very young men, since few of them outside the ruling clans would have tribal titles, it is clear that the majority of mature men must possess tribal titles and that among them must be a large number of commoners. Informants state that formerly there were fewer tribal titles, that new ones have been invented and issued in order that the chiefs might profit by the title-payment feasts, and that most commoners in times past had only section titles. Nevertheless, a significant number of commoners has always achieved titles in the two tribal series; and in such achievement the principle of clan seniority cannot operate, for the commoner clans, though some are held to be worthier than others, have no title series considered to belong exclusively to them. Though a commoner normally has a higher title than another man who is his junior in blood in the same clan, he has no particular status in relation to a man in another commoner clan, except with reference to the title each of them holds. The status of a man of high title is for the most part ascribed, for with the exceptions already noted it comes to him in the main through birth. But the status of a holder of one of the lesser titles is largely achieved, for he gains his title through certain types of activities, in competition for prestige against his fellow commoners. It is through such competition that merit for promotion is judged—the judges being primarily the Nahnken (for tribal titles) and the section head (for section titles).

Promotions come about in part through bringing to feasts for presentation to chiefs larger and better and more frequent food offerings than other men, thus demonstrating industry, ability, loyalty, and affection toward the chiefs. But more important than presentations at feasts are the direct offerings of first fruits (*nohpwei*) and the occasional gifts of food between first fruits (*kaiak* or *uhmw en kaiak*). All of these types of presentation are known as Service (*uhpa,* literally "to stand underneath"). Perhaps even more important than regular offerings is the bringing of a valuable article, such as the fermented contents of a large breadfruit pit, to the Nahnmwarki on a special occasion, as when an important visitor comes from another tribe and the Nahnmwarki wishes to make some display at a feast in the visitor's honor. All of these acts are stored in the memories of the chiefs (in Net nowadays recorded in writing) and duly rewarded when vacant titles arise.

A man who has a tribal title may perform Service direct to the Nahnmwarki and Nahnken and thus gain prestige. A man who has only a section title, unless it is that of the head of the section, cannot do this; but he can present articles to the head or to any man with a tribal title who, he sees, lacks enough goods to offer to the Nahnmwarki or Nahnken at the time of a feast; the recipient then presents the goods as his own but in the course of the feast praises his benefactor to the Nahnmwarki or Nahnken. The section head also reports to the Nahnmwarki and Nahnken on the quality of performance at Service of his various subjects.

Activities of all sorts performed for and on behalf of the Nahnmwarki, including communal labor, proper expression of obedience, etiquette, deference and the various forms of Service, but not including warfare, are called Great Work (*taulap*). All of these things are the due of the Nahnmwarki; in native theory promotions are earned not so much for gifts to the Nahnmwarki as for looking after the property of the tribe; all valuables—large yams, large kava bushes, fine mats, etc.—belong to the Nahnmwarki, and offerings made on specified and other occasions are not truly presents but merely delivering up, when called upon or when occasion requires, what is rightfully the Nahnmwarki's. Warfare on behalf of the Nahnmwarki constituted a second type of activity. It was called Little Work (*tautik*). Both of these activities are considered in making decisions about promotions though warfare, of course, is now a thing of the past.

Great Work is regarded as everyday, humdrum work and easy; Little Work though brief in duration as difficult. Some informants say that Great Work counted most in Kiti while Little Work was more important in Madolenihmw, but others assert that Little Work counted most everywhere. The literal meanings of the terms make it difficult to evaluate these opinions; probably the suffixes, great and little respectively, refer not to the relative worth of the two types of service but to the period of their duration. Little Work, in any case, produced the more spectacular results. A man might be jumped from a low title to one as high as A3 [68] or B3 through valiant deeds, if he were a commoner; or up to A2 or B2 if he belonged to the proper clan. There were even instances when a successful war leader, upon return from battle, dethroned the Nahnmwarki or Nahnken and took over the office. One informant includes under the term Little Work the division by chiefs of the food offerings made to them at feasts and redistribution among the people, but several others deny the application of the term to this custom. (Such return is more properly *kepin koanoat. Koanoat,* as discussed elsewhere, is the special honorific for food which is applicable to the Nahnmwarki and some other chiefs, but it is also extended to redistribution of feast goods as well as to any acts of generosity by the Nahnmwarki, such as the giving out of titles, land, or anything else, including a daughter to a noble husband, in return for Service.)

The war pattern has already been discussed. Remaining to be discussed is Great Work, and more particularly Service, as expressed through first fruits, feasts, and other presentations.

## FIRST FRUITS

First fruits offerings to chiefs, as distinguished from food offerings made at the regular feasts, are called *nohpwei.* Since some types of food are offered more than once, only the first of these is strictly speaking, first fruits, and this particular *nohpwei* is called *mwohn dipwisou.* After the first fruits offering for any plant food is made, the commoners are free themselves to partake of that food and any variety of it.

In general, first fruits are offered to the Nahnmwarki, Nahnken, and the section head, and unless otherwise indicated the term "chief" as used in the descriptions of first fruits to follow applies to each of these three. But if a man of higher title than the section head lives in a particular section, it is he instead of the head who has the right to receive the first fruits, and the section head is sometimes ignored in this regard. People who live in the same section as the Nahnmwarki or Nahnken need offer only two first fruits for a particular product, one to the Nahnmwarki and one to the Nahnken, and need not offer a third to the section head as other people should do.

Many informants state that formerly only the sections belonging to the Nahnmwarki gave first fruits to him and only those belonging to the Nahnken gave to him; other informants deny this. This difference of opinion is no doubt due to the changes effected by successive European influences. The German land deeds which, in giving the lands to individual owners, authorized the giving of an honor feast annually to the Nahnmwarki failed to mention the Nahnken, thereby affecting the pattern of food offering. In Net today, for example, both Nahnmwarki and Nahnken receive first fruits from those who hold to the old customs regardless of where they live, but many give only to one or the other, and some to neither. The concept is often verbalized that first fruits are a rental for the use of the land, and since the chiefs no longer own the land many people consider that no rent is due.

---

[68] A5, according to some.

The various tribes were formerly divided into political subdivisions larger than the sections and some of the chiefs who headed these areas seem also to have been entitled to food offerings. Nowadays, large landholders, such as chief A6 of Kiti, receive first fruits regularly from their tenants, while the A1 and B1 of Kiti, having only a small amount of land of their own, receive first fruits only in times of plenty.

The formal presentation of offerings to the Nahnmwarki and Nahnken is not made directly by household heads but through the section head, who receives such offerings and transmits them appropriately, retaining those that have been made to him directly.

Anciently, failure to present first fruits resulted in loss of title and land, as well as banishment, but today there is no compulsion, although titles are still taken away. But it was acceptable for a man who had nothing of a particular food to offer to present another food as a symbolic substitute. Those who retain the old customs still offer some of the first fruits, particularly those described under the names *kehmei, lihli, idihd,* and *kotekehp;* but others have fallen into complete desuetude. It is undoubtedly correct to say that only a minority of Ponapeans nowadays adhere to the old practices. One semiacculturated informant who used to offer first fruits but has given it up argues that his title is a low one, hence he gets little back from the chiefs when yams are redistributed at feasts and he therefore looks upon contributions to the chiefs as an economic loss to him; this attitude is to be directly linked with the money economy that has been introduced into Ponape since the missionary and whaling days. Another man states that his mother bought the land he has now, he did not get it in fief from the chief in the manner practiced before the issuance of the deeds in German times, hence he feels no compulsion to pay in kind for the use of the land.

The first fruits (*nohpwei*) are to be distinguished from the feasts (*kamadipw*) in that they are simple presentations of food, whereas the latter are more formal occasions. Where cooking is involved, the objects offered as first fruits are usually prepared by each man in his privately owned, family cookhouse and presented to the chief at the chief's house; whereas feasts are held in the community house, where the food is communally cooked. A number of other differences are described later.

The various first fruits occasions by name are as follows:

1. Yams (*kehp*):
   a. *kotekehp* (*kote,* to cut; *kehp,* yam). This is the first of the first fruits of the yam season (*isol*). The vines are cut from the immature yam, which is then baked in the family cookhouse. The yam must come from a new garden. The whole yam must be brought, undivided, to the chief. Any variety of yam will do except "southern yams" (*kehpineir*). Commoners present what they can afford; a section head presents to the Nahnmwarki and Nahnken a definite number of yams, which varies from one tribe to another; in Net it is five. Supposed to occur in October.
   b. *idihd* (to grate). When the yams are mature, two or three are dug up, skinned, and grated on a piece of tin (formerly on a rough stone found in salt water), then mixed with coconut cream. Grated yam, when prepared for private consumption, is tied up into a leaf of *Cyrtosperma* (*mwahng*) to make a loaf and baked in the cookhouse; the food is then called Bundle (*koruk*). But for presentation to the chief it is baked in a banana leaf, when it is called *raisok.* Both may also be called *idihd,* the name of the first fruit. The food is normally presented in a basket made of a section of coconut leaf (a *kiam*). A commoner may present a small basket, but a section head presents one of three sizes, containing (in Net) five, eight, or 11 baked loaves; or sometimes, instead, he presents a basket made of an entire coconut leaf (a *pahini*). Sometimes the dish is made of *Cyrtosperma,* bananas (of any kind except *utuniap* or *karat*), arrowroot, or manioc; or bananas may be mixed with manioc or yams, when the dish is called *repwrepw.* This first fruit presentation comes in December.
   c. *deulimau* (*deu,* to fill; *limau,* five). This also consists of grated yams baked in the cookhouse, but it is wrapped in *Cyrtosperma* leaves and is always presented in five loaves, carried to the chief by two bearers in a long basket slung under a pole. This first fruit was never obligatory, but was made in February by anyone who could afford it.
2. Breadfruit (*mahi* or *mei*):
   The various first fruits involving breadfruit are collectively called *karihmei* or *mwohnmei* (the latter is also the name of a particular one of these first fruits).
   a. *karisimei* (*karis,* to pluck; *mei,* breadfruit). Green breadfruit is picked with the stem and leaves attached, baked in the cookhouse, and taken to the chief. This has not been observed for about 15 years in Net. Occurs in early May.[69]
   b. *kehmei* (from *ka,* to bite or chew?). A type of breadfruit containing seeds (*meikohl*) is used. Baked in the cookhouse. May, June, and July.

[69] Hambruch (1932 II, p. 227) records this in April, but regards it as a feast, not a first fruit.

c. *mwohnmei* (*mwoh,* first). Mature breadfruit baked and taken to the chief. Late May through July.

d. *lihli* or *mwohlihli* (*mwoh,* first). This is the most important first fruit involving breadfruit. The people of an entire section bring great quantities of breadfruit to the community house, where the Nahnmwarki is in attendance, and the fruit is there baked and pounded, and coconut cream squeezed over it. This first fruit partakes also of the nature of a feast, since it involves pigs and kava as well as the community house. Held in July and occasionally later. (See further remarks on *lihli,* p. 80).

e. *uhmw en pahini* or *dokapahini,* names used in Net; probably the same as *dokemei* in Kiti (*uhmw,* stone oven; *dok,* to spear or punch a hole; *pahini,* the whole coconut leaf). A hole is punched in the eye of the breadfruit, water and sometimes a *Macaranga kanehirae* (*ahpwid*) leaf put in the hole, and the fruit left overnight to ripen artificially. Then it is baked in the cookhouse or occasionally in the community house. A long basket is made from the whole coconut leaf and some 30 to 50 baked breadfruit are carried in it to the chief at his house. Not done by a section but by every man who is rich enough. Occurs in July and August.

f. *uhmw en inihn* (*uhmw,* stone oven; *inihn,* to roast on a fire). Until this first fruit is presented, breadfruit must always be baked in the stone oven, as they are on this occasion too, but after this they may be roasted over an open fire. The breadfruit are prepared in the community house in the presence of the chief.

g. *song en mar,* name used in Net; same as *pokolopwon* in Kiti (*song,* to taste; *mar,* pit-breadfruit; *poko,* to roll into a ball; *lopwon,* a ball of baked pit-breadfruit). Done individually; each man bakes some fresh breadfruit together with pit-breadfruit in his cookhouse and takes a small basketful to the chief. August and September.

h. *sakalap* (*sak,* to eat; *lap,* much, big). Breadfruit artificially ripened, as in 2e, above, then baked in the cookhouse and carried to the chief in a basket made from the whole coconut leaf. September.

i. *uhmw en luhwen mei* (*uhmw,* stone oven; *luhwe,* remainder; *mei,* breadfruit). This is made from the last breadfruit of the season; the people of a whole section bake the fruit in a stone oven in the community house with the chief in attendance and with pigs and kava simultaneously prepared (according to Net informants) or in the cookhouse (according to Kiti informants). These particulars in Net would cause this occasion to be classed as a feast rather than first fruits if one follows the definitions informants give; nevertheless Net people call this first fruits. Held in September or October.

A Madolenihmw informant gives also *mwohndelemei* as a first fruit, when a food called *delemei* is offered. This is made from artificially ripened breadfruit, which is pounded, heated with hot stones, and added to coconut cream squeezed into a wooden vessel. Other informants do not consider *delemei* to be a first fruit offering but agree that it is presented to chiefs. Some informants also list *kaiak* as a first fruit, but others state that it is merely an occasional gift occurring between the various first fruits and consists of the best portions from food of all sorts prepared at family ovens as part of regular family meals.[70] The information about *sakalap* (2h, above) comes from a single Kiti informant, and was not checked with other informants.

3. Kava (*sakau*):

a. *wisik pwehl* (*wisik,* to carry; *pwehl,* earth). The first kava bush dug from a new kava garden is brought to the chief.

b. *sahrpahn sakau* (*sahr,* to remove; *pah,* under). After the kava has grown high, the lower parts are trimmed off and brought to the chief.

4. Bananas (*uht*). The first fruit is called *mwohn uht.* Offered to chiefs in breadfruit season. A Madolenihmw informant says only *mangat* bananas may be offered; a Net informant says *utuniap* and *karat* are offered; another Net informant says that all three of these, the only types of bananas which ought to be baked in a stone oven, are traditional offerings, but that nowadays the first of every sort of banana from a new garden should be offered.[71] When bananas are intended for use by commoners, the stalk is cut off close to the top of the bunch, but for a chief care is taken to leave a long stalk with two young leaves attached.

5. Pineapple. The first fruit, which had its origins only in German times, is called *mwohn painapal;* pineapples are not native. It comes in the bread-

[70] Gulick's vocabulary gives *kaiak* as "food prepared at the natives' homes and taken to a chief; better food than that usually prepared at a feast," thus agreeing with the second group of informants.

[71] Offerable types of *mangat* are *mangat* proper, *mangat en alohkapw, epohn, ihpali en pohnpei, ihpali en Saipan;* types of *utuniap* offerable are *utuniap* and *utumwas; karat* types are *karat* proper, *karat kohlo,* and *karat en pahlil.* Other than these three, which are considered native and are baked in the stone oven, the numerous imported varieties are prepared as "ainpot" (from English, iron pot), i.e., by boiling, a nonaboriginal method.

fruit season. The stems and leaves must be left attached. The largest fruit are packed five to a basket and brought to the chief.

6. Mango (*kehngid*). The first fruit is *mwohn kehngid;* it comes in breadfruit season. The fruit are laid along with separated leaves and branches in the long coconut-leaf basket (*pahini*) and carried by two men with a carrying pole to the chief; the basket holds several hundred fruit. Two varieties of mango may be used, *kehngid en pohnpei* and *kehngid en salong,* also the sports developed from each of these in recent times, *kiewek en kehngid en pohnpei* and *kiewek en kehngid en salong.*
7. Pandanus (*kipar* or *deipw*). The first fruit is *mwohn deipw* and comes in the breadfruit season. The fruit is presented uncooked. As with bananas, a long stem and two leaves are left attached, but unlike bananas, pandanus is offered in a basket. All types may be offered. Pandanus, however, is rarely offered except in Madolenihmw.
8. Sugar cane (*sehu*). The first fruit is *mwohn sehu.* Presented at any time whenever the cane is of sufficient size. The leaves may not be removed; this is true for all three purposes for which sugar cane is presented to a chief: first fruits (*nohpwei*), begging pardon for an offense (*tohmw*), and invitation to a feast (*luk*). All six varieties of sugar cane may be offered, as well as *sehu ahlek,* which is a kind of reed somewhat resembling sugar cane, but no one of these may be offered by itself.
9. Polynesian chestnut, *Inocarpus edulis* (*merepw*). May be offered only under a basketful of pit-breadfruit or of *kehp palahi,* a sweet yam.
10. Taro (*sawa*). Only the varieties *pahmaru, pahnta* and *keiwetik* may properly be offered to chiefs. though *kuhwet* has also been recorded.
11. *Dioscorea bulbifera* (*palahi*). A wild yam. The first fruit is *mwohn palahi* and is made in December. The yams are baked in a stone oven one night, then skinned with the fingernails and brought in a coconut-leaf basket to a brook and placed on a flat basketry tray (called a *pwaht en palahi*), 1 to 3 feet square, made of *Saccharum spontaneum* (*ahlek*) leaves; the sides are built up of a sort of fern (*mahrek*), which is not woven into the tray but worked up around its edges. A supply of running water is fed into the tray from the brook by means of a flume constructed of overlapping half-cylinders from the concentric layers of banana tree trunks (Net informant) or bamboo (Madolenihmw informant). The yams are kneaded with the hands and, after the bitter quality leaches out, the fern is removed and the tray placed with its contents (now called *kedepw*) into a coconut-leaf basket and presented to the chief as first fruits; in this condition it is described as ice cold and is nowadays regarded as a rare and great delicacy. It may be baked again after leaching. On the occasion of this presentation, five places are laid on the main platform of the community house, each place being a sort of platter consisting of 10 breadfruit leaves and two leaves of *Campnosperma brevipetiolata* (*dohng*). Four of these places form the corners of a square, the fifth is in the center of the square. Two spoons are made by slicing chords through the husk of a young coconut and the official in charge of food distribution at feasts (the *soun ne*) uses these to scoop out a portion of the food from the center of the tray, which he places on the central leaf platter. The second scoop is taken from the lower right corner of the tray and placed on the corresponding platter; then the lower left, upper right, and upper left corners are similarly treated in that order. These five scoops are presented to the chief, who retains only the central one, the others are distributed to the highest men of title present. The remainder of the dish is scooped up according to no particular plan and distributed among the rest of the people, whose leaf platters contain no particular number of leaves. The ritual of division corresponds closely to that used for a dog or turtle.

In the old days this dish was prepared by women on order of the high chiefs. Nowadays it is made primarily for invalids and is offered as first fruits only when there is enough left over after the invalid has partaken of it. It is considered difficult and time-consuming to make; the tray alone requires considerable labor. Formerly it was sometimes a substitute for *idihd* (yam first fruits 1b).

## Lihli

The making of *lihli,* mentioned above as breadfruit first fruits 2d, is sufficiently important and sufficiently associated with ceremony and deferential customs to merit its description at length. The dish consists usually of baked and pounded breadfruit covered with coconut cream. It is offered as one of the principal first fruits to the Nahnmwarki by the people of each section. Sometimes it is also made for the Nahnken. When these requirements are satisfied, it is then made for the head of each section, following which anyone can eat of it. It is made perhaps five or ten times yearly. The dish can also be made of banana (*lihli uht*) or taro (*lihli sawa*),[72] and sometimes

[72] Bascom (1965, p. 40) also includes *Cyrtosperma* (*lihli mwahng*) but the writer's informants say that only Pingelap, Ngatik, and Mokil people make this dish.

bananas and breadfruit, or bananas and taro are mixed (*lihli repwrepw*).

The following account is based in large part on a *lihli* preparation arranged for the observation of the writer by the A6 of Net and ceremonially held for the Nahnken of Net in December 1947:

A wood fire is made and stones heaped over it to make a roughly square oven with vertical walls instead of the usual dome-shaped stone oven made for other occasions. Whole breadfruit are piled on top of the hot stones and no covering leaves added, while in the ordinary stone oven the coals are raked out, the hot stones built up again, and halved breadfruit piled on the stones with leaves over them; the result is that breadfruit in an ordinary stone oven are baked in a steamy atmosphere, but for *lihli* they bake in the open, are turned over several times in the process, and the skin becomes charred (Plate 2a). This charred surface is peeled away by two men (designated as *soun rar*); they use a flat, oblong piece of hibiscus wood (*mehn rar*) to pry off the char, holding the hot fruit with half a coconut shell (Plate 2b). The hot breadfruit are then carried to the *lihli* maker (*soun li*),[73] who pounds them on a flat stone (*peitehl,* the same type of stone used for kava) with a wooden pounder (*pein rar*) of *Morinda citrifolia* (*weipwul*)[74] (Plate 3a). The flat stone will have previously been cleaned by pounding a coconut husk on it and then washing with water. Close to the *lihli* maker is a bucket or wooden vessel of water into which he dips his hand so that he can remove the hot core and seeds without burning himself; he also wets the striking surface of the pounder with his hand from time to time to prevent the breadfruit from sticking. He must work very fast, since the *lihli* is supposed to be still too hot to eat when it is finished. A girl or boy sits near him and fans him, so that he does not sweat. He prepares four breadfruit at one time, and the resulting loaf-shaped mass is put on a banana leaf that had been previously seared in the fire to waterproof it; this is placed on top of another similarly treated banana leaf (Plate 3b) and then laid in a certain type of coconut-leaf basket (*ilail*) which is carried to the coconut-cream maker (*soun piah*).[75] The man who carries it holds the basket in both arms, with its stemward end (as determined by the direction of growth of the pinnae from which the basket was woven) and the banana-leaf stems to his left.

A Madolenihmw informant says two or three baked breadfruit are used for each loaf, sometimes five for a large one. A Kiti informant says that four are used, but that for the Nahnmwarki and Nahnken only four halves are used to make one *lihli* loaf, the other halves are put aside for the commoners. As observed on this occasion in Net, four whole breadfruit were used.

The coconut-cream maker has meanwhile been grating coconut meat and has a heap of it piled in front of him on a banana leaf. He now piles some of it on a mass of young coconut[76] husk fiber, which he twists to squeeze out the coconut cream over the loaf of *lihli* held up before him.

Both *lihli* maker and coconut-cream maker wear a headband of two coconut pinnae with the ends twisted together and turned up over the ears (a *sedei;* this is also used for divining and for what Hambruch calls "Botschaft" leaves) (Plate 5a). The *lihli* maker must be bare to the waist. He sits on two banana leaves and holds another in his lap so that his kilt and the hair on his stomach do not show to the women present. Neither he nor the coconut-cream maker may speak, laugh, or cough during their work, lest a fleck of spittle fall on the food they are preparing. There is no calling out or notification that the *lihli* is ready, since quiet must be maintained.

Four *lihli* loaves are prepared, one apiece for the Nahnmwarki and Nahnken and their respective wives, before whom they are laid. The stems of the two banana leaves and the stemward end of the basket that holds each loaf are to the left of the recipient. In Madolenihmw six loaves are prepared, as described below. Additional loaves are prepared without ceremony for the men who prepare the oven, remove the char, pound the breadfruit, and make the cream to partake of after the chiefs have eaten.

Before the coconuts can be grated the water from them is put into a kind of cup (*putemei*) made of an *Alocasia macrorrhiza* (*sepwikin*) leaf. The cup is made by sewing up the leaf around its edges with the rib of a coconut pinna (see Plate 5a); it is brought to the Nahnmwarki, on the main platform of the community house, in one of the special *lihli* baskets (*ilail*) previously mentioned.[77]

To the Nahnmwarki's wife is also carried one of the special baskets, containing a number of objects: one baked and peeled, but not pounded, breadfruit; the two halves of a ripe coconut; an implement of wood (*mehn rar*) for coring the breadfruit like those used by the men who remove the char; and a piece of coconut husk, shaped somewhat like a club, used to tap and soften the breadfruit (a *mehn pok*). The whole (called a *meirar*) is presented, like the other baskets, with the stem end to the left. It is

[73] This person on Ponape is always a man, but Ponapean informants say that on Truk and the Mortlocks, where a similar dish is prepared, a woman may officiate.

[74] The wooden pounder was used on the occasion being described, but a pounder of white coral, *takai mei*, is said to be preferable.

[75] From *piahia,* to squeeze out coconut cream; this term is not used for straining kava or any other plant.

[76] On the occasion witnessed by the writer; but all informants questioned say that the straining apparatus should be strips of bast from the hibiscus tree.

[77] The sketches in Hambruch (1932 II, Abb. 158, p. 372) are of an *ilail* basket and a leaf cup from Madolenihmw; both are made somewhat differently from those seen on this occasion.

said also to be given to any of the other people entitled to receive *lihli* who do not like coconut cream and therefore abstain from it.

The special *ilail* baskets are made during the baking of the breadfruit by the high chiefs and the visitors on the main platform of the community house. A whole coconut leaf is brought by a man of lower title to the chiefs and split in half down the rachis; in Net 19 pinnae are counted from the stem end of the leaf, counting the first three as number one, then each succeeding pair as a unit, so that the actual count is only nine, and this section is then lopped off; then another 19 pinnae are counted and cut, and so on, to the distal end of the leaf. Each section is given to a titled man to weave into a basket. In Net there are said to be six types of these baskets; among them are *pwat en kole* (Plate 4b), *oaralap, ulung en nahnpwatak,* and *pweiwer.* They are made differently in each tribe and (traditionally) on Ant atoll. They are made only for *lihli,* and differ from the ordinary coconut-leaf general utility basket (*kiam*) in that the latter is made from the full width of the leaf while for these the leaf is split in two down the rachis.

In Kiti, informants give as the types of *ilail* baskets:

1. *Ilail en soupeidi,* for the Nahnmwarki and Nahnken. Two pinnae remain inside the basket, unplaited; if the *lihli* is to be carried home, these two pinnae are tied together to hold the basket tightly together and prevent the coconut cream from flowing away. For only this type of basket the two banana leaves in which the *lihli* is put must be cut from the tree at the point where the stalk of the leaf joins the trunk; for the other types they are cut where the stalk merges into the blade of the leaf. Also, the leaf blade is torn loose from the central rib and pushed back up the distance of one hand's breadth by running the hand up the stalk against the blade.
2. *Ilail en likend,* for the wives of the Nahnmwarki and Nahnken. This is made in the same way as the previous type, but the banana leaves have no stalk attached, nor is the blade torn back.
3. *Ilail en soun lih,* for the *lihli* maker. On the underside of the basket are four unplaited pinnae, two on each side; each pair is tied in a knot, which prevents the basket from sliding when the *lihli* maker eats *lihli,* for he eats it with his hands, whereas the Nahnmwarki and Nahnken and their wives use spoons of coconut husk made by cutting a section through the outer husk on the plane of a chord.
4. *Ilail en soun piah,* for the coconut-cream maker. Three pairs of pinnae are left unplaited on the upper side of the basket, one at each end and one in the middle. Each time the man whose duty it is to make the coconut cream wrings it out of the fibers he wipes his hands on one pinna, then tears it off and discards it. Six pinnae are required, since in Kiti (and also in Madolenihmw) six *lihli* are made for ceremonial presentation to high persons prior to general eating of *lihli* by the masses: one for the Nahnmwarki and Nahnken; one for their wives; one for the A2, A3, and B2; one for their wives; one for the other high chiefs present; and one for their wives.
5. *Ilail en soun rar,* for the men who remove the char. One end of the basket is rounded, one end left pointed with the ends of the pinnae not tied together as with the other baskets; this end is used to clean off the char-peeling implement, which is then used as a spoon to eat the *lihli.*

## Other First Fruits

Tobacco, beans, manioc, *Cyrtosperma* (*mwahng*), cucumbers, corn, sweet potatoes, watermelons, and onions are occasionally presented as first fruits; onions were recorded only once, in section 3 of Net. All of these except *Cyrtosperma* are European-introduced plant species. They are offered only from new gardens, as with the first of the yam first fruits.

A number of animals are also offered to chiefs, and the offerings are called by the same name (*nohpwei*) as first fruits. That for a turtle is called *mwohn par;* both common species of turtle are offered, the hawksbill [78] (*sapwake*) and the green turtle (*kalahp*); a rare sea-creature, *malipwur,* which some informants identify as a turtle, possibly mythological only, is also considered to be a chiefly gift. A coconut-eating crab, *omp,* which occurs on the sandy islets off Madolenihmw, is similarly offered. Fish presented to chiefs, however, are given simply as their due and are not called *nohpwei.* Large specimens of *Serranus* (*mwanger:* several species of giant grouper), *dep, moat,* and *Gymnothorax* (*lahpwid:* several species of sea eel) are occasionally presented nowadays; all *merer* caught are supposed to be offered; wrasse (*kemeik*) are presented to the chiefs at the third feast given on the occasion of the dedication of a new seine of the largest kind (see below). Failure to offer the chiefs their due results in supernaturally caused disease, as described elsewhere. In the prestige competition for political advancement these presentations, though neither first fruits nor feasts, count as Service too.

## Ceremonial Presentation of Fish

Certain fish that are offered to high chiefs to be eaten raw are presented with slits made in them according to

[78] Some informants deny that the hawksbill need be offered to chiefs.

special patterns, which differ according to the species of fish and from tribe to tribe. Failure to prepare fish in this way would cause much offense to the chiefs who are the recipients. Cooked fish are not slit except (at least in Madolenihmw) for very large ones; but when they are baked for presentation to a high chief the fins and tail are left out of the fire so that these portions will not fall off; otherwise they are not considered fit for presentation.

In Net there are seven methods of slitting fish, each applied to a number of species of fish (see Figure 3):

1. Four slits are made transversely on each side, evenly spaced between the base of the tail and a point close to the gills. Then the fish is presented whole. Species: *Pseudoscarus* sp. (*mwommei*), *pakas.* (The identical pattern was seen on a *pakas* fish hanging outside the B1's house in Madolenihmw too.)
2. The head is cut off, and ten transverse cuts are made on each side, evenly spaced from the base of the pectoral fin to the anal fin; then a longitudinal slit (a) is made above the gills, connecting with the first transverse slit at a point near its upper end and curving upward and forward to meet the equivalent cut on the other side. For presentation to a high chief the three slices between the third and sixth slits are freed at their dorsal ends and laid back downward on each side (b), the three slices between the sixth and ninth slits are similarly laid upward (c). The twelve slices thus produced, counting both sides of the fish, are for the delectation of the high chiefs, the rest of the fish is for commoners. Species: *Caranx* sp. (*arong*) (Figure 3A).
3. After scaling, six transverse cuts are made on each side, the first at the base of the pectoral fin, the sixth about halfway to the tail. The three slices between the third and sixth cuts are removed entirely from each side, except for their most ventral portions, and presented to the high chiefs (these portions shown shaded in the sketch); the rest of the fish is for the commoners. Species: wrasse (*kemeik*) (Figure 3B).
4. The fish is first scaled; then one transverse slit is made at the base of the pectoral fin; from the ventral end of this slit another slit curves upward and posteriorly, then runs laterally along the flank and curves back down again to a point about midway along the length of the fish (a). Also from the ventral end of the first slit the belly is slit all the way to the anal fin. Four more parallel slits are made from the base of the first dorsal fin and running down the flank, somewhat diagonally forward, until they meet the slit that runs laterally along the flank. These slits are duplicated on the other side, and the fish is presented whole to high chiefs. Species: mullet (*ah*) (Figure 3C).
5. Eight parallel transverse cuts are made on both sides, from the base of the pectoral fin to a point near the precaudal constriction. Presented whole to high chiefs. Species: *kioak, kereker* (Figure 3D).
6. The two spines (a) on each side near the base of the tail are cut off, also the ventral and dorsal fins. Then the skin from the gill slits to the precaudal constriction is laid back, inside out, on both sides, over the tail (b). Six parallel transverse slits are made, the first at the base of the pectoral fin, the last before the anal fin; the first, third, and fifth of these are cut through to the bone, the second, fourth, and sixth only into the flesh. The whole goes to the chiefs. Species: *pwulak* (Figure 3E).
7. A portion of the back and stomach (marked a and b in the figure) and the head are given the chiefs; between the back and stomach portions four parallel transverse slits are made and the four slices that result are cut out and given to the commoners, along with the rest of the fish. Species: *merer* (Figure 3F).

A number of other fish that bear a resemblance to one or another of these seven types and which are eaten raw are treated in identical manner. In other tribes than Net different methods of slitting are used. The methods are not common knowledge, but are known particularly to the master fisherman (*soused*). There are other ceremonial details connected with presentation of fish, which again vary from tribe to tribe; for example, when *toik* fish are presented to the A1 of Madolenihmw they must be wrapped in leaves in a certain manner and offered to him in special kinds of baskets.

All of the foregoing applies only to fish caught in a new net, except for such fish as *merer*, which are always presented to high chiefs, new net or old.

## FEASTS FOR CHIEFS

### The Major Feasts

To an outsider, the multiplicity of feasts on Ponape and the development of the feasting complex seem almost hypertrophied in comparison with the rest of the culture. Yet we shall see how closely they are linked with the political organization, not to mention their importance in the economy.

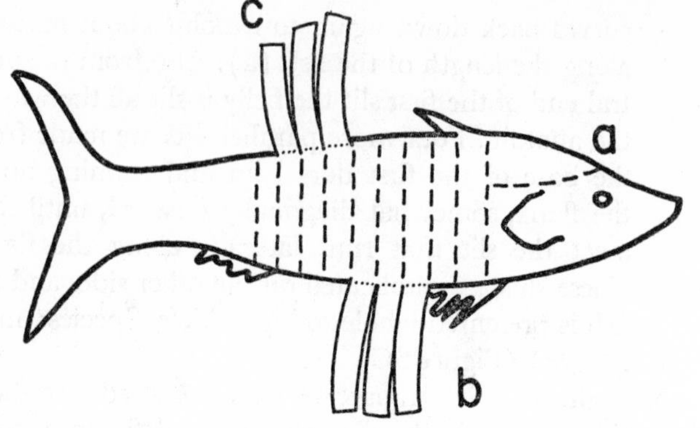


A. ARONG

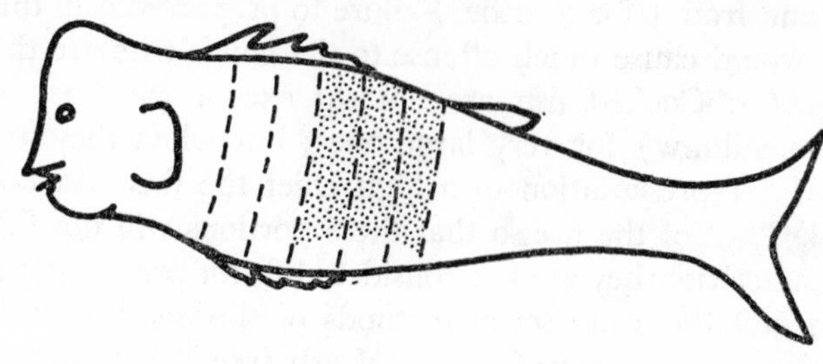

B. KEMEIK

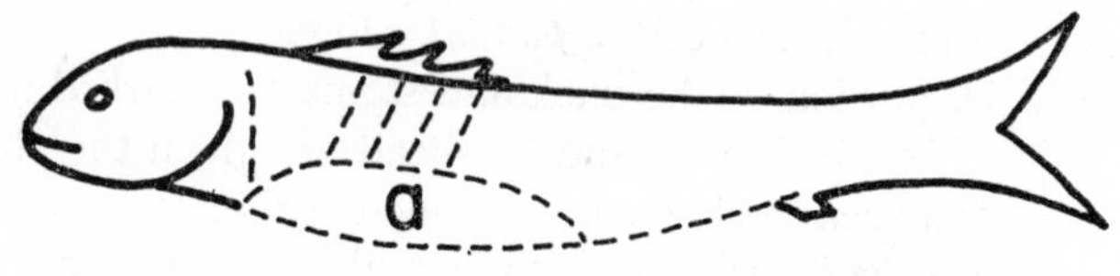


C. AH

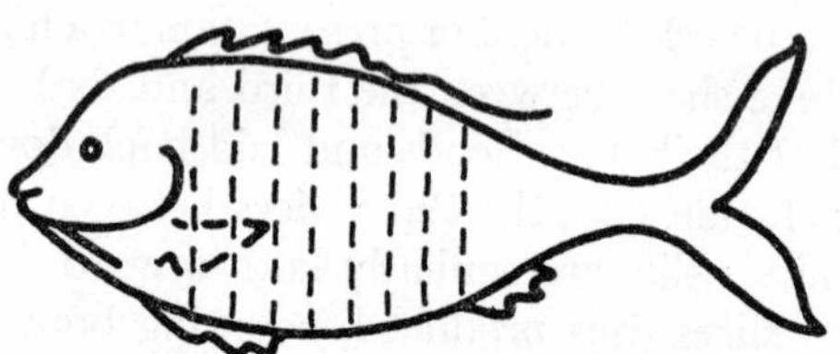

D. KIOAK

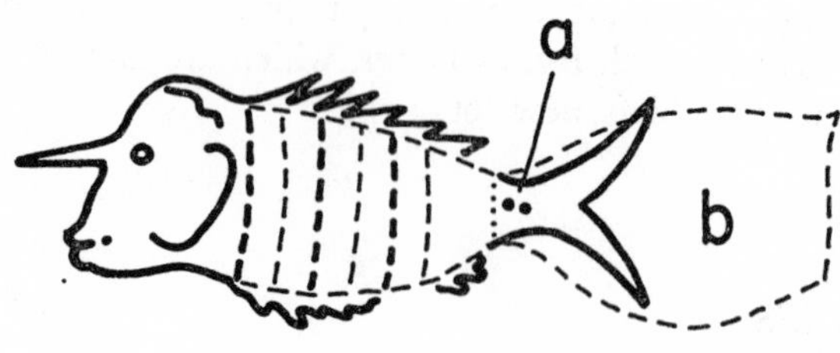


E. PWULAK

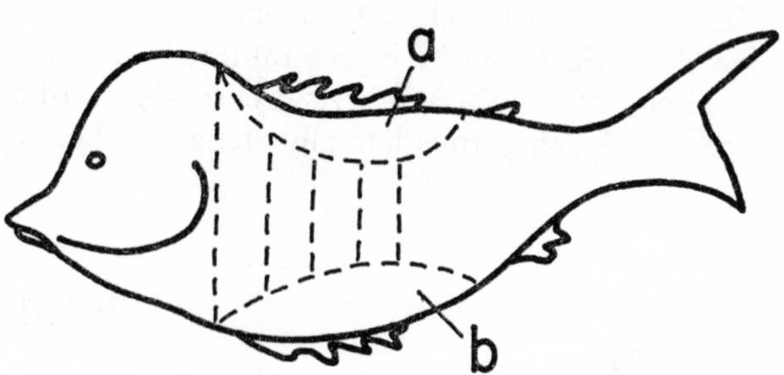


F. MERER

FIGURE 3.—Variations in the slitting of fish for ceremonial presentation to high chiefs.

Feasts of most kinds are known loosely as *kamadipw,* though the people sometimes distinguish the most important ones as *kamadipw* proper. The important feasts are always held in the community house in the presence of the chiefs. All feasts involve the preparation and drinking of kava. Theoretically also a major feast always involves the use of yams, while first fruits are concerned with all types of food plants, particularly breadfruit, and need not include yams. But these native definitions and distinctions are not always strictly sustained in practice. The feasts are by name as follows, in the calendrical order in which they were formerly held:

a. Start of Yam Season (*ire ihsol*). Two Kiti informants give the time it is held as January; a Net informant and one from Madolenihmw say March; another Net informant says any time from October to May, depending upon the condition of the yams. It is supposed to follow the first fruits called *kotekehp.* When the feasts were sharply curtailed by the German regime, the deeds to land that were issued provided that an honor feast (*kamadipw en wahu*) would be provided once a year to the Nahnmwarki, and this feast is today reckoned as the old Start of Yam Season feast. Each tribe made the feast in sequence to the Nahnmwarki, Nahnken, A2 and B2, and each section made one for its head. At this feast yams of any variety may be brought for presentation.

b. Counting Cookhouses (*wad wonuhmw*). Given in February (Kiti informant) or April (Net informant). The Nahnmwarki and Nahnken each formerly went about from section to section, accompanied by a wife and some attendants, to visit every section head and every important man and was feasted once yearly in this manner. The feast was made in the family cookhouse. Some informants state that each section gave one feast, others that every important family head gave one. One Kiti informant also says that each farmstead would give the feast and invite the other seven farmsteads that supposedly constituted a single section. (See p. 93 for the theoretical 8-fold divisions of sections.) Rarely given nowadays; occasionally accompanies the title-payment feast (*iraramwar*).

c. Twisting Coir Twine (*dakadak dipenihd*). This feast was given for the Nahnmwarki and Nahnken separately (Madolenihmw informant, any time; Kiti informant, in September) and was considered the biggest feast of all. It was held in the community house. The old men would sit and prepare twine for the chief by rolling coir on the thigh, while the young people would make a stone oven and prepare the yams, pigs, and kava. The feast is no longer given (see Figure 4).

d. *Kapei tehnrip* (*kapei,* ?; *tehnrip,* the banana or breadfruit leaves used on this occasion). This is probably the same as the feast called in Madolenihmw *tehnkulop.* The contents of a whole pit of fermented breadfruit were brought to the community house and placed on banana or breadfruit leaves. Each person present took a piece and kneaded it on a smooth stone, then made it into a loaf about 3 feet long, 6 inches high, 8–12 inches wide, which he wrapped in banana leaves and put in the stone oven to bake. The feast was given in the community house, separately for the Nahnmwarki and Nahnken.

e. Oven of Whole Yams (*uhmw en kehp pwon*). Yams baked whole, then divided. For the Nahnmwarki and Nahnken separately, given by the whole tribe at one time; for lesser chiefs by the people of their sections. Formerly made in the community house, nowadays generally in the family cookhouse and brought to the A1 and B1.

f. Oven of Half Yams (*uhmw en pali en kehp*). Similar to feast e, above, but the yams are baked after breaking them up.

The above six feasts are the most important. Supposedly these feasts involve yams, never breadfruit, despite the obvious discrepancies that are apparent in the descriptions. A number of less important feasts, however, are often included in the category of *kamadipw* and may involve breadfruit. Some informants include the feasts for new buildings, new canoes, new fishing nets, etc., under this heading of *kamadipw.* A Madolenihmw informant adds to the list above a feast called *koummot,* which is the same as feast b, above, except that the chief comes to visit without formal invitation. A Kiti informant adds *kaitihsol,*[79] given in May at the end of the yam season and held in the community house. Among the smaller feasts are *tiepwel,* given to a Nahnmwarki when he recovers from an illness; *uhmw en mwirilik* or *mwiririk,* the death feast; *iraramwar,* a payment feast for a new title; *tohmw,* a feast of apology or propitiation (already discussed in

---

[79] The Luelen manuscript gives this term (meaning literally "no more scarcity," referring to the scarce period between breadfruit seasons when yams must substitute) as the last of four yam first fruits; the first two are my yam first fruits 1a and 1b; the third one he writes "um en tanpuat" (which can be translated as Oven of Leaf Basket).

detail); family feasts; feasts given to visitors; and a number of others described below.[80]

## Other Feasts

While Great Work is done and titles thereby earned principally through the forms of Service thus far discussed, a man's reputation is also affected by the degree of his generosity exhibited at other types of feasts, not classified under Service but at some of which chiefs receive shares of offerings also. These are therefore discussed as part of the prestige competition complex.

For a new seine three feasts are given, called collectively *oulaid;* most people do not refer to them as *kamadipw.* The first of these is Seine Commencement (*simas uhk*). The man who has ordered the net prepares food in a stone oven and pounds kava and brings these to the netmaker (*sou uhk*) at the beginning of his work. The net is made in two halves, and on the day that the netmaker joins the halves and has ready the floats another feast is made, Seine Joining (*kohpene uhk*) or Seine Binding Together (*patpene uhk*). The fishermen of the section meanwhile have for several days been assembled in the community house, from which women have been excluded, awaiting the proper tides; sexual activity is forbidden during this time. The day after this feast the fishermen go fishing, taking with them the food they have received at the feast, and when they return, the third of the series of feasts, called *laidkapw,*[81] is made. The three feasts are made for all three of the types of seines used on Ponape, but only *laidkapw* is made for the four types of hand nets.

The fishing undertaken on these occasions is always done for 4 days in succession. In Net, for a new small seine (*uhketik*), the fish caught on the first day are brought to a community house where the *laidkapw* feast is held for the Nahnmwarki; the second day the same feast is given to the Nahnken, at the community house closest to his residence; the third day to the A2 and B2; the fourth day to the A3 and B3. For A2, B2, A3, and B3 the feast need not be held in a community house. In Net today the Nahnken and Nahnmwarki are father and son, and one feast is held for both. For the larger seines (*uhkelap* and *sokesok*) the *laidkapw* feast is held all 4 days for the Nahnmwarki and always in the community house; the lower chiefs attend, of course. The *laidkapw* feasts for the three types of seines and the two larger types of hand nets (*naikelap* and *naik en dokedok*) are tribal feasts. Those for the two smaller hand nets (*luhkouk* and *naiketik*) are section feasts, may be held elsewhere than in the community house, and the head of the section in which the new net has been made may function in place of the tribal titleholders.

At such feasts the fish that are distributed are considered to be an exchange for the agricultural food brought and prepared in the stone oven by the farmers and are equally divided among them. All the land produce, except that offered to the chiefs, is given to the fishermen, who retain none of the fish; the largest share goes to the master fisherman. This exchange is known as *soawa.* But if the fishing has been unlucky, the sacred staff (*ketia sarawi*) used by the master fisherman for religious purposes is brought into the community house where the chiefs and the farmers are assembled waiting for the catch, the staff is taken to symbolize the wanting fish, and the food from the stone oven is divided among all present. The assemblage occurs when the signal of the returning fishermen is heard; this signal consists of long blasts on the conch trumpets, similar to those formerly given for a dead commoner.

At the time of these feasts the section head and the tribal chiefs who dwell in the section must be present, and no fish can be sent to their houses; if they are not there they have to be summoned before the feast can proceed. Besides the fish consumed at the feast many are distributed to be carried home. The first fish caught (*mwamwenieng*) is always given to the highest chief present. Additional offerings depend on the size of the catch and whether any of the royal fishes have been caught. Large fishes are given singly to the chiefs; medium-sized ones are tied in bundles of three, small ones in bundles of five, and so presented.

While all of the foregoing activities are centered about the occasion of the new net, there is ample opportunity for an ambitious man to exhibit his prowess as a farmer or fisherman, to demonstrate fealty to the chiefs by lavishness of offerings and by appropriate deference, and thus to further his political advancement.

A considerable religious element formerly entered into these feasts. How much of it survives it is difficult to say, though in the practices surrounding fishing more pagan customs continue than in any other phase of Ponapean

---

[80] Hambruch (1932 II, p. 227f.) gives a different sequence of first fruits and feasts. His list follows (the parenthetical notes refer to my lists as given above):

*Breadfruit first fruits:*

1. *puatsemê'i*
2. *mê'i áui*
3. *pai i ni* (first fruits 2e)
4. *lili* (first fruits 2d)
5. *tsakalap* (first fruits 2h)
6. *kamemem*
7. *tautau*
8. *um en lu en méi* (first fruits 2i)

*Yam first fruits:*

1. *puke men puel*
2. *puke lo pun* (first fruits 2g)
3. *kotsé kep'* (first fruits la)
4. *itiz* (first fruits lb)
5. *um en peli en kep'* (feast f)
6. *um en kep' uong* (feast e)

*Feasts:*

1. *irê'isol* (feast a)
2. *takatak tipenit* (feast c)
3. *kê'itisol* (see text above)
4. *karisimê'i* (first fruits 2a)

[81] This feast is also known as *kapas* and *pasalaid* to different informants. Strictly speaking, *kapas* refers to the farmers of the section who prepare the stone ovens for this feast, not to the fishermen.

PLATE 1

Abandoned house site and burial cairns. *a*, Stone platform of an abandoned house site on Sokehs Island. *b*, Burial cairns for the Soukise at Paler in Wene.

Preparation of breadfruit for *lihli*. *a*, The oven of stones with the breadfruit on top. *b*, Peeling the breadfruit after baking by holding it with half a coconut shell and prying off the charred exterior with a piece of hibiscus wood.

PLATE 3

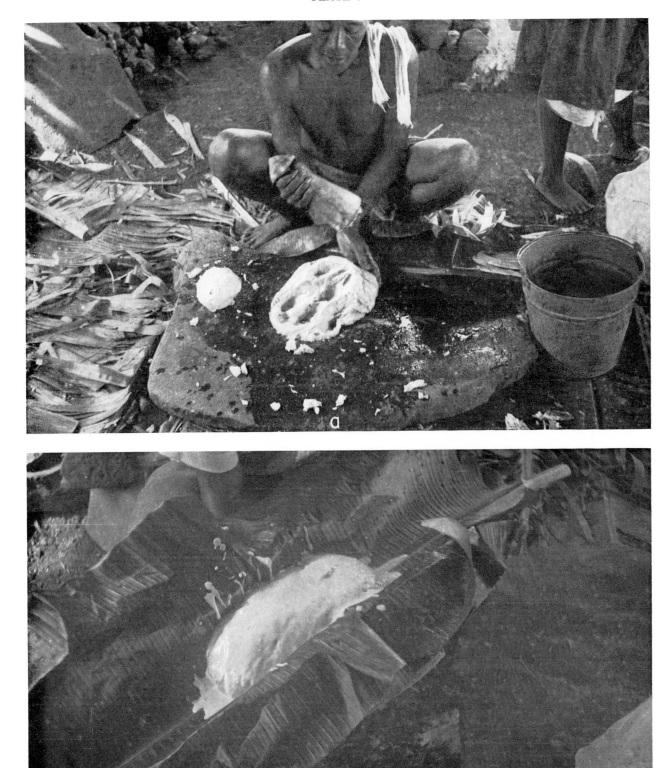

Preparation of breadfruit for *lihli*. *a,* Pounding the peeled, cooked breadfruit with a wooden pounder on a flat stone of the same type used to pound kava. *b,* The finished *lihli* of pounded breadfruit and coconut cream.

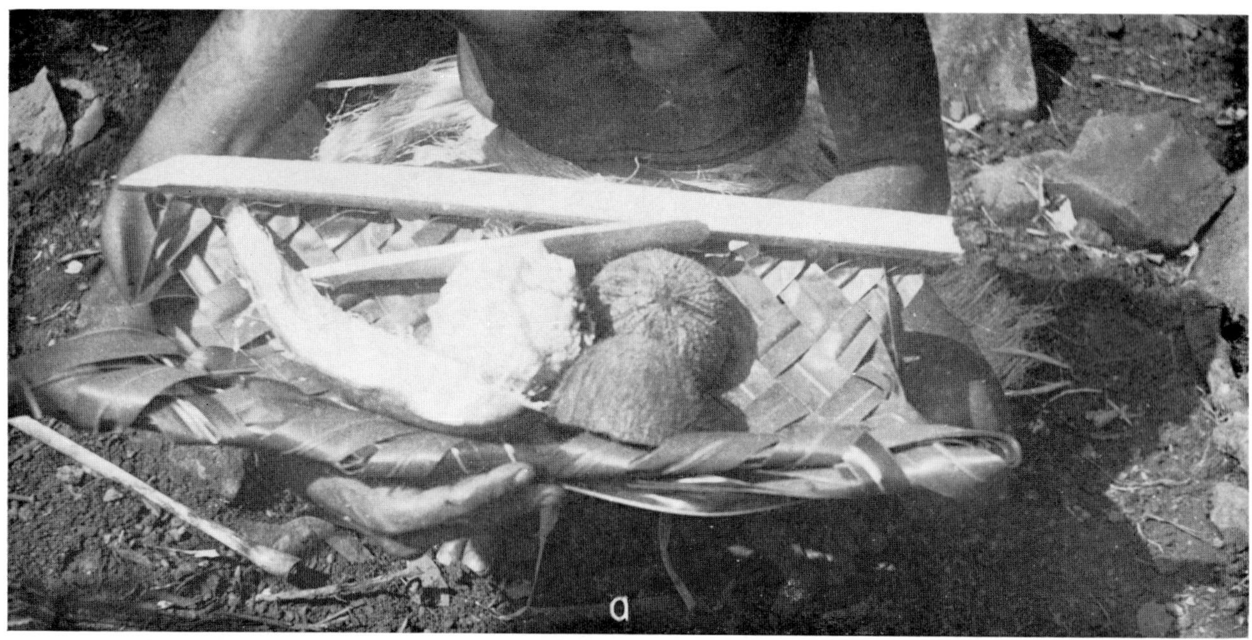

Ceremonial food preparation. *a*, A *meirar* (see p. 81, for explanation). *b*, One of the six types of coconut-leaf baskets used for *lihli* in Net—this type known as *pwat en kole*.

PLATE 5

Ceremonial food preparation. *a*, The *lihli* maker preparing a taro-leaf cup; he wears a headband of two coconut pinnae twisted together. *b*, Roasted dog in ceremonial wrapping held by author.

PLATE 6

Community houses. *a,* Side view of the community house at Tamworohi, Madolenihmw, showing various acculturative elements. *b,* Front view of the community house at Temwen, Madolenihmw.

PLATE 7

Servitors in community house and chief's belt. *a*, The main platform of a community house in Net. Leaning against the wall is the B1 of Net; to his right, drinking a cup of kava, is a visiting chief from Sokehs; to his left, in the foreground, is the B1's wife. Each has a servitor; the B1's servitor is seen in typical posture. *b*, Chief's belt, worn by the B6 of Madolenihmw.

Transporting sugar cane and kava. *a*, Sugar-cane bearers in procession at dedication of a new community house in Kahmar, Net. *b*, Kava plants piled up before pounding.

PLATE 11

Kava-drinking ceremony. *a*, Master of kava ceremony handing cup of kava to chief's servitor. *b*, Servitor handing kava to chief. Note conventional sitting posture and position of arms.

Preparation of kava. *a*, Old stone for pounding kava found at Nan Madol ruins. *b*, Pounding the kava roots. *c*, Twisting the hibiscus-bast strainer to wring out the kava. *d*, Combing out the bast strainer with the fingers to prepare it for laying on the stone so that macerated root fibers can be placed on it before twisting.

culture, except possibly in medicinal practices. At each of the three feasts for a seine the netmaker formerly made the Kava Holding (*sapwsakau*) ritual as in the title-promotion ceremony, except that in the formula used while holding up the cup of kava the name of the fishing deity, Nahnullap, was substituted for the title being conferred. At the first two feasts the accompanying prayer, made by the netmaker to Nahnullap and uttered in the community house, bore the name of the two respective feasts. The Kava Holding and prayer made when the fishermen returned with their catch, before the third feast was held, were given not in the community house but at the landing place and called Landed (*pasedo*); it was accompanied by kava drinking. A fourth Kava Holding and prayer, called Alighted (*keredi*), occurred in the community house very early in the morning on the day of the third feast, before going fishing.

Before commencing work on the net, the netmaker gathered four sticks of hibiscus wood, each about 2-spans long, and stripped off their inner bark. These four lengths he then folded and tied into sacred bundles of bast (*sohpe sarawi*), which were put into a basket, weighted down with stones, and sunk in shallow water. At this time there was Kava Holding and prayer to Nahnullap again.

For a new canoe there are again three feasts. The first feast, Canoe Payment (*kating en wahr*), is held the first day of the shaping of the hull, the man who is having the canoe made thereby paying the artisans. A chief must be present, otherwise the Nahnmwarki would in former days come and destroy the canoe. When the lashing is to be put on the outrigger, a second feast, Canoe Lashing Payment (*kating en inoau wahr*), is held; a chief should again be present but is not always on this occasion. When the canoe is finished and has been taken out for fishing, the people left behind make a stone oven and the food therefrom is exchanged with the fish that the fishermen bring back, while all drink kava; this feast (*katepeik*) is similar to the *laidkapw* feast for a new net. The Nahnmwarki himself is obliged to attend on this day. (A *katepeik* feast observed in Kiti, however, was given to the A6, on whose land the tree from which the hull was fashioned had been felled; the Nahnmwarki was not present. The farmers on this occasion brought breadfruit, pit-breadfruit, and kava as their part.) The three feasts are also known collectively as *katepeik*.

A new dwelling house (*imwalap*) calls for two feasts, together known as Cause to Enter (*kapidelong*). When the framework is in place, a feast called Visit Together (*kakahnpene*) is given by the owner to the master carpenter (*souse*) and the people of the section who have come to help. When the house is finished, another feast, again called Cause to Enter, is given at which the Nahnmwarki or Nahnken attends; no one may enter the new house until one or the other chief has done so, otherwise a disease of divine origin (a *riahla*) befalls the tempter of fate. In Kiti the dedication of a new house is called *kapenpilong*.

A new community house requires four feasts, called collectively Cleanse Maggots (*isimwas*). The first job in building is to dig two holes for the main central posts; when this is done, a feast known as Erect Framework (*sereda*) is held. When the roof is put on, a second feast, Black Smoke (*editoal*; i.e., the roof is to be blackened by smoke), is given. When the floor is laid, there is a third feast, Floor Payment (*kating en taht*). When all is finished, a fourth feast, called Cleanse Maggots again, is held. (The word *isi* probably could also be translated as to singe, and *mwas* can also apply to foul matter; the implication of the whole expression is that the building is lustrated by these feasts and by the attendance and prayers of the high chiefs.)

The expression Cleanse Maggots is sometimes used loosely to cover the ceremonies for both dwelling house and community house. On both occasions the Nahnmwarki or Nahnken anciently came with his priests and prayed to his clan gods, in order to avoid the possibility of the divine disease; then the final feast would follow. Today the situation is not essentially altered. Though there is less communal effort in the building of private houses and more individual payment of carpenters, the old customs of communal work are still preserved in building the community house; and in the dedication of both types of buildings the Nahnmwarki or Nahnken attends, and Christian ministers pray that the house be protected from evil.

The deference exhibited toward men of higher rank is evident again in the arrangement of these feasts. In 1947 a family that numbered among its members the B4, the B11, and the Soukeperoa of Net completed their new community house in section 14 and should have staged their dedication feast; but they deferred to the A2, who was also building a community house, and waited until he had finished and dedicated it before they held their ceremonies.

One of the greatest feasts of all was formerly given to fishermen of a type of bonito (*weliwel*), who came to Ponape from the nearby atoll of Ant. Only the Ant people caught these fish; they quartered them, partially baked them in a stone oven, removed all the bones (as the Kapingamarangi people are said to do today), then dried them on a rack in the sun till they were very hard and would keep for as long as a year. The Soulik en And, who was the high chief of the atoll, and his people then brought them in baskets to Kiti, whose overlordship was acknowledged by Ant. If the Soulik did not come, the Ant people were accorded the honors in his place; they were anointed by the Kiti women, took the highest place on the

298-818—68——9

main platform of the community house, and were presented with all sorts of valuables—mats, sennit, dogs, yams, kava, etc. In return they presented the fish. The feast was known as Feast of the Food of Ant (*kamadipw en sak en And*). The schools of bonito are said to come only once a year, hence this feast was an annual affair. It persisted until the time of the Nahnmwarki Paul of Kiti. Elsewhere in Ponape such a feast made for fishermen is called Feast of the Canoe Bottom (*kamadipw kepinwahr*, referring to the fish brought ashore on the floor of the canoe). This is a different feast from that given fishermen for the catch from a new net or from a new canoe.

On the occasion of the visit of a Nahnmwarki of one tribe to the Nahnmwarki of another, the host would give a big feast that lasted for 2 or more days. Thereupon the visitors would return home and shortly afterward the visit would be reciprocated, and a feast as large or larger was given in return. The feast was known as Travel Feast (*kamadipw en seiloak;* see p. 71). Each party felt it necessary to make the trip in force, usually some thirty or more canoes accompanying the chief, so precarious was the state of peace at any time.

Before a war party set out it held an affair known as Oven of Smoke (*uhmw en edied*). On 4 successive days the men feasted together; this was called *kepwenek*. Then, the day before hostilities began, they gave a departure feast to the women and children, called also Oven of Smoke. For the feasts they killed rats, dogs, and in later times pigs, but the warriors partook very scantily of flesh, subsisting largely on kava and coconut meat, while they made their plans for battle. The portions of flesh distributed were about as large as a man's thumb. A brave warrior was supposed to take the field with an empty stomach, for if he were slain his body would often be slashed open by the enemy and his stomach contents examined. If they consisted of half-digested food, he was an object of contempt, but if there was found only coconut or the hard, black kernels which kava is said to form in the stomach, he was held to have met death with honor.

Some informants say that the stomach contents of a slain stranger were always examined in order to ascertain whether he had come for warlike purpose, in which case the stomach would be empty or contain only the kernels. One informant gives as the reason for abstaining from food when going to war the shame one would feel at having one's faeces seen. These attitudes also explain the incident in the story of the conqueror Isohkelekel who, en route to Ponape from Kusaie before his battle with the Saudeleur, stopped at Ant, where the Soulik of that atoll prepared a feast consisting of 333 breadfruit seeds, one seed for each of the warriors in the party.

A ceremonial cannibalism was also involved in these practices. Some 60 years ago, according to an eyewitness, four men from Sokehs made a raid on Mwahnd peidak (section 15) in Uh. They were killed and their bodies opened by the section head, Soudel. Only kava and coconut were found, so they were proved brave men. When the Wasai of Sokehs heard of it "he was happy that they had cared so well for his people." But the Soudel also ate the hearts of the dead men, "to show his own people how brave he was and so that Sokehs would hear about it and know he didn't fear them." [82]

On the occasion of the act of aggrandizement called Knotted Basket (see p. 63), when a chief of high rank drove a man of lower title from a piece of land that he coveted, the inhabitants thereof would give their new lord a feast, which bore the same name, Knotted Basket.

A number of feasts are called Family Feasts (*kamadipw en peneinei*), though they may involve more than relatives if the persons concerned are of high rank. Among these is included the Death Feast (*uhmw en mwirilik* or *mwiririk* [83]). This is regarded in the prestige complex as a man's farewell gesture. All his yams are dug up, except a few that are reserved for the use of his family, and are displayed at the feast. Although the relatives contribute some food too, the dead man is supposed to contribute more in order "to show what he has done during his life." Though there is ceremonial mourning at the bier of the dead man in his house, there is little sign of grief at the feast itself, which is held in a community house. The mourning period, which may last six months or a year, involves considerable unconventional behavior, but none of this is displayed at the feast.

A similar feast is called a Last Farewell (*kamwirumwur*). It is given by a man who thinks he is about to die and has his people take all of his property to make the feast, except what he sets aside for his heirs to keep. The feast is a gesture of loyalty to the Nahnmwarki as well as a display of property, for the Nahnmwarki attends and receives all the feast goods. Such feasts have been made up to recent times.

The birthday feast (*kamadipw en ipwidi*) is not native, but stems from the influence of the American Board missionaries; this is true also of the birth feast (*kamadipw en ipwipw*) for most people, although the Nahnmwarki and Nahnken did in ancient times give a feast for a newborn

[82] O'Connell (1836, pp. 181–182) also refers to "tasting an enemy's heart," but further says that genuine cannibalism occurred on nearby Pakin. Pakin is an atoll that today is considered to be a section of the tribe of Sokehs. Since about 1905, it has been inhabited by a small colony of Mortlock Islanders, but there is no question that in O'Connell's time its people and culture were Ponapean. (He identifies Pakin, which he spells Pokeen, as Wellington Island, which is modern Mokil, but it is obvious that he did this by misreading a map.) I questioned six different Ponapeans on this matter; all agreed that true cannibalism would have been impossible.

[83] Gulick seems to limit this practice to chiefs, since he defines "muririk" as "a chief's farewell, bidding goodbye."

child. Usually the birthday feast today is made by high-born or rich parents for their young and adolescent children; one such feast on a large scale was given in 1947 by the Nahnmwarki of Sokehs for his son on the occasion of the latter's eighteenth birthday. But sometimes these are only family affairs; the writer attended a birth feast for the great-grandson of the Nahnken of Madolenihmw at which he was the only guest, all others present were close relatives. The arrangements were very informal, consisting simply of the drinking of kava, not from the traditional half coconut shells but out of china bowls; the kava roots were pounded under a shelter made of a tarpaulin and palm branches laid over clotheslines next to the house; and the kava was drunk not in a community house but in the dwelling.

The marriage feast is called *kamadipw en kopwopwoud* (or *pwopwoud*). At the feast in former days the bride sat on the side platform of the community house. If she was a girl of high rank and was to be the Nahnmwarki's wife, the Nahnken would go to her and anoint her head, back, and chest with sweet-smelling coconut oil; then he would say to her, "I have anointed you, you are the Nahnmwarki's wife," and would put an *elin seir* wreath (see p. 41) on her head and lead her up to the main platform of the community house, where she would take her seat, and other women would come to sit in the traditional attitude of her servitors. For a Nahnken's bride the Nahnmwarki would perform the reciprocal office. If the pair were commoners, the man's parents would do the anointing and crowning. The feast might be held the same day that the marriage was agreed upon between the parents or maternal uncles of the couple, or it might be delayed a day or two to allow distant relatives to assemble. It was given by the boy's parents, who would bring the girl back with them from her parents as soon as the marriage arrangements were made. Sometimes it would be preceded by another feast made by the father of the girl immediately following the agreement; this was called Feast of Asking in Marriage (*kamadipw en pekpek pwopwoud*). The marriage feast was then given by the boy's parents on their return with the bride, and might also be called Feast of Returning a Gift for a Kindness (*kamadipw en dupuk en kahdak*). Nowadays the marriage feast follows upon the church wedding; usually there are two feasts, the bridegroom's family making one on the day after the wedding, the bride's family reciprocating on the next day.

In token of recognition of adulthood, at about the age of 16, the family formerly gave boys and girls a feast called Feast of Bathing (*kamadipw en kadepwedepw*). The reference is to the 4-day period during which bathing was proscribed, following the tattooing done on both sexes and the semicastration practiced on adolescent boys. At the end of the 4-day period the young people bathed and were anointed with oil, after which the feast was given; thereafter they were recognized as eligible for marriage. The feast is defunct, along with tattooing and semicastration.

The foregoing descriptions are based largely upon informants' accounts. Whatever may have been the practice in former times, the theoretical distinctions between the various types of feasts and first-fruit offerings are not today always maintained. Differences tend to become obliterated and details vary considerably from occasion to occasion. A *kotekehp* (see p. 78) type of first fruits in Net attended by the writer in 1947 was given in August instead of in October, as it theoretically should have been; first yams, but also sugar cane, were brought to the Nahnken of Net by some 20 people of two sections; and at the same time kava was brought to be pounded and drunk, as at a regular feast. On the same day the Nahnmwarki, who is the Nahnken's son, was similarly honored. The affair was also referred to as a Tasting of Things Growing Underground (*song mehnpwel*), because of the yams, though sugar cane obviously does not come under this category. The yams were brought by the men, the sugar cane by the women; these two foods are supposed to be divided on this sexual basis, according to which sex looks after their care. In September the writer attended an affair held by the people of Sapwtakai, Kiti, for the A6 of Kiti, on whose land they live. It was referred to as the *idihd* (see p. 78) type of first fruits, though *idihd* is supposed to come in December. At the same time they brought kava and a pig they had cooked in their family cookhouse and the kava was drunk in the nearby community house, giving the affair the character of a feast instead of the first-fruits presentation it was alleged to be.

The feasts exchanged between individuals or between political subdivisions—to be discussed in the next section—are also sometimes difficult to distinguish from the feasts offered to the chief. A generous chief, such as the present A6 of Kiti to whom many feasts are given, retains only a small portion of the yams he is offered and usually bestows most of the rest on one of the visitors from other tribes, who will have brought nothing themselves, or on representatives of a particular section. The recipient accepts if he feels able to return the feast at a later date. The return feast is given again to the A6, but most of the offerings end up in the hands of the sponsor or sponsors of the first feast. In such a case only a small part of the food offered at these two feasts accrues to other visitors or to the chief in honor of whom they are nominally given; economically, if not ceremonially, the two feasts consist essentially of two men or groups of men exchanging garden products with one another. Such feasts then differ very little from the reciprocal feasts to be shortly described, where two men exchanged friendly feasts directly with one another instead of through a chief. (The reciprocal exchange does not affect the pigs and kava, some of which are consumed at the feast, the remainder divided among all persons present.)

In Net nowadays the chiefs have systematized the feasts and caused a number of different kinds to be offered simultaneously. One feast witnessed by the writer combined a dedication of a new community house (*isimwas*) and an honor feast (*kamadipw en wahu*) given by several sections together; another was given by 12 men as an honor feast and by three others in payment for new titles (*iraramwar*); still a third feast combined a new-house dedication, an honor feast, and a feast for payment by three more men for their new titles.

## COMPETITIVE FEASTS[84]

As described earlier (p. 77), competition for enhancement in prestige and rank is centered on Great Work (and, in earlier days, Little Work, or warfare, as well). Great Work consists of communal labor, obedience, deference, and all other forms of activity regarded as appropriate on behalf of the Nahnmwarki, but especially Service. Service is basically the presentation of food to the Nahnmwarki at every possible opportunity: regular first fruits, regular feasts, periodical gifts, and presentations on special occasions. All these various activities are carried on competitively, and they and all forms of general competition are collectively called Serving Together (*uhpene*). The competition is between every man and all his peers simultaneously, each striving to outdo the others by showing that he is the most industrious, the most skillful in growing large yams, the most generous in making offerings, the most devoted to the chiefs. Thus he gains merit and earns titles.

Serving Together is to be distinguished from Displaying Together (*selepene*), which is something quite different, by native theory. The latter is not a general struggle among all men but is a direct contention between two individuals, two groups of relatives, or two groups of coresidents. It is not directly concerned with personal ambition for political advancement but with besting another man or group in order to avenge a slight, or upon order of a chief, or simply for ostentation and ego gratification. The feasting is done not to make offerings to chiefs but, as the means of expression of rivalry, to exchange goods with rivals.

It is true that in the Display Together type of competition the winner inevitably gains favor in the eyes of the chiefs and thereby facilitates his rise; his ensuing fame is certain to reach their notice; and if they are present at the feast the chiefs receive food offerings, as at the other types of feasts. The Display Together occasions are therefore, like the Serve Together ones, part of the machinery of political advancement. But this is not their overt purpose, and whatever promotions come about in consequence of them are incidental.

Three kinds of feasts are usually classed as Display Together, although the first of these three, the Yam Head feast, is by some people excluded from this category. The Yam Head feast is called in Ponapean *mes en pek* (*mes:* face, front; *pek:* cut) in reference to the heads of the yams, which at the feast are cut off and distributed to be replanted by their recipients. Because of this replanting the feast has an alternative name, To Cause to Increase (*kaparapar*). Ponapeans speak of this kind of Display Together as a friendly feast, in contrast to the other two types, which are demonstrations that closely parallel the potlatch of other parts of the world. But there is nevertheless a strong element of rivalry, with the man who has brought the largest and the most yams thereby deriving personal satisfaction and elevating his prestige in the eyes of other persons. Such feasts are still made nowadays. Joseph, the present Nahnken of Net, describes his competition with the old Nahnken, Paulino, at this type of feast as friendly but yet competitive, each striving to outdo the other. Paulino would visit Joseph (who was then B3) apparently purely from motives of sociability, and a feast would be given in his honor. Paulino would then return home and send his people back to fetch and divide among themselves the presents of food; then he would invite Joseph to visit him for a return feast. The motive for the Nahnken in this sort of competition could not have been ambition, for he could go no higher in the hierarchy of titles; but a lifelong habit of pitting oneself against other men in every sort of social situation is a difficult one to discard even when no further advantage is gained by its exercise. Moreover, quite apart from political ambition, he could still augment his prestige, publicize his wealth, and gratify his ego by consistently besting other men. The farewell feast previously mentioned, given by a man who is about to die, is of a parallel character; the spirit of ostentatious display and competitiveness is carried to the very grave.

Sturges, in 1854, describes the same kind of friendly competition between the A1 and B1, who feasted each

[84] Though written in the present tense most of this section, except for the references to friendly feasts, applies to the past.

other alternately, each striving to excel the other. He refers to these feasts as "national entertainments," which continued for days, to distinguish them from the feasts to a chief by his own people that were held nearly every day, and he is appalled by the quantity of work and time devoted by the commoners to their preparation.

The pervasive dualism so characteristic of Ponapean society is revealed in the annual canoe ceremonies, now long in abeyance. In each tribe every section, about January, became completely absorbed in the building of a new canoe, of the elaborately carved chief's type. Everyone worked day and night, under the direction of the local section head. Those people not working on the hull, outriggers, and end-pieces were kept busy preparing the varicolored twine for the decorative lashings. Others formed bands of singers and dancers and practiced for weeks, under teachers, and prepared the dance paddles, costumes, and other paraphernalia for their performances. In April the canoes were launched, amidst religious ceremonies. Any canoe not ready at the appointed day had to be abandoned where it lay or destroyed, and the delinquent section head was punished.

All five tribes followed these practices, but the ceremonies in Madolenihmw were regarded as the most important. At least in Kiti all the people of the B1 took their canoes to him, and those of the A1 to him. Then both parties collected at the B1's place and competed in canoe races, in dances held on canoes lashed together to form a raft, and in other performances. After this they assembled at the B1's community house and the B1, who had chosen some canoes to keep as his own, distributed the others to the people and to visitors from elsewhere (with the expectation of return when the visitors held their own ceremonies). The same ceremonies and exchanges were then held a few days later at the headquarters of the A1, where his canoes had been gathered; here the two rival parties competed again.

At this distance in time it is hardly possible to relate these canoe ceremonies very precisely to the political system, but it seems evident that they were basically a prestige competition between the highest chiefs; presumably the lower chiefs gained merit in proportion to the successfulness of their canoe building and dance performances, just as they do today in their contributions to feasts. Similar celebrations are described at Madolenihmw by Gulick, but here the competition seems to have been primarily between A1 and A2, and the religious element bulks larger; esoteric performances accompanied the presentations of the new canoes, various rites were conducted at several localities among the artificial islands of Nan Madol, including the feeding of turtle entrails by priests to a sacred eel kept at one of these islands, religious ceremonies were held for each chief of importance, and new titles were conferred.

The friendly feast and the other paired festivities just described are similar to the feast made by the two halves of a section for each other, which is discussed later; this is again a competition but on an amicable level. But on a different plane are the two other Display Together feasts, which may be labeled as the potlatch. They usually result from a disparaging remark to the effect that someone has no yams or pigs or kava; more rarely, when someone has been seen to violate the secrecy of a yam plantation by sneaking in to observe what possessions the owner has.

Between two sections a Display Together competitive feast is called a Making a Variety of Things (*kourepwerepw*). Between two halves of a tribe it is called Lifting a Taboo from the Land (*kousarensapw*, referring to the freeing of the people from the taboo against digging yams periodically enjoined by the chiefs); this term is also applied to competitive feasts between some other geographical areas as well. The two types of feast are similar except that in theory somewhat different standards of victory are applied; at the Taboo Lifting it is quantity of yams that counts most, while at the Variety Making it is the variety of yams that is important. In contrast to both of these, in the prestige competition at ordinary feasts, Serving Together, it is the size of the yam, not quantity or kind, that is supposed to gain most merit. Actually a new variety of yam seems to win at any type of competition; the names of the feasts are loosely applied and difficult to distinguish in practice.[85]

The potlatches thus differ from the friendly and ordinary feasts not only in intensity of competitive feeling but in rules and standards. At the friendly feast only yams are concerned, while in the true potlatch every possession the contestants have may be entered. At Serving Together, standards with yams are based not only on the size of the yam but also on the number of vines. But at a potlatch a large yam with only one vine counts more than one with many vines. With sugar cane it is the length of the stalk that counts at any type of competition. With kava the important point is its age and the number of its branches; a certain fern which grows on old plants is artificially encouraged in order to enhance their apparent age. Age counts also with pit-breadfruit.

A castrated and fattened dog is one of the most important articles one may offer a chief at a feast or enter in competition at a potlatch. Today dogs are rarely seen

[85] This is indicated by two alternative terms for Making a Variety of Things (*kourepwerepw*) that occur in the writer's notes in recording accounts of the same event: *uhpene en kousapw* and *selepene en kousapw*. These terms translate as Serving Together between Sections and Displaying Together between Sections. I have previously given native definitions that would categorize Making a Variety of Things as one kind of Display Together, which is set against Serve Together as a contrasting group of feasts; yet in my notes on this occasion my informants treat all three as synonyms.

at feasts, though this is true more because of their scarcity than because of Western attitudes. Dogs are well treated and considered almost like children. They sometimes sleep on their master's mat. A fight between dogs is frequently the occasion for a quarrel between their masters. But a man who offered several dogs at a feast was greatly admired, and desire for prestige usually outweighed affection toward the animals. Pigs are likewise castrated and fattened, but the important thing with this animal is the length of its tusks; even more significant than a boar with long tusks is a female that is past bearing and has become very fat.

In any type of feast breadfruit, bananas, and coconuts do not count. Articles are rated in order of prestige value as follows: yams, kava, dogs, pigs, and pit-breadfruit.

In the potlatch, the side that has been insulted by disparaging remarks or by being spied upon calls on all its resources for the preparation of the feast, to which it invites the challengers. Sometimes there is no challenge or cause for challenge, the competitive feast being ordered by a chief in order to ascertain which side is superior. The contest may be between two men, two families, two subclans, two sections, two tribes, two halves of one section or tribe, or any other kinship or political grouping. When political or geographical units compete, they transcend clan or kinship ties across which they may cut; and vice versa.

The challenged side kills all its pigs and brings yams and kava and whatever valuables it may have. The articles are displayed, then given ostentatiously to the challenging side, which accepts them if it feels it can outdo the challenged party at the return feast, held the next day or so; otherwise it rejects the gifts and acknowledges defeat. The guests at this first feast may also indicate acceptance by "lifting" the feast; that is, they take over the officiating and division of the food; apparently failure to do so may, in at least some situations, indicate acknowledgment of defeat. "Lifting" may occur even at a so-called friendly feast; and occasionally other types of feasts are given the aspect of a potlatch by the issuance of a challenge and the "lifting" of the feast then and there. Many outsiders attend the feast and will join the victors in putting to scorn the party which has admitted defeat. Often taunting results in actual fighting.

When a competition has resulted from a quarrel between two men, the relatives of each man gather to urge them on; and if the relatives of one contestant see that he cannot match the other, they will exhort him not to accept defeat; instead one may take up the challenge in his place. If this happens the relatives of his antagonist join in also, and eventually large numbers of people may become involved, all digging up their yams to display their abundance. But if only the two original contestants are the active participants, the relatives abstain from contributing. Should one party acknowledge that it has been bested and retire in disgrace it would make an attempt to come back on a future day.

The news of such a contest spreads rapidly and spectators come in large numbers. Often the Nahnmwarki and Nahnken come to stop it, to halt the digging up of all the yams and to prevent possible bloodshed. In such a case each side would present to the Nahnmwarki a large yam, a large kava bush, and a large pig; this would indicate their equality and formally end the matter.

When the competition has been ordered between the two halves of a tribe by the Nahnmwarki, and sometimes on other such occasions, the Nahnmwarki and Nahnken attend and are the formal recipients of all the objects brought for display. They retain what they wish and the remainder is given to the challengers, who then present the return feast. The exchange of goods is, then, between the two contestants, and the attending chiefs only function as part of the machinery of the exchange. A feast given by command of the chiefs in this fashion may be either friendly or inimical; if friendly, each side supposedly gives what it wishes and it does not matter which gives most; such a feast is called a tribal feast (*kamadipw en wehi*) instead of Lifting a Taboo (*kousarensapw*). But in actual practice it is difficult to make a distinction. The descriptions of the feasts formerly held between the two halves of Madolenihmw (*pali en kepidau paliet,* consisting of sections 1–13, and *pali en kepidau palio,* sections 14–28) suggest that they varied considerably. Sometimes the Nahnmwarki would lead one side and the Nahnken the other; sometimes they would be both on one side and other chiefs would head the other side. It is possible that such variability reflected jockeying for political position and that this in turn would be expressed in greater or lesser overtness of hostility, hence giving a variable aspect to such feasts.

At a Taboo Lifting feast the first competitor sets the style, so to speak, and the challenger at the return feast will bring yams of the same size, small or large, depending on what size the challenged party brought, but will try to outdo him in quantity. The same applies to kava. Where the standards of competition involve kinds, rather than quantities or size, a single specimen of a new kind of yam not possessed by the challenger will give victory, regardless of whatever else has been brought.

At Service there is also competition to bring most but there is no taunting, only good-natured joking. A man might say in jest, "I have more than you," and everyone laughs. Ponapean habits of personal modesty preclude one's making such a remark except in joke. If one man tells another, "Your yam is the largest," the second man laughs and denies it, and says, "It is all I have." A man who is pointed out as having brought the largest yam feels proud but will point to someone else as champion.

Yet he will make sure that his modesty does not obscure his prowess in the eyes of the attending chiefs.

The foregoing descriptions are ideal patterns. Some instances of remembered potlatches reveal that there is considerable variation in detail in actual practice:

In German times a Taboo Lifting feast was held on the occasion of the construction of wharves at section 19 and at Wene, in Kiti; first section 19 gave a feast and presented all the food to the Nahnmwarki, who kept a small part of it and presented the remainder to the Nahnken; the Nahnken then divided it among his people, who were the Wene party. Then the Wene people gave the reciprocal feast and this time the Nahnmwarki divided the objects among his people, the party from section 19.

On another occasion in Kiti during the same period the Nahnmwarki ordered a Taboo Lifting competition between the two halves of Kiti, simply to see which side could produce the most.

About 1890 a Taboo Lifting was held between the B3 of Madolenihmw, who headed sections 20–22, and Toses, who led the people of section 23. It originated in a quarrel over yams. Toses, as the aggrieved party, gave the first feast, in his section; he made ten stone ovens in a large community house and brought all the food he could accumulate. Nearly every oven contained a different type of yam; two of them were of the type called *aunsona,* after the title of its discoverer, and were so large that they required 20 men each to carry them. The B3 had no yams of this type and therefore conceded defeat without giving a return feast; instead he returned all the articles that had been presented him by Toses. Both sides obeyed the strict injunction of Paul, the Nahnmwarki, to keep the peace, and no fighting resulted. Although this feast was called a Taboo Lifting, the standard applied was kind, not quantity, hence it conforms more closely to the definition of a Making a Variety of Things feast and illustrates the difficulty of attempting to adhere to native theoretical distinctions.

A Taboo Lifting was held in 1900 between Augustine of section 2, Madolenihmw, and his classificatory mother's brother, whose children had taunted Augustine over his supposed lack of yams for feasting. Augustine, his elder brother, and his three children competed against the mother's brother and about ten other relatives; he brought to the feast 100 *kehp en namwu* yams of 2-man size, 300 smaller yams, 300 kava plants, 30 pigs, and a cow, and Augustine boasts that he still had yams left in the ground after all this. The mother's brother did not attend the feast, having heard of the great quantities of food brought by Augustine and realizing that he could not win; his relatives came, however, and shouted insults, but departed without fighting, owing to the Nahnmwarki's edict. There was no return feast. Nearly 50 years later Augustine still laughs at the discomfited challengers.

A competition some time before 1870 took place between Kiti proper and Wene. It involved only kava, no yams. It was an abortive affair, for the Kiti people sent observers by night to spy out the amount of kava the Wene people had and on receiving the report decided that they could not successfully compete, so withdrew their challenge.

Under Nahnmwarki Paul of Madolenihmw (before 1900) a competition arose between sections 6 and 8. The people of section 6 vilified those of section 8, spreading gossip that the latter had no yams. The insulted party began to dig up all its yams, but Paul came to them and stopped it because he was afraid of a fight afterward.

Some time prior to 1870 the section 8 people spread gossip that the people of Lohd (now two sections, 27 and 28) had no yams or kava worth mentioning. Lohd thereupon dug up all its yams and made a feast; the people from section 8 came, accepted all the food, and 2 days later gave a return feast. When everything was counted, it turned out that the Lohd people had won, and they mocked their opponents, who "got a bad name." The losers were angry, but the Nahnken, who was from Lohd, and the A2, who lived in section 8, prevented any fighting.

No actual record of a fight following a competitive feast was obtained. It is possible that this is because of Christian influence, for missionaries have been active in Ponape since shortly after 1850.

Despite the German and Japanese prohibitions a Making a Variety feast was held in section 23, Net, just before World War II, with half of section 23 pitted against the other half. The division had no relation to kinship but purely to geography. It was caused in the usual manner, by one party decrying the poverty in possessions of the other. The side headed by the A5 of Net won by producing a large 2-man yam with only one vine, which is more difficult to grow than one with several vines.

Pairing off in competition tended in some areas to become institutionalized. Thus sections 1 and 2 of Net, which are islands within the lagoon, used to compete regularly. In theory (at least in Kiti) there was a regular division of the sections into eight subdivisions at the annual Start of Yam Season and Twisting Coir Twine feasts (see p. 85) given to the Nahnmwarki and other high chiefs of each tribe and section, and perhaps at every regular feast. These eight divisions were called Ovens (*uhmw*), from the fact that each of them prepared one stone oven, and in the pages to follow the word is used in this meaning. Sometimes these ovens appear to be identical with farmsteads (*peliensapw*), and are called alternatively farmstead or oven, but sometimes not. They were arrayed in two sides, the sides themselves sometimes called Taboo Lifting, like the name of the competitive feast, and competed against each other in providing yams, kava, and pigs. At these feasts the two sides competed simultaneously instead of on successive days. Such regular affairs were not usually followed by fighting.

This sort of competition, though it lacked the overt hostility of the formal potlatch, illustrates the fact that the theoretical distinctions in the native mind between friendly feasts and competitive feasts and between Serving Together and Displaying Together are not always clear-cut in practice. The Twisting Coir Twine feast was previously described as feast c in the regular cycle, hence part of the Serve Together complex. But descriptions of this feast as held in section 19 of Kiti in former days cause one to doubt these neat classifications. The people of the eight farmsteads in this section were ranged on two sides, each side consisting of four farmsteads. In the community house four ovens would be lined up on one side of the central, ground-level area, four more on the other, a farmstead head in charge of each oven (see Figure 4). A kava pounding stone would be prepared by each side. Then each farmstead would start its own oven going and exchange yams with a particular farmstead on the other side. For example, if farmstead No. 1 on one side had 100 yams in its pile it might bake perhaps 20, give another 20 to the Nahnmwarki, and present the remaining 60 to farmstead No. 1 on the other side. The recipient farmstead would reciprocate by giving the donor what it had left in its pile after its presentation to the Nahnmwarki. The Nahnmwarki (or other chief for whom the feast was being held) would distribute much of what was given to him to the other high-titled men present. It can readily be seen that more than one idea is involved here; generosity in presentation direct to the chiefs in order to win prestige and perhaps a promotion in the hierarchy of titles for the head of the farmstead that made the best showing; and direct competition with another political subdivision in order to show superiority and gain renown, but also, indirectly, to win promotions through the reflection of prestige on the side that dominated.

Informants often refer to this 8-fold division or to eight ovens in connection with paired competitions within the section, and they speak also of eight ovens when there was competition between larger areas (though in this situation it must have been something larger than a farmstead that provided one oven). But where information is available the ideal number eight is not always manifest. A part of Uh, consisting of sections 3 to 9, in the past would make a Start of Yam Season feast at which there were 12, not eight, ovens. These 12 were arranged into two sides called *lepilong* and *lepiei*. The feast was given for four days, to the A1, B1, A2, and B2 in that order. The pairing was as follows (the six named areas are all farmsteads of section 7):

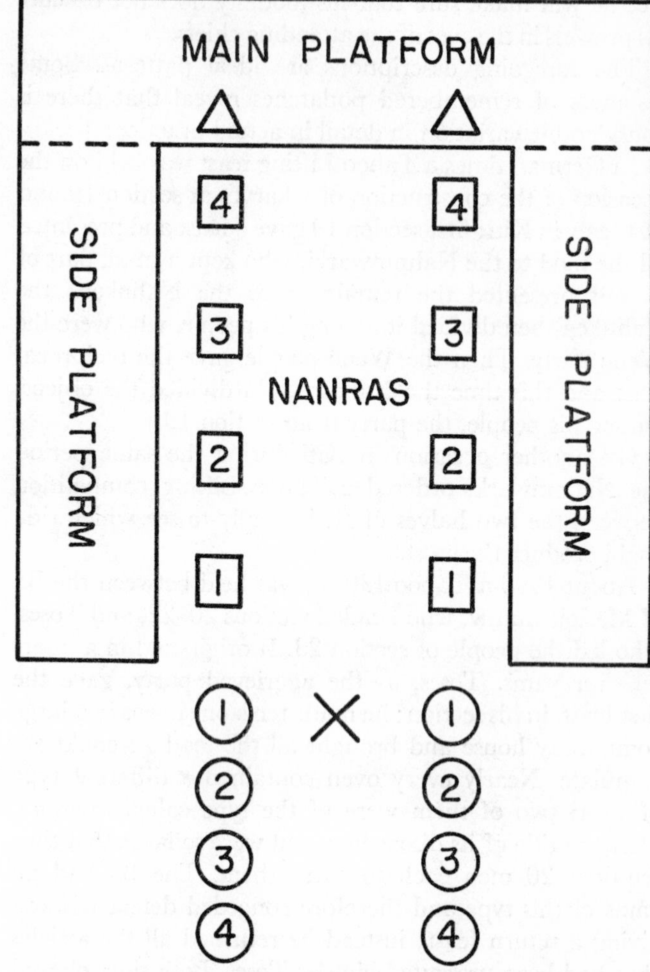


FIGURE 4.—A Twisting Coir Twine feast in the community house of section 19, Kiti. Numbers in squares represent the stone ovens of the eight farmsteads of section 19; farmstead No. 1 on one side competes and exchanges with farmstead No. 1 of the other side, and so on. Numbers in circles represent the piles of yams belonging to each farmstead, left outside the community house for display. "X" marks the heap of pigs brought by all the farmsteads, placed here before singeing off the hair on the hot stones from the ovens. The triangles on the main platform represent the location of the two principal kava stones, where kava is pounded until the ovens are cleared away, when more kava stones are placed in two rows in the central area (*nanras*). One kava stone and a row of ovens are under charge of the Kroun Wein, X1 of the section, the other stone and row under the Nahnawa en Rohnkiti, the Y1 chief. Overseer of all is Oun Kiti, formerly highest tribal titleholder in the section.

| | | |
|---|---|---|
| Section 8 | vs. | Section 6 |
| Section 9 | vs. | Section 3 |
| Pohnkeimw | vs. | Peien Uh |
| Keimwin | vs. | Lukoapoas |
| Nanseinpwel | vs. | Section 5 |
| Sewihso | vs. | Section 4 |

Informants say that this Start of Yam Season feast was then followed by another, similar one, which they call Taboo Lifting. It is not at all certain that this was the same kind of feast previously referred to as Taboo Lifting; it is also possible that what the informants are describing is the same Start of Yam Season feast but somehow given a more competitive aspect. At any rate, the same pairing of the same 12 units occurred, and it seems to have been a regular affair, not depending on a challenge; sometimes it ended in fighting. In contrast to Kiti, the two sides did not compete simultaneously, the recipient returned the feast the next day.

The other sections of Uh (1, 2, and 10–15) staged their Start of Yam Season feasts separately. In section 13 of Uh there were again 12 farmsteads, which were matched thus:

| *lepilong* | | *lepiei* |
|---|---|---|
| Peidi | vs. | Sep |
| Pohnpihr | vs. | Soukiro |
| Sewihso | vs. | Peilong en rohi |
| Apweiakpeilong | vs. | Nindol |
| Apweiakpeiei | vs. | Likomwpweilong |
| Nanepwok | vs. | Likomwpweiei |

The expressed native theory that there were eight farmsteads in a section fails thus to be borne out everywhere. The twelve farmsteads of section 13 just listed have been in existence since at least during informants' early years (as far back as 1880), as have the six of section 7 previously mentioned. Elsewhere irregularities in number may in part be due to the effects of the German issuance of deeds during the first decade of the 20th century. On such deeds the various holdings that were awarded as private property, when they were contiguous, were entered as a single piece of land and collectively called by the native name of one of those holdings; thus references nowadays to named areas may become confused. Depopulation in some areas has also affected the number of ovens that can be made. But Net informants deny any general eight-oven or six-oven pattern and say that there may even be an odd number of farmsteads in a section. The B2 of Net, for example, recalls that there were ten ovens at Start of Yam Season in section 1 some 30 years ago and there are 16 today at its modern substitute, the honor feast. Each farmstead was occupied by one extended family, hence it is obvious that the subdivisions must have varied in number from time to time. But where the number eight was held to, as it seems to have been in Kiti, there must have been grouping of families together in order to achieve the ideal number of ovens, and a farmstead could not always have corresponded to one oven. Or it may be that the word *peliensapw* is not always to be taken literally as meaning a family farmstead but may indicate a political subdivision with which farmsteads tended to, but did not always, coincide.

In Kiti, at least, the ceremonial exchanges between the farmsteads occurred also at those first fruit ceremonies that involved assemblage in the community house. The rivalry in attempting to outdo others in food presentation at such affairs persists today, but only in a minor degree. In Kiti there was the same ranging of the ovens on two sides, but the exchanges, at least in some places, were between any two farmsteads on opposite sides, not between members of designated pairs. In section 16 of Kiti the ovens were arranged as follows:

| | |
|---|---|
| Pokil | Pohnangieng |
| Kepinuluhl | Pohnangkiok |
| Tonkiap[86] | Pahlap |
| Karki | Soupir |

In section 15 of Kiti:

| *Kepinsemwei* | *Kepilerohi* |
|---|---|
| Kepinsemwei | Nanmangil |
| Tonemwok | Alamas |
| Reiwei | Kepihle |
| Kias | Kepinta |

In section 26 of Kiti:

| *uhmw peiuhpa* | *uhmw peiuhpowe* |
|---|---|
| (i.e., four lower ovens) | (i.e., four upper ovens) |
| Pohnkulu | Dol en samaki |
| Loahngenkiti | Eipwa |
| Ta wenapa | Imwindol |
| Longorik | Madol |

But section 29 of Kiti has only two farmsteads (i.e., two ovens): the northern half of the section is Dionpwo, the southern is Lehpwel; informants say that this was true anciently also. Section 5 of Kiti likewise has two farmsteads, Sounsom and Ipal, each divided into six *mwokot* (a term used rather variably in different areas, but here signifying a subdivision of a farmstead); each *mwokot* provided one oven, as follows:

| *Sounsom* | *Ipal* |
|---|---|
| Nantipw | Alapowei |
| Sapwet | Pohntui |
| Nanpahlap | Paler |
| Doleni | Pohsomwak |
| Panor | Dopari |
| Pohniong | Pahnkomwo |

It seems clear that in this section the term farmstead is being used for the two halves of the section that exist elsewhere but are usually unnamed, and that *mwokot* is here equivalent to farmstead as previously used.

[86] Given as Panios by another informant.

298-818—68——10

In Awak, the present-day sections 1 and 2 of Uh, the ancient organization was six ovens, three on a side:

| | |
|---|---|
| Pelienpil | Paremitik |
| Sewihso riau | Mesenpal |
| Matar | Panol [87] |

Following the German redistribution of lands the two sides in Awak became organized into 12 ovens, four on one side, eight on the other, as follows:

| | |
|---|---|
| Kopwun | Peimore |
| Wel | Panpei |
| Meikido | Nanwou |
| Dierekpwel | Nankepiniak |
| | Alukeren |
| | Penietik |
| | Tipwenpohnore |
| | Panipa |

Just how this apparently unbalanced division functioned in food exchanges is not clear; another informant gives eight unnamed ovens instead of 12.

Although these 2-fold divisions pitted geographical areas against one another, political and kinship ties were also involved. For example, in section 29 of Kiti it was the X1 of the section, the Nahnsahu en Sewihso, who led the people of Lehpwel farmstead in competition against the people of Dionpwo farmstead headed by the Y1, the Nahnkroun Sewihso. The followers of each of the two chiefs tended to be his clansmates within the section. In section 15 of Kiti the four ovens in Kepilerohi were similarly headed by the X1, the four in Kepinsemwei by the Y1. Each separate oven might be headed by a designated section titleholder belonging to one or the other line of titles within the section. In Awak, Uh, this was organized as follows:

*Under the X1* (Soulik en Awak)

| | |
|---|---|
| Pelienpil | under the Lepenien Awak |
| Sewihso riau | under the Sidin Awak |
| Matar | under the Soulik en Awak |

*Under the Y1* (Kroun en Awak)

| | |
|---|---|
| Paremitik | under the Kroun en Awak |
| Mesenpal | under the Koaroahm en Awak |
| Panol | under the Soumadau en Awak |

Since the three titles on each side (especially in Uh) belong to the same line of chiefs and usually to the same family, the competition within the section is essentially between two kinship units and is of a somewhat different cast from that between political units larger than sections and different also from the prestige competition of individuals. When more than one section is involved, several kinship units may be in competition, and kinship ties may cut across political and residential bonds instead of reinforcing them as they do within the section. There are, however, no data as to intensity of competitive feeling at the different levels of competitive exchange, so we can make no generalizations concerning the reality to the native of this distinction. Again, in the presentation of food to the chiefs at ordinary feasts the individual strives to augment his prestige by surpassing the efforts of all other individuals; whereas in group competitions personal ambition must be temporarily submerged in the communal cause; but the distinction is not clear-cut, for in the individual offering a man is often helped by his relatives in his efforts to prove himself worthy of a promotion, and in the communal offering the individual's contribution to the oven is noted by all persons present and his reputation is thereby affected.

# THE FEAST PATTERN

## The Community House and Seating Arrangements

Feasts of most types are held in the *nahs,* which is variously referred to in the published literature as community house, meeting house, canoe house, feast house and all-men's house. Any of these terms is applicable, since the building serves all these purposes, except the last, which is an error based upon a false analogy with the bachelor's house of the central and western Carolines. In this work the term community house is consistently employed. The building varies somewhat in architecture, but the most developed form is a structure containing platforms on three sides, in the shape of a U with the front left open. The central, ground-level area (the *nanras*), enclosed on three sides by the platforms, is the place where kava is pounded and the stone ovens (*uhmw*) are made. The main, rear platform (*lampahntamw*) is somewhat higher than the two side platforms (*mongentik*) and is sometimes stepped (Plates 6a and 6b).

On the main platform of the community house sit the *soupeidi,* or Those Who Face Downwards, an expression whose various meanings have already been discussed. The term *soupeidi* derives from this seating arrangement, since the people it refers to sit facing the front of the building, while everyone else sits on a lower level and faces them.

In Kiti the Nahnmwarki sits forward of the rear central post of the main platform (the post itself bears the name

[87] Mesenpal and Panol constitute modern section 1 of Uh, the other four ovens making up modern section 2.

*soupeidi*), with his servitors in front of and facing him. The B2 sits alongside him in front of the next post to his right and the Nahnken in front of the next post to his left; to the left of the Nahnken the A2 may sit, though not always.[88] The point of this arrangement is that men of lower title in the same line as the Nahnmwarki do not sit near him, and juniors to the Nahnken in the B-line do not sit near that chief. Farther to the right of the B2 sits the Nahnmwarki's wife, and to her right sits the Nahnken's wife.[89] In front of each of these persons sits his servitor or servitors, but still on the main platform. Nowadays in Kiti, Oliver, who is the A6 but who holds one of the titles properly belonging to the Nahnmwarki, namely Rohsa, may sit in the B2's place; he is in the A-line but belongs to clan 18 rather than to clan 4 (the A-clan) or clan 11 (the B-clan). In Kiti the A2's position is not definite, since his duties often take him down into the central area where the other holders of A-titles are working. He often sits to the left of the B1, but he can also sit elsewhere on the main platform, as long as he is not near the Nahnmwarki.

In Net, according to the Nahnken of this tribe, the Nahnmwarki and Nahnken should sit on the right of the main platform, their wives on their left; but the position of the Nahnmwarki relative to that of the Nahnken and the positions of their wives relative to each other do not matter (Plate 7a). As observed at feasts in Net the Nahnmwarki actually sits in the center of the platform, as in Kiti, with the Nahnken and the visitors from other tribes to his right, his wife to his left and the Nahnken's wife to the left of her. The A2 in Net does not get on the main platform but should sit and work at the last kava stone in the right row of stones; he is not supposed to move about. The A3 has duties that keep him on the right platform. The A4 must, like the A2, stay in the central area and work, when the Nahnmwarki is present (although the present A4 is one of the assistant food dividers). The B-line chiefs, being Royal Children, are permitted to move about as they please. The present B2 in Net is the principal divider of the food and has duties that keep him standing on the main platform, so his proper place was not observed. The main assistants of the B2 of Net, the A4, A6 and B4, likewise have special duties, though these are not duties that adhere to these titles but to the particular men who at present possess them. On the left side platform, from the Nahnmwarki's point of view, sit the women; on the right platform sit the men who are not working in the central area; but this division is not always enforced, and at some feasts, when the women do not fill up their side, a number of men sit there too.

In Madolenihmw the Nahnmwarki, instead of sitting in the center, sits toward the right side of the main platform, with the Nahnken more toward the center, to his left, contrary to the practice elsewhere. To the left of the Nahnken sits the Nahnmwarki's wife, and leftward of her the Nahnken's wife. All of these sit facing forward. The A2 in this tribe sits toward the rear end of the left platform, facing Those Who Face Downwards; behind him, about midway down the platform, is the position of the A3; and behind the A3, toward the front end, is the A5, who must stand in order to perform his duty, the overseeing of the work in the central area. If the A5 is absent, the A4 may be positioned here. On the right side platform in Madolenihmw the B2 sits in a position about one-third of the way to the front, and the B3 is at the front end of this platform; the B3, like the A5, must stand, for it is up to these two chiefs to see that no one else stands up straight so that his head will be higher than the heads of Those Who Face Downwards, that the people on the side platforms do not sit with their legs outstretched or apart, that their legs or skirts do not hang over the heavy beam forming the inner edge of the side platform, that everyone speaks quietly and does not use commoner speech, and that all maintain the various forms of respect due the high chiefs.[90]

The right platform in Madolenihmw, as in Kiti but unlike Net, is the feminine side, although the B2 and B3 and sometimes other men sit here too.[91] The B2 is in charge of the division of the food, as the bearer of this title seems formerly to have been in all of Ponape in his capacity of chief priest. Whoever wishes to go out to fetch breadfruit or firewood must first get his permission, and the breadfruit picker or the axe must first be shown to him. After the food is baked, it is brought to him in baskets and he pulls the slip-knot of hibiscus fiber that fastens the baskets shut; then, in former days, he would give a prayer. After this, his assistants help him divide the food. Only then might food go to the Nahnmwarki or Nahnken.

Much of the foregoing ritual is rarely seen today, and the seating arrangements are not always taken seriously.

---

88 Hambruch (1932 II, p. 17) has a diagram of a feast in Wene (part of Kiti) that shows this arrangement of Nahnmwarki and Nahnken. The B2 is absent and the A2 is to the right of the Nahnmwarki, but the community house in which the feast was held belonged to A2, which may have affected the seating arrangements.

89 In Hambruch's diagram of the Wene seating arrangements the only high-ranking woman present is the wife of the A2, who was the host at this occasion. She is seated to the left of the Nahnken.

90 Hambruch's sketch of the Wene arrangements shows the B3 at the front end of the left instead of the right platform as in Madolenihmw, and the A3 at the front end of the right platform instead of midway down the left platform. These two chiefs are described as guards. The reversal of position with respect to the side platforms is no doubt connected with the fact that the position of the two sexes on the side platforms is also reversed as compared with Madolenihmw.

91 But the sketch in Hambruch of the feast in Wene shows the women on the left. It is of interest, also, that at a motion picture shown at Kolonia and attended by many Net people, the men, without any apparent direction, all took seats on the right, the women on the left.

The prayer by the B2 was his function as priest. The B4 is also said to have "blessed" food before the highest chief ate; he was the second priest.

In addition to the high chiefs a number of other persons are entitled to sit on the main platform of the community house. Among these is the Lepen Moar in Madolenihmw, who is not a member of either ruling clan but owes his special position to certain feats performed in war by an ancient holder of the title. In Net the Lepen Net and the Nahnsoused, whose titles were formerly those of the A1 and B1 but are now bestowed on other men, still receive high honors along with the Nahnmwarki and Nahnken, whose titles have replaced theirs. Also visitors from other tribes take their places beside the high chiefs, regardless of the position of their titles, if they come in official status. Many of the X1 titles rank very high and their holders may sit alongside the Nahnmwarki.

There is a tendency for the people who sit on the side platforms to arrange themselves by rank, those with higher titles sitting toward the rear, the commoners toward the front; but this is anything but a rigid ordering. Bascom (1965, p. 29) states that the Nahnmwarki and other chiefs in the A-line sit in order along one side of the building, while the Nahnken and B-chiefs sit on the other, but neither informants nor observation bore this out; in fact, it would be impossible, for nearly all men of the A-line must be working in the central area when the Nahnmwarki is present. Other than this requirement there are no assigned positions for the lower titleholders in either line except for those already specified. There is only a faint resemblance to the kava circle of Western Polynesia.

When a titled man from one tribe comes to a feast in another tribe, his clansmates residing in the second tribe, who are normally commoners there, move up closer to the main platform. If the visitor is a Nahnmwarki or Nahnken or comes as his representative he sits facing forward on the main platform alongside the local high chiefs; but if he has a lower title and is visiting for his own purposes, he faces up toward those chiefs.

Besides the Royal Children, the Nahnmwarki's sons-in-law, even if they belong to his own clan and thus have A-titles, may move about and may sit on the main platform (but not facing forward) if they wish. This is because, like the Royal Children, they are considered as his children.

As noted previously, the A2 takes the Nahnmwarki's place when the latter is absent, the A3 takes it if both of his superiors are absent, and so on; similarly, in the B-line, the order of the series is followed. At a section feast, unless a person with a high tribal title is present, the X1 takes the place of honor. If the A2 takes the Nahnmwarki's place, the other members of the A-clan may move up closer to the rear.

Only the highest Royal Children, particularly the actual children of a Nahnmwarki or Nahnken, may climb up at the front ends (the *karatak en seriiso*) of the two side platforms. Sons use the masculine side, daughters the feminine side. This custom is attributed to the similar behavior of the first Nahnken of Madolenihmw in the legend of Isohkelekel. The two rear doors (*wahnihmw en lampahntamw* in Kiti, *wahnmeimei* in Net) and the first side door on each side opening onto the main platform are reserved for the use of Those Who Face Downwards. Holders of lower A-titles and male commoners must come through the large front entrance and climb onto the side platforms from the central area. Women of any rank may enter by the side doors on the feminine side platform, but on the masculine side the side doors may be used only by Royal Children.

## Feasting Procedure and Ceremonial

The preparation of the food at feasts is carried on in the central, ground-level arena of the community house, below the three platforms. It is entirely the work of men. A number of stone ovens are arranged in two parallel rows along the length of that area. The oven is not the same as the earth oven of other parts of Oceania but is a surface structure. A layer of basalt rocks is made on the ground or in a shallow depression. On top of this is piled firewood, then more rocks are heaped on to form a dome-shaped structure. When the rocks are hot, the oven is taken apart with wooden tongs, the coals and ashes are raked out, and the stones are built up again over the food. The food is wrapped in leaves, but halved or quartered animals are laid in place, and this is followed by layers of hot stones. Then yams and any other vegetables being prepared are laid on the stones; over these are placed leaves, usually of banana; then the pig or pigs or other animals are laid in place, and this is followed by layers of more leaves—banana, *ieuieu,* and coconut palm leaves are often used in successive layers, or sometimes old mats. The edges of the leaves around the oven may be weighted down to keep in the steam (Plate 8a).

For carrying most small articles to feasts the carrying basket (*kiam*) made from a section of a coconut leaf is used. Articles may also be tied to each end of a carrying pole (*ini*) which is borne on one shoulder, or tied to its middle and carried on the shoulders of two men in file. A long basket (*kiam ro*) made of the whole coconut leaf (*pahini,* also used as the alternative name of the basket) is carried slung from a carrying pole with one man at each end. For large quantities of food a litter of wood (*peikini*) with coconut leaves laid over it is carried by 6 to 10 men with two poles; such a contrivance can hold hundreds of breadfruit, 10 or 20 bunches of bananas, 20 or 30 small yams, or 5 or 10 pigs. In place of the litter a "nest" (*pahs*) can be slung between two poles (Plates 8b, 8c, 8d, 9a, 9b).

Articles carried to a feast are designated according to the number of men required to carry them. A 1-man yam is a *kehptapan* or, if very small, a *kehptikitik*. A kava bush small enough to be carried by one man is a *sakau kepaik*. A yam that requires two men is a *kei*, while a kava plant of this size is a *ro*. The term *ro* may also be used for yams, but *kei* is not used with kava. In Net, *kei* is applied to a yam that requires two to four men. For a yam or kava plant carried by four or more men (six or more in Net) the term applied is *pahs* (the same as the carrying device). The number of men required for very heavy yams, as given by various informants, may run over 30; one informant gives the hardly credible figure of 50. On one occasion, in December 1947, at a funeral feast in Madolenihmw, a 5-year-old yam was carried in a "nest" by 30 men. Even 2-year-old yams are often large enough for this carrying device. The poles are heavy and there is also a tendency to add superfluous porters in order to magnify the impression of opulence on the part of the donor of the yam; nevertheless such large yams must weigh very considerably to require so many bearers. Though the writer had no scales with which to verify his guess, he judged the average weight of five 2-man yams at one feast to be about 50 or 60 pounds, which would be at least 25 pounds per porter. A yam that required 30 porters would, on this basis, weigh an incredible amount, but I have no hesitation in saying that Ponapeans can grow yams weighing 200 pounds or more.

For distribution at the feast among the people the large uncooked yams are broken up into their component tubers (*kutor*). There are usually 2 to 10 tubers to a yam of the 2-man size, depending on its kind.

Pigs and dogs are brought to feasts slung under carrying poles, the legs tied over the poles with hibiscus fiber; or they may be brought on litters if there are several of them. The pole is slipped out and the animal is killed by stabbing in the heart with a machete; dogs may also be killed by having their throats cut. The hair is singed off by pulling the carcass back and forth over the hot stones scattered about when the stone oven is opened, or coconut-leaf brands may be applied to the animal; then the skin is scraped with a machete. A single ventral slit is made and the entrails drawn. The ceremonial preparation of dogs described and illustrated by Hambruch (1932 II, pp. 246–252) was not seen in 1947–48, due to an epidemic that had virtually wiped out the canine population. (See Plate 5b, a photograph taken in 1963 of a roasted dog in a coconut-leaf basket; its preparation was not witnessed.)

Usually, while the food is being prepared in the oven, one or two kava stones are pounded for the early kava, known variously as morning kava (*sakau en menseng*), quick kava (*sakau en ahmwadang*), and kava of the rising sun (*sakau en kapwarisou*). Formerly these stones were on the main platform, and the kava produced from them was made only for the Nahnmwarki, Nahnken, and their attendants, but this is seldom seen nowadays; usually the stones are in the central area, just below the main platform. The hibiscus carrying pole, on which a kava bush is brought for this early pounding, is thrown out of one of the doors of the main platform.

In the middle of the main platform, built into the stone foundations, there was formerly a pit about six feet square and two feet deep (*nanpehs or nanparas*). Here a fire was kept burning, from which were lit the fires for the stone ovens.

Sugar cane (*sehu*) is brought to a feast either in single stalks or in a whole clump (*uhnsehu*) joined at the roots, which is then divided into separate stalks. Single stalks are carried on a man's shoulder, the large clumps on litters (Plate 10a). Like kava, sugar cane is carried root foremost. If sugar cane is brought, it is carried by the women as well as the men, for "sugar cane is women's work." The litters are placed with the root ends of the cane on the main platform, the other ends in the central area. One large litter may be shoved up into the rafters. The women who bear the sugar cane are much less inhibited than the men who follow them with kava and they whoop and give the ululating yell (*kadakadek*) common through the Carolines; I have seen them occasionally breaking into solo dances. Some of the cane is cut up and distributed; in Net the persons of high title present, male and female, get two pieces each, one piece of four sections and one of eight. The remainder of the cane is distributed whole, according to rank.

After this distribution the ovens are opened and their baked contents are removed and distributed according to rules described below. The kava is then brought in, in a singing procession, after which the kava pounding stones are set up (Plate 10b).

If dances are held at the feast, the side platforms may be used or a special structure may be built out from them. But dances are seldom associated with the feasts nowadays.

When the feast is over, the portions of food that have been distributed are carried home, the uncooked yam tubers to be replanted, the cooked foods often to be recooked. The Nahnmwarki's share should be carried to his home by someone from the opposite line of titles, who takes commoners along with him to act as porters. The wife of a generous Nahnmwarki will give perhaps half of the food to the bearers, hence there are eager volunteers for this duty; a complaint against the present chiefs of Net is that they are too stingy to live up to this custom and their bearers go unrewarded.

The baked pig carcasses are taken from the opened oven and brought up to the main platform to be cut up on coconut leaves. In Madolenihmw the pig is placed on its stomach before it is carved. First the head is taken off, cutting from the left side. Then two longitudinal gashes are made along the loin, from neck to rump, first along the left, then the right side. After this the pig is turned on its back and the left front leg, including the shoulder, is cut off; then the left rear leg; then a belly strip on the left side of the ventral slit made before cooking for drawing the entrails. Next the flank is sliced, from the ventral slit to the loin cut, into a number of pieces; these include the ribs. Then the whole operation is repeated for the right side. The remaining part, the back between the two loin cuts, is chopped into several portions.

Elsewhere than Madolenihmw the pig is placed on its back before it is cut. Butchering procedure in Kiti is similar to that in Madolenihmw, though the writer has seen the two belly strips removed first, even before the head, and the flank sliced up after the front leg is cut off and before the rear leg is removed; this in spite of the expressly stated procedure. Occasionally, also, the butchering begins with the right side. In Net the right side is the proper side to begin with, but if there are two men carving pigs at a feast, one begins with the right side, the other with the left side.

In the preparation of a turtle the intestines are first removed without separating the carapaces and are baked in the oven without any container for some 15 or 20 minutes. The baked intestines are considered a great delicacy, despite their overpowering odor. At the feast they are served on breadfruit leaves to the highest chiefs and their wives. The turtle itself is baked in the stone oven for about an hour; after it is removed from the oven the portion of the right front leg that protrudes from the shell is cut off, then the right rear, then the left front and left rear legs. (This is the procedure observed in Net.) After this the lower carapace is removed and a certain portion behind the right foreleg is cut away, followed in order by the same portion from the left foreleg. A large portion of the carcass is then removed from between the hind legs, followed by the large front shoulder muscles, and then what is left of the legs and shoulders themselves in the same order of right front, right rear, left front, and left rear; with these portions comes most of the rest of the body of the turtle.

At a feast a turtle should be cut up before the pigs, so that it can be served hot; they are baked together in one oven. A large group of eager observers usually gathers around to watch the butchering, since it is considered a difficult job and there is much less opportunity to witness its execution than there is with pigs or even dogs.

Formerly, a taro leaf full of water had to be nearby for washing the hands and the knife; nowadays, any container serves. The palm leaves on which the butchering takes place are supposed to be thrown out of the doors leading into the back of the main platform; if they are bloody, the side doors may be used. In Madolenihmw the breadfruit-leaf platters upon which the portions of meat are placed have their stems attached, but elsewhere the stems are supposed to be removed. The men who cut up the pigs and distribute the parts are required not to wear shirts.

## Division of Food

The official divider of the food (the *soun nehne* or *soun ne*) is appointed to his task by the Nahnmwarki and Nahnken. One man from each line of titles is appointed because only if he is a member of the opposite line may he stand with his head higher than that of a high chief. At one feast observed in Kiti, when the Nahnmwarki was present, there was no man in the B-line present who was considered skilled enough to undertake the job of divider, so the A3 functioned. But being in the same line as the Nahnmwarki he could not stand in the divider's usual place on the main platform, for the Nahnmwarki was seated there. The central area was too full of people and kava pounding stones to permit him to stand there and function effectively. So he stood outside of the building, in the rain, and called out the titles of the recipients of the various portions from that position.

Also two women, one from each line, divide the women's share of the food. In a section feast there are likewise two functionaries, although their assumption of duties is more informal. In Net, at a large feast, the B2 and A4 function; at smaller feasts the B4 and A6; the Oundol en Ririn is also a qualified food divider. The duties of the divider are not incumbent on the holders of these particular titles, even though the B2, as chief priest, was anciently the chief functionary and tends still to be so in each tribe. Until a few years ago the present Lependeleur of Net was a food divider of that tribe, but he proved unsatisfactory and was replaced by the Oundol en Ririn. It is considered a difficult and delicate job, for it is easy to offend a titleholder by not giving him a portion commensurate with his position.

In the division of the pigs each man's portion is raised up by the divider while he calls out the recipient's title. Thus, at a feast where there are a number of pigs, the largest pig is held up while the official loudly calls "koanoat Nahnmwarki"; the second largest pig is assigned to the Nahnken by a call of "sahk Nahnken." (See p. 45 for explanation of these honorific terms for food.) This procedure is called *pwekpwek*. The pig or portion of pig is not handed over to the person designated but is taken by commoners to the front of the community house and hung there in baskets from the main stringer. For men of lower titles portions are hung elsewhere in the building. The third portion, which goes to the A2 (the Wasai), is announced as "Wasai kepin koanoat." If the Nahnmwarki is not present the Nahnken takes the first share and that of the A2 is called "sahk Wasai." It does not matter which divider apportions the food, but if he belongs to the A-line and the Nahnmwarki is present he cannot shout out the proper words, the divider of the Nahnken line must do it instead; and likewise, the official of the opposite line must function in this manner for the Nahnken. The female functionaries call "pwenieu Nahnalek" and "sahk Nahnkeniei" for the wife (Nahnalek) of the Nahnmwarki and the wife (Nahnkeniei) of the Nahnken respectively, and their baskets are also suspended.

In Kiti if there are enough pigs the order of division is as follows: Nahnmwarki, Nahnken, Nahnmwarki's wife, Nahnken's wife, chiefs A2, B2, A3, B3, A4, and B4, alternating thus between the A and B lines. Beyond this whole pigs are not distributed, only portions. Some of the section heads and some of the holders of priestly titles that rank high may, however, in the distribution of pigs, come ahead of the tribal chiefs just listed, as explained earlier, except for A1 and B1. Also nowadays the A6 of Kiti, Oliver Nanpei, comes just after the Nahnken, because of his special position as the wealthiest and most powerful man in Ponape, and because of his extra title of Rohsa, which is normally another title of the Nahnmwarki of Kiti but has been awarded to Oliver. When Oliver attends a feast in Uh (where he is also A6) or Madolenihmw, he is said to receive first honors, ahead of even the Nahnmwarki or Nahnken.

In Net the order of division is supposed to be Nahnmwarki, Nahnken, Lepen Net, Nahnsoused, A2, Souruko, Soulik en Daun, B2. This tribe has apparently interleaved the old Net titles (see p. 19) with the new ones that have been copied after the other tribes. But in quite recent times there has been disruption of this ideal order; thus Soulik en Daun is a title that is supposed to belong to the A-line but is now held by the Nahnken himself as a secondary title; the title Lepen Net, which was formerly that of the A1 instead of the title Nahnmwarki and belonged to clan 7, is nowadays held by a man who is a member of clan 6, hence in the B-line, and he follows the A2 in food distribution.

The order of division is also interrupted in all tribes by the presence of visitors (*tohn kapar*) from other tribes, who share very generously in the food distribution. If there are only two pigs and only one visitor from another tribe is present, he is supposed to get one of the pigs.

If there is only one large pig, it goes entirely to the Nahnmwarki, except for the legs and ribs. In Net the right foreleg goes to the Nahnken, the left foreleg to the Nahnmwarki's wife, the right hind leg to the Nahnken's wife; the other leg and ribs go to holders of lesser titles. But if there is only one pig a benevolent-minded Nahnmwarki should tell the divider to divide his portion among the people. In Kiti the belly strip from the left side is laid on a leaf and put before the Nahnmwarki; he may redistribute it if he wishes. Another portion from the left side is similarly given the Nahnken. In Net the equivalent portions for the Nahnmwarki and Nahnken are ribs, from either side. These portions are in addition to those received in the distribution procedure called *pwekpwek* (see p. 100), and they are intended to be eaten at the feast; most of the rest of the meat is taken home and recooked, since there is actually little eating at a feast. Eating is considered improper when kava drinking, the principal activity at a feast, is going on.

In Kiti all of the left forelegs remain hanging in baskets during the division; after the division is made they are taken down and the Nahnmwarki disposes of them as he pleases. He usually gives some to each of the holders of the first 12 titles in the two lines and divides what is left with the Nahnken, taking his own share home. Besides the left forelegs, the head belongs to the Nahnmwarki and the portion of the back immediately behind the neck to the Nahnken.

Actual procedure varies widely. Records were kept of three feasts in Net; at one, of three large and seven small pigs, the Nahnmwarki received the head, back, and right foreleg and shoulder of the largest, and his wife the two hind legs; the Nahnken, who is the Nahnmwarki's father, received one whole pig and another left foreleg, and his wife received two hind legs. This left only the remaining portions of one large pig and the seven small pigs for division among more than 80 people. At a second feast, where some 80 or 90 people were present, the two largest pigs went to the Nahnmwarki and Nahnken, and a leg apiece from other pigs to their wives; three pigs were divided among the visitors from the other four tribes; the remaining six pigs were left for the other people. At the third feast, one whole pig was given alive to the Nahnmwarki as well as the head and back of the largest pig; one leg apiece from this pig went to the wives of the Nahnmwarki and Nahnken; the second largest pig was given to the Nahnken; four pigs were given to the visitors from the other four tribes; three pigs were eaten; and the remaining five pigs and the remaining portions of the largest pig were divided among the rest of the people.

The food divider is in theory autonomous as far as the performance of his duties is concerned, just as is the kava distributor (*soun dei sakau*). His job is to apportion the meat and vegetable food baked in the stone ovens and such food as sugar cane, which does not have a high prestige value. The B2 of Net, who is the principal divider (and also kava distributor) of that tribe, asserts that he would dispute with the Nahnmwarki or Nahnken if they attempted to interfere with his proper functions. To be sure, at small gatherings the writer has seen chiefs of various ranks issue sotto voce instructions to the man, appointed only for the occasion, who did the dividing, or even countermand an apportionment that displeased them. But over the uncooked yams, which constitute by far the largest part of the yams brought to a feast, the divider has no authority except to present one such yam to the visitors from each of the four other tribes. The uncooked yams all belong to the Nahnmwarki and Nahnken, for they have been presented to them; they retain or distribute them as they please, the food divider follows their instructions with regard to them as well as with their rightful portions of the cooked articles. Hence there is considerable opportunity for generosity or niggardliness to make themselves evident, as there is in connection with pigs. The five present Nahnmwarkis are ranked according to public opinion in the following descending scale of generosity; Kiti, Uh, Madolenihmw, Net, Sokehs; and the Nahnkens as follows: Madolenihmw, Kiti, Uh, Net, Sokehs. The Nahnken of Madolenihmw is considered particularly generous, and is said to keep practically nothing for himself. At the other extreme, the Nahnmwarki and Nahnken of Net are noted for their greediness, which is held to stem from their acquaintance with western concepts of money economy. In Sokehs most of the chiefs are out-islanders and do not follow Ponapean feasting patterns.

The divider makes two primary divisions of all the uncooked yams: one heap is the Nahnmwarki's, the other the Nahnken's. Then he further divides them according to the wishes of these two chiefs, the best and largest yams being usually retained by them. Men of lower titles in the A-line receive their shares from the Nahnmwarki's heap, those in the B-line from the Nahnken's. Commoners receive what may be left over after the division.

However, commoners have a device for augmenting their meager portions, known as yam seizing (*doar* or *doarekehp*). During the division of food the young people will occasionally make a rush for the yams and seize what they can and carry them off. The divider will scold at them but usually only half-heartedly, and the Nahnmwarki and Nahnken "cannot scold because the yams will be planted and brought to another feast when they have grown." Most people are ashamed to do this sort of thing, but the elders will often whisper to their youngsters at the propitious moment to dash up and grab their share. The practice is generally frowned upon, but the high chiefs in their ascribed role of generous and paternalistic despots are supposed to overlook it. A grievance against the Net chiefs is that they have forbidden the custom. It applies only to yams, but a similar practice, known as *simw,* occurs at the death feasts when the mourners, especially the women, suddenly swarm over all the feast goods and carry off both cooked and uncooked yams, kava, pigs, etc.

Cooked yams for consumption are distributed also according to rank. Visitors do not fare so well here as they do with uncooked, planting yams and with pork; at a feast in Kiti attended by the writer a basket of cooked yams apiece was presented to the Nahnmwarki, the A2, the B2, and to the A6 (Oliver Nanpei); the Nahnken was absent; but the visitor from Sokehs, the B3 of that tribe, received only a single cooked yam, like holders of other, lesser titles.

## Kava

There are several versions of the legendary origin of kava. One of them attributes the discovery to a rat, which nibbled at the root and whose actions were observed while under the influence of the plant; thus the effect of consuming the plant was learned. This story is found also in Western Polynesia, Fiji, and on Pentecost in the New Hebrides. Another story gives credit to Wuhtanengar, a native of section 10 in Uh, who was taken when an old man by the god Luhk to the mythical land in the south, Air, where he became young again and shed the skin off his footsole; the skin grew into a kava plant and a bit of its root, pounded in heaven, fell to earth in section 10; there it took root and grew. Another version combines both themes. Hambruch (1932 II, p. 103) gives a similar story, substituting the island of Kusaie for the land of Air, and he and Christian record still other accounts.

Kava does not grow everywhere, but it is easy to tend; it is necessary to clean around it only once a month. The plant is grown from cuttings, usually from the young branches of an old bush brought to a feast. The cuttings are made two joints long if the branch is more than an inch in diameter, four joints if less; they are severed diagonally, between the nodes. They are planted about one yard apart in cleared ground prepared first with a digging stick; later they are thinned out to two or more yards; but single plants may be seen sometimes growing in a thicket of other species of plants. The cutting is stuck into the ground somewhat diagonally to bury one node. Usually two cuttings are planted in the same spot to produce a large plant. If they cannot be planted the same day they are cut they are bound into bundles and soaked in water by day, left in the dewy grass at night. A kava garden is called a *kemenseng.* A small one contains a hundred plants, a large one five or six hundred. A large garden is a great source of pride but is usually kept very secret, for fear of witchcraft which will cause the plants to dry up.

Those men who are regular kava drinkers eat nothing before partaking. The high chiefs also are not supposed to eat before drinking kava, a rule not applicable to commoners. At most feasts a little food (*kepsakau*) is served before the kava is prepared; this is eaten by the nonindulgers[92] and the moderate drinkers. After each drink something is taken to palliate the unpleasant aftertaste; this may be a sip of water, a morsel of pineapple, raw fish, sugar cane, a puff at a cigarette, or any of a large number of other things. Whether the drink induces salivation or because of the disagreeable taste, many persons find it necessary to spit frequently between draughts; cracks between floor boards are used for this purpose. The slime from the fresh hibiscus bast used as a strainer also produces spitting.

The immediate effect of the drink is a numbing of the lips and tongue; speech becomes thick, though the head remains clear. Eventually control is lost of the lower limbs, and men who have overindulged must be carried home. After returning from kava drinking to one's house, food is eaten in ample quantities but it must be eaten slowly to experience the full effect of the kava. The result is a deep and sound sleep. The next morning, while some persons seem to remain unaffected, others complain of a hangover, have little appetite, and slight noises seem to be intolerably magnified in volume. The writer observed none of the effects on the eyes and skin attributed to intemperate use of kava in parts of Polynesia, although Hambruch (1917, p. 113) describes overindulgers whose skins looked as though they were sprinkled with a yellow-green powder. Possibly the Ponapean variety of the plant produces a chemically different drink. Natives believe that kava is beneficial to the health, and that heavy drinkers do not contract gonorrhea; whether this is an aboriginal belief was not verified, and it is possible that they acquired the idea from the Germans, who listed kava in their pharmacopoeia, or the Japanese, who are said to have manufactured pills from kava as a specific against gonorrhea. The Japanese are supposed to have bought several thousand yen worth of kava annually for shipment to Osaka to be reduced to pills; one native chief states that he sold 540 yen worth in one sale. Some of the pills found their way back to Ponape for sale to the Japanese there. Dr. Girschner, the physician on Ponape in German times, is said to have drunk kava every time the ship arrived, which it did semiannually, in the belief that it prevented the cough the ship would bring. Hambruch (1932 II, p. 64) states that kava was taken as an abortifacient, but informants deny this.

In later Japanese times and especially in the war years, when natives were impressed as laborers, there was little opportunity for feasting and for cultivating kava; thus in 1947 kava was relatively scarce; but this was a temporary condition. During the war a large bush of kava, large enough to be carried by ten men, was worth a hundred yen. In 1947 many people were buying kava for use at feasts or privately. Enough kava for one stone, which would be about half of the roots from an average bush, sold for $5; a large bush, providing enough roots for five to 10 stones, was worth $50 or more. (Twenty people can drink for a whole evening of the kava produced at one stone.) By 1963 kava was much more plentiful.

Earlier, the Protestant missionaries had made a determined effort to eradicate the drink and the customs associated with it. One Nahnmwarki convert in the 1870s is said to have uprooted large quantities of the plant. Nevertheless, Joe Kehoe, an American trader in the 1880s and 1890s, according to Christian, found it profitable to export kava from Ponape to Fiji, so it must still have been in plentiful supply. By 1910 when Hambruch was at Ponape its use had greatly declined, and he predicted that it would soon disappear entirely. But the efforts of the missionaries were destined to fail; they achieved permanent results only on Kusaie, the only other Micronesian island where kava and the complex of traits accompanying it existed aboriginally.

## Kava and Feasting

At a traditional feast, with full development of ceremonial, the kava bushes are carried to the community house in a procession of men singing a type of song called *ngis* and blowing conch trumpets. There is much noise and talk and frequent emission of the typical falsetto ululation of Ponape. The plants, carried root foremost, are brought up to the main platform, where the Nahnmwarki sits under two taro leaves bound to a post that provide spiritual protection. The kava plants are placed with the roots and the ends of the carrying poles and litters on the edge of the platform, the branches down in the central area.

The kava bushes are frequently decorated with ornamental plants. Large bushes carried on a litter may have a stalk of croton or breadfruit inserted in them. A fernlike plant (*tehnlik*) that climbs on kava branches is artificially encouraged on the growing bush by tying it on the new shoots annually. A man is proud of a kava plant he brings to a feast when each branch (very old plants may have as many as 100 or 150 branches) bears this fern. The practice, of course, is somewhat akin to that of adding unnecessary bearers to a litter in order to exaggerate the apparent weight of the yam, kava plant, or whatever object of prestige value is being carried. People consider it evidence of a man's wealth to be able to keep a kava bush without having to use it till it is old and very large.

When the plants are removed from the main platform to be pounded the roots are cut off and the stems taken away for replanting. The earth is knocked off the roots but there is no washing. The roots are not dried, as in

[92] The Christian Endeavor movement has made a considerable number of converts among the Protestants; its members are pledged not to dance, smoke, or drink.

parts of Polynesia, but used fresh. In very large plants the lowest part of the stem can also be used. One whole bush was formerly placed in the beams above the main platform of the community house as an offering to the spirit of the building,[93] and no one might remove it except the Mwarekehtik ("little Nahnmwarki," A12 to A16 in different tribes), who alone has the privilege of reaching for it above the Nahnmwarki's head. But this is seldom seen nowadays.

The roots after being cut into small pieces are placed on the pounding stones and, especially at a large feast, they are covered over with taro leaves until the signal is given to begin pounding. The taro leaves are then placed on the ground around the stone so that any kava that falls on them will not get dirty.

The pounding stones (*peitehl*) are large, flat or slightly hollowed, basalt slabs, irregular in outline and three or four feet in diameter (Plate 12a). They are propped off the ground by coconut husks, which help to bring out the clear, bell-like tone produced during the pounding. The pounders (*moahl*) used on them are cobblestones large enough for one hand to grasp conveniently.

During the first part of the feast the stone ovens are arranged in the community house in two rows, from front to back between the side platforms, and occupy most of the central area, leaving room only for two kava stones at the front of each row, in line with the ovens, just below the main platform. These four stones are active in the preliminary kava preparation, called *audida,* before the ovens are opened. (This is apart from the "early" kava, *sakau en menseng,* mentioned previously.) After the food is divided and the ovens are cleared away, more kava stones of indefinite number are set up behind the first two stones of each row in place of the ovens, and the second stage of the kava preparation, called *audsapahl,* begins. But when kava is drunk privately the arrangements are much less formal than in the feasting situation and a single stone may be set up, perhaps outside of a dwelling or in a cookhouse. Occasionally nowadays a sheet of iron is seen in place of a stone in such circumstances.

Sometimes the four stones of the first phase are not seen, and *audida* does not commence until all the ovens are cleared away.

The leader of the kava ceremony (the *soun dei sakau*) is usually a man of high title. In Net nowadays the B2 is, because of his abilities, designated for the job, but it does not seem that there is a connection with a particular title. In Madolenihmw he is said always to be a lesser Royal Child. The major requirement is that he be well informed on the proper procedure. He may not sit but stands continuously at the central post of the main platform with his back to the notables who sit on this platform, facing the workers and calling out the various steps in the kava ritual; there is no prompting from any of the chiefs behind him. If someone drinks without his permission, he may knock the cup out of the man's hands; if any faux pas occurs, he scolds the guilty person publicly. A person called up from the central area to drink a cupful must come promptly. The filled cup is supposed to be passed up to the leader by the kava pounders and he distributes it according to a sequence that, as will be detailed, differs from one tribe to another. In Uh he gives the cup directly to the Nahnmwarki, but elsewhere he is supposed to give it to one of the servitors sitting around the Nahnmwarki who passes it on to the latter[94] (Plates 11a, 11b). With "early" kava, however, at least in Madolenihmw, he always hands the cup to the Nahnmwarki; the servitor sits in the usual position but is bypassed. The writer has also sometimes seen one of the pounders pass a cup directly to a servitor instead of to the leader.

There is no passing of the kava cup from one man to another; a man drinks and hands the cup back to his servitor, to be refilled and passed to another. A man who can drink a whole cupful is greatly admired. (This is indeed a feat, for the roots are pounded fresh and the drink is strong; the first pressings, which contain slime from the hibiscus-bast strainer,[95] are of high flavor; and whatever earth adheres to the roots adds its own quality to the concoction. The writer found that in Samoa, where the dried root produces a weaker and more watery fluid, he could easily drink a whole cup of kava but he could manage only a few sips of the Ponapean variety.) It is considered good form to refuse a cup of kava when it is first offered and to point to someone else as the proper recipient, in keeping with the Ponapean pattern of modesty. This may explain the failure of a very rigid sequence of serving to develop. The Polynesian traits of macerating the root by chewing instead of pounding, the use of a mixing bowl, the kava circle, the formalized motions of preparing and serving the drink, and the custom of pouring some of the liquid on the ground or flicking a drop into the air as an offering to the gods are all absent on Ponape (though libations poured on the ground are mentioned in some of the early literature).

[93] Hambruch (1932 II, p. 136) has a reference to an offering of kava in this manner to a deity at a regular priestly ceremony in Kiti.

[94] Fischer's notes seem to imply that direct passing of kava to the Nahnmwarki in Uh occurs only at the kava first fruits and applies only to the first four cups.

[95] The use of fresh hibiscus bast for the strainer, which results in the slime in the first cups, is said to have begun about 1915. Sigismundo, who was later Nahnmwarki of Kiti, was the first to experiment with it, and it caught on because it produced a stronger drink and because it was less work to prepare the bast, which hitherto had to be scraped with clam shells and then dried. Even earlier the strainer is said to have been made of the "cloth" from the base of the coconut leaf. But hibiscus bark was in use in the 1850s (Gulick, 1858c, p. 27).

There are, or formerly were, a number of minor officials with duties connected with kava ritual. One of them, the Sapadan Sau,[96] for example, was charged with cleaning the stones used in the community house. Another official stands outside of the building and awaits the bringers of the hibiscus poles used for making the bast strainers. The kava workers (the *tohn wie sakau*) are commoners and holders of lesser A-titles.

During the process of pounding, water is added to the roots from time to time by means of a half coconut shell, which is replenished by dipping into a vessel of water (formerly the Ponapean boat-shaped *kasak,* of wood; nowadays, often, a bucket). Although the stone on which the pounding is done is flat, there is little spilling over, for the shredded roots absorb most of the water. When the roots are well macerated their fluid content is wrung out by means of the hibiscus-bast strainer. Previously poles of hibiscus will have been brought and the bast stripped off and distributed among the workers. The bast in lengths of three or four feet is knotted in the middle to form a bundle (*nimakale*)[97] and keep the fibers from parting. This bundle is the strainer. Generally two such bundles of bast are apportioned to each stone. The bundle is combed out with the fingers and laid out flat on the stone, doubled, with the knot at one end. Then the macerated kava root is heaped along the surface of the bast and two of the four workers each take one of these strainers, twist the ends to enclose the kava in a cylinder of bast, then raise it above the stone and wring it out tightly over a cup made of a half coconut shell (*ngarangar*[98]). The other two workers each hold one such cup in which they catch the streams of liquid that run out. These two men are called respectively *longpeik* and *soupeik.* When not in use the cups should be kept in a *doulong,* which is a stick of hibiscus wood driven in the ground close by the stone, split in four from the upper end to about its middle, with two wedges to hold the four parts separate so that the vessel can rest in the spread upper end; but it is seldom seen nowadays. Although the formal motions of Polynesia in straining and wringing are lacking, certain other behaviors are required, such as keeping the two hands at the same level and keeping the back of the fist turned up, and the workers are supposed to maintain proper decorum and not wear European clothing (Plates 12b, 12c, 12d).

### Kava Ritual

Pounding of kava in the community house is done in unison and according to various rhythms. At one stone four workers normally do the pounding. Two of these men will pound *wokpekid,* which is a rocking motion of the hand, hitting alternately with each end of the pounder projecting from the sides of the closed fist; the others pound *tempil,* a straight up-and-down motion. The term for pounding, *sukusuk,* includes both of these beats, but Kiti informants apply it also to the method called *wokpekid* elsewhere. *Wokpekid* is a sort of minor beat, heard throughout the strong, steady tempo of *tempil;* it is said to be not native in origin but an imitation of the sound produced by the coopers aboard the whaling vessels of the last century; it is used when there are a large number of kava stones being pounded at one time.[99]

The pounding, as observed in Net, begins with *reidi,* a 4-note beat consisting of three short and one long beats. This is done only once,[100] on a bare part of stone. Then there is a short pause, after which pounding of the root begins in earnest, with some of the men pounding *tempil,* some *wokpekid,* on each of the stones. The rhythmic pounding on the bare stone is not done for the "early" kava. When the kava roots are well pounded, another tempo begins called *sokemwahu;* this consists of three pairs of short beats followed by slow single beats that quicken rapidly and continue for a variable length of time, depending on the degree of maceration of the kava. This is repeated three times more, making four such rhythms in all; but the fourth time I have occasionally heard four instead of three pairs of short beats. *Sokemwahu* is the signal whereby people outside the community house are supposed to know that the kava is almost ready and that the Nahnmwarki is within. When the kava is all pounded, there is a final rhythm called *kohdi;* this is again on the bare stone and consists of seven rapid beats, followed by a short pause, two rapid beats, another pause, two long beats, a pause, two rapid, and one long. After this the wringing-out of the kava begins.

In Kiti the *reidi* rhythm is used again to end the pounding.[101] In Awak, Uh, the final rhythm is called *pedidi,* but it was not ascertained whether this is the same rhythm as that called *kohdi* in Net. If the Nahnmwarki and

[96] Hahl (1901, p. 3) refers to him as a priest, as does Hambruch (1932 II, pp. 131–132). Hambruch gives a whole series of priestly titles, each assigned some duty in connection with kava preparation and feasting.

[97] Given as kǒtš by Hambruch (1932 II, p. 246) and by some of my informants, but I also recorded the word *kot* as an alternative name of the bast itself.

[98] A half coconut shell is used as a container for all sorts of liquids, especially medicines, but except when it is used for kava it is called a *pohndal.* (Some of Hambruch's texts, however, use this latter term for kava cup.) These cups are highly polished with a stone. Occasionally a china bowl is used nowadays, but informants say the flavor is then inferior.

[99] Hambruch (1932 II, p. 246) refers to *wokpekid* as "Begleitmusik beim Stampfen" and to *tempil* as "Dämpfen der Musik."

[100] Hambruch (1932 II, p. 242) gives this same rhythm, but more than once, as occurring only if the Nahnmwarki is present, and a different rhythm if only a lower chief is present.

[101] Hambruch (1932 II, p. 246) likewise calls this "Schlussmusik."

Nahnken have still not entered the community house when the pounding is almost finished, the kava makers pound *reidi,* the beginning rhythm, until these chiefs appear, then they pound *pedidi.*[102] If the kava is almost ready, and the men who have been dispatched to get the hibiscus bast, used for wringing out the drink, have not returned, the workers pound a beat called *pepain,* to hasten the gatherers. (But Net informants deny any special rhythm to make the hibiscus gatherers hurry.)

All of the stages in the pounding are directed by the leader of the kava ritual (the *soun dei sakau*) who stands on the main platform of the community house and calls out the various tempos; for example, he will call out "kohdi" and, at the same time, signal by dropping his arm from its raised position. There is no leading of the actual rhythm, the pounders taking up the tempo from each other (or, at least as observed in Madolenihmw, from the pounders around a particular stone), but one of the pounders sometimes signals for the final long beat.

There are said to have been special rhythms when kava was made for drinking by a shaman before he became possessed by a spirit, and other rhythms on various religious occasions. There were apparently also various rhythms for playing on the Ponapean drum (*aip*) for different ceremonies, including the kava ritual, and songs to accompany the rhythms on both the stones and the drum. These, along with the drum, are long extinct.

While the kava is being pounded, a party of men will have been dispatched to gather the hibiscus bast (*dipenkeleu*) in order to make the strainers. If they are late in returning, in addition to the playing of the special rhythm the leader calls to the man who has been stationed at the central pole of the front entrance to the community house and this man (in Madolenihmw) calls to the laggards, "kohteilong, kohteimwahu, kumwa tangakihdo dipenkeleu." (The first two words are antique phraseology; the translation is approximately "come-of-heaven, come-of-good, you bring-running hibiscus-bast.") The men answer, "nindalawa, ninpalawa, ninpaleiu, iet se samwehr," the last portion of this meaning "Here we come." [103] An Uh informant states that the man who does the calling out must be a Royal Child, since only Royal Children can raise their voices at a public assemblage, and that he stands in the *soun,* the space beyond the front opening of the community house. The call, in Uh, is given as "ninpalawa, nikoneieu, nipoikot"; this is largely untranslatable. In the Luelen manuscript, which has special reference to Kiti, the call and response are given as one and are in Luelen's spelling as follows: "Kotei ina, kotei ilang; nintaleue, nipaleue, nipalio; kotei ina, kotei ilang." My translators give the first and third phrases as "wringer of the earth, wringer of heaven," making "kot" to mean "hibiscus bast wringer," instead of "come" as my Madolenihmw informants gave it.

Each wringing from the pounded kava roots of the first pounding has its distinctive name, as given in Table 5. The term *audida,* referred to previously as denoting the first part of the kava ceremonial, seems to be used collectively in Kiti only for the first four wringings, but elsewhere for all the wringings made from the first pounding. In Kiti the fifth to eighth wringings are called *sapwe* (meaning "end"). Fischer, who does not give the term *audida,* uses *sapwe* for the fourth wringing alone in Uh, which I also got as an alternative term in Madolenihmw (see Table 5).

These various stages of the ceremony, and the remarks on first and second poundings, and various wringings from the various poundings, should not be confused with the references previously made to "early" kava. At least four expressions are used that have to do with the time of the day during which the ceremony is held. The early kava (known variously, as already mentioned, as morning kava, quick kava, and the kava of the rising sun) has its counterparts later in the day: noon kava (literally kava under the sun), evening kava (literally kava of the setting sun), and night kava (literally kava under flame, i.e., illuminated by fires). I am not certain that there is any essential difference between the last three occasions except for the time of day when they occur, but early kava, which is regarded as more important, has some unique features. For example, in rolling up the bast strainer to enclose the macerated roots, one hand holding the end of the strainer must be kept palm up, while the other hand does the rolling. In twisting the strainer to express the liquid the hand continues to be held palm up, and the strainer must not loop over the back of that hand, which is allowed only to be raised and lowered vertically during the straining. The strainer cannot be allowed to form more than one loop. After the cup is filled the server takes it in both hands and walks to the Nahnmwarki in a kind of zigzag step, alternate steps taken sideways, at the same time muttering a prayer (though this last is seldom heard today). He then kneels before the Nahnmwarki, who receives the cup with both hands directly from the server instead of through his attendant, holding it up high and, formerly, uttering some magic words.

A small part of the macerated root from the first pounding is put aside before the juice is expressed for

---

[102] Hambruch (idem) refers to this as "Eingangsmusik." But he also, in one text (1932 II, p. 239) by a chief of Net, translates what appears to be the same word as a pause in the pounding rhythm, and in another text (1932 II, p. 241) by the same man, as the conclusion of the pounding. The "entrance music" he (1917, p. 111) gives quite differently from any rhythm I recorded; it contains four different kinds of beats.

[103] The second word, *ninpalawa,* is said to refer to *inipal,* the natural cloth from the base of the coconut leaf, which is used in wringing out infusions of medicines today and supposedly was also used for kava anciently instead of the hibiscus bast used today.

TABLE 5.—*Stages of kava ceremonial*

| Net | Kiti | Madolenihmw | Uh [a] |
|---|---|---|---|
| 1. pwel (beginning) en sakau | 1. pwel en sakau | 1. pwel en sakau | 1. pwilin sakau |
| 2. are (second) en sakau | 2. are en sakau | 2. are en sakau | 2. arien sakau |
| 3. esil (third) en sakau | 3. esil en sakau | 3. esil en sakau | 3. esilin sakau |
| 4. epeng (fourth) en sakau | 4. epeng en sakau [b] | 4. epeng en sakau [c] | 4. sapwen (end of) sakau |
| | | | (5. dipen keleu) |
| 5. alim (fifth) en sakau | 5. pwel en sakau | | |
| 6. aun (sixth) en sakau | 6. are en sakau | | |
| dipenkeleu | | | |
| | 7. esil en sakau | | |
| 7. wong lopwon | 8. lopwon, wong lopwon | 5. lopwon | 6. wung lupwun |
| | | | 7. pelien (mate of) wung lupwun |
| | | | (8. dipen keleu) |
| dipenkeleu | | | 9. wung kep |
| 8. wong kep | | 6. kep | 10. pelien wung kep |
| | | | (11. dipen keleu) |
| dipenkeleu | | | |
| 9. wong luh | 9. luh, wong luh | 7. luh | 12. luh |
| dipenkeleu | | | |

[a] Information on Uh from Fischer's notes.

[b] In Wene, the eastern part of Kiti, this fourth stage is called *kapahrek.* This difference is attributed to the deposing of the Nahnmwarki of Kiti, in the war with Pehleng, described previously and the subsequent defeat of Pehleng by the Soukise of Wene; but exactly why the kava terminology was affected is not clear.

[c] Also recorded as *sapwe,* as Fischer gives it for Uh.

the first cup. This ball of root fibers is known as *lopwon.*[104] It is not used until the cup known as *wong lopwon* (*wong,* to wring) is made. Madolenihmw informants say it is used only for this cup; according to Kiti informants a little of it is added to each wringing after that cup also. After *lopwon* come the cups known as *kep* [105] and *luh,*[106] but Kiti informants referred to several cups following *lopwon,* all known as *luh* or *wong luh.*

The term *dipenkeleu* properly means hibiscus bast, the material of the kava straining device. In Table 5, however, it is used metaphorically to mean general drinking by commoners; a cup of kava is requested by a commoner by his asking for *dipenkeleu.* In Fischer's list from Uh the term occurs as the name of certain cups in the series, but in my list from Net it is indicated only as stages between cups; informants from Kiti and Madolenihmw probably did not consider it worthy of mention.

There is no pounding again until the stages of *audida* have been completed and the shredded kava roots yield only a weak drink. At this point the master of the kava ceremony calls out, *"audsapahl,"* the name of the second major phase of the ceremonial, and fresh roots are brought up for the second pounding.[107] This call was recorded in Kiti, Net, and Madolenihmw, but at the same time the name of the second pounding in Kiti was given as *kopur sakau.* Net informants state that *audsapahl,* with ritual pounding and calling out of stages with the same names as those in *audida,* occurs only if the Nahnmwarki is still present; otherwise there is general drinking of the fresh kava but without ritual pounding or calling of stages. In Madolenihmw it was further recorded that when the drink becomes weak again the master of the ceremony calls *"wong par,"* and this cup is followed by *kodie,* the last cup, which is brought to the Nahnmwarki. The term *kodie* was not recorded in Net, but it appears in a text taken by Hambruch (1932 II, p. 240) from a Net chief, where it means the last cup, brought to the high priest. Also in Kiti the term *luhwala* was recorded as a small part of the macerated root from the second pounding put aside before the wringing commences, equivalent to the *lopwon* from the first pounding; when the Nahnmwarki signifies that he has had enough the *luhwala* is put into the bast strainer and the cup from this straining, given to the Nahnmwarki, is called *luhwala en sakau.*[108] When all is finished the term used in Kiti is *kodie,* but it does not seem to apply, as in Madolenihmw, to a particular cup. After the Nahnmwarki leaves there is general drinking among commoners again, without any particular order of serving and with no formalities.

The order of serving varies from tribe to tribe as much as do the other details of the ceremonial. In Kiti the first

[104] Hambruch (idem) uses what may be the same word (*lupong*) to mean "Becher für die Adeligen."

[105] *Kep* refers to the bottom of the cup. Hambruch (idem) uses a similar word (*kap*) for the last cup from the first pounding.

[106] *Luh* (remainder) is given by Hambruch (idem) as "neugewonnene Kawa."

[107] Hambruch (idem) gives *audsapahl* the meaning "neue Kawa ist zur alten getan."

[108] Hambruch (idem) gives "luela" as "der letzter Becher des Gelages."

wringing, *pwel en sakau,* is for the Nahnmwarki. All the cups, one from each stone, go to him. He drinks the cup from the main stone, the *soumoahl,* and directs that the others be given to other titled men and to his attendants, beginning with the A2 but without particular concern with order of rank thereafter. The A2, whose duties in this tribe usually require him to be in the central area when the A1 is present, stands at the wall of the platform and drinks there when his cup is called. The second cups, *are en sakau,* go to the Nahnken. He drinks the first of these, presents the second to the Nahnmwarki, and divides the others among the other titled men, in no particular order. The third cups go to the Nahnmwarki and Nahnken and the fourth to the wife of the Nahnmwarki, who distributes them to the wives of other high chiefs. (In Madolenihmw the fourth as well as the first cups are supposed to go to the Nahnmwarki.) The fifth cups, called again *pwel en sakau* as the beginning of the second series of four pressings, go to the Nahnmwarki, the sixth to the Nahnken, the seventh to the Nahnmwarki's wife, and the eighth, *lopwon,* to the Nahnmwarki again.

In Uh, according to Fischer, the distribution is in 12 stages as follows:

1. Nahnmwarki
2. Nahnken
3. Nahnmwarki's wife
4. A2
5. general drinking
6. Nahnmwarki
7. Nahnken
8. general drinking
9. Nahnmwarki
10. Nahnken
11. general drinking
12. Nahnmwarki

In Net the first cups go to Nahnmwarki and Nahnken, the second to their wives, the third to A2 and B2, the fourth again to Nahnmwarki and Nahnken; later distributions were not recorded.

In Kiti the cups brought to the Nahnmwarki are said to be from the stone called *soumoahl,* which is located at the middle of the rear end of the central area, below the middle front post of the main platform; to each side of it is another stone, each of which is the first of a row of stones extending to the front of the building. The writer, however, saw no *soumoahl* in use at any of the feasts he attended. One Kiti informant states that the *soumoahl* was formerly on the front edge of the main platform, to the right of center from the Nahnmwarki's point of view; and to the left of center was another stone, the *konaku.* Whether these are the same stones used for the "early" kava was not determined. At competitive feasts each of these two stones would be manned by the leaders of the opposing sides, and they would be operated during the time that the central area was filled with stone ovens; later, when the ovens were cleared away, the conventional double row of kava stones would be set up. Madolenihmw informants call the principal stone the *upeileng,* and locate it on the main platform, at its front center; if there are two steps in this platform (or three, as often in Sokehs) it is on the lowest and frontmost one. In the central area and close to the main platform in Madolenihmw are two stones that are the first of the two rows previously mentioned; the one to the right (looking toward the rear) is the *konaku,* and this is considered as the Nahnken's stone, just as the *upeileng* is the Nahnmwarki's; the stone to the left is the *upeiu,* and belongs to the lower chiefs. The second stone in the left row is somewhat closer to the left platform than the others in that row and is called *upeimwahu;* this stone is said to lead all the others in the rhythmic pounding, although this was not observed. When the leader calls to the *upeimwahu* workers to bring kava to the main platform, all the others follow the lead. None of the other stones have special names.[109]

The stones used as pounders or hand-mullers on the *upeileng* also bear names. In Madolenihmw they are called *moahleileng* (muller of heaven) and *moahlesang katau* (muller from Kusaie). Those used on the *konaku* stone are called *sairiha* and *katariha.* No other names were obtained.[110]

Consonant with the special place kava holds in Ponapean life and with its ceremonial and political importance, there is, in connection with its use, a considerable development of special vocabulary and honorific terms. The following expressions, collected in Madolenihmw, are only a part of this vocabulary. If during the pounding some bits of kava root spray in the direction of the Nahnmwarki, this occurrence is called *diper en leng;* if they fly in the opposite direction, the term is *diper en mes;* if sideways, *diper en pwel;* there are two other terms to signify other directions. The stream of kava from the bast wringers is called *kapeirek* (this is possibly the same term as that used in Wene for the fourth wringing). If it flows from the upper side of the fist, it is called *dingiding* ("drop") *en kapeirek;* if it flows from the lower side, it is *kereker* ("flow") *en kapeirek.* When a man receives kava plants from the Nahnmwarki to take home, the gift is called *lipwenepwenial.* The ordinary name for the housefly is *loahng,* but if one falls into the vessel of kava, it is called *soutol;* if a second fly falls in, it is given the name *dolakati.* (Only the kava workers or the man who

[109] Fischer records two names of stones at Uh, the principal one *soumoahl,* the other *litemwahu.* I also recorded, for "early" kava in Madolenihmw, the Nahnmwarki's stone as *pelenkatu,* the Nahnken's as *pelenmwahu,* both of them located on the main platform of the community house.

[110] Fischer's notes record, at Takaieu in Uh, the names *moahlasan katau* and *moahlihna* for mullers.

presents the vessel to the Nahnmwarki may remove the fly.)

## The Role of Kava in Ponapean Culture

Kava was once very important in the native religion. Hahl (1901, p. 2) says "Der Darbringung des Gebets geht der feierliche Umtrunk der Kawa voraus . . ." and (1902, p. 97) refers to kava as "stets eine heilige Sache." According to Hambruch (1932 II, p. 232), "Ohne der Kawa . . . ist weder eine kultische Feier noch ein Folks- oder Familienfest denkbar. . . ." And the missionary Sturges, writing in 1856, says "To this people kava is the only means of communication with their spirits; they hold a cup of this drink, always in their hands, when addressing the object of prayer. . . . Kava here is what the cross is to the Christian; it fell from heaven and is the only means of obtaining a hearing there."

Diviners would formerly diagnose illness and forecast the future by scrying in a vessel of kava. In 1947 only one man could be found who admitted knowledge of this technique. A shaman, just before becoming possessed, would squat and hold a cup of kava aloft in both hands while he muttered spells. Priests also would offer kava to the gods in this manner. This form of offering to gods and spirits has already been described in another context as Kava Holding (*sapwsakau*). Formerly also a few drops might be poured on the ground as a libation, in the Polynesian manner.[111]

Kava Holding is still done by fishermen, who, along with the native doctors, have retained more aboriginal religious practices than any other group of people. A fisherman, the evening before going fishing and again upon his return, would drink kava and hold the cup in the fashion described while uttering prayers to the various fishing deities.

[111] See also Hambruch (1932 II, p. 240); Christian (1899, pp. 96, 191); Hahl (1902, p. 96). Gulick (1872, p. 6) gives the word *auramei*, to prepare a vessel of kava "by the first expression of juice into it (a sort of dedication, though unattended by religious ceremonies)." He reports that when foreign ships were first seen the natives fled into the interior and "the priests drank kava for 'the spirits' until the dreaded objects disappeared."

The ceremony and protocol connected with kava drinking have been described previously as they were observed and as recorded from modern informants. There seem to have been, however, some quite different arrangements in connection with secret esoteric life, when priests of various ranks instead of chiefs took the places of honor; Hambruch (1932 II, pp. 133–134) illustrates one such assemblage of priests at Wene, in which the details diverge markedly from those recounted in the previous section.

Kava is also part of the ritual of promotion to a higher title and has an important role in the prestige competition, as has already been described. It is also the greatest single inducement toward the granting of pardon for some offense at the feast of propitiation. A Nahnmwarki or Nahnken is supposed not to be able to reject a cup of kava offered him on such an occasion, though he may resist temporarily. In the words of the Nahnken of Net, "kava is our treasure."

Kava was and still is to a considerable extent considered to be associated with high rank. Formerly members of the royalty and nobility considered drinking kava their exclusive prerogative and no commoner could drink it by himself but had to present first fruits to the high chiefs in order to be able to drink with them. A few section chiefs, those who were of the family of the Nahnmwarki or Nahnken, were permitted to drink alone, but even this was rare; also people might come and drink with an elder sister of a Nahnmwarki or Nahnken, or with a clansmate senior to either of them or with a son of either. Women of very high status could drink, but to other women kava was practically forbidden. Some of the priests might drink alone; in Net the Krou en Doropwop, who was the priest at a regular celebration to the god Daukatau, was one of those who could drink kava (as well as eat the chiefly food, turtle) in the absence of a high chief. Kava was one of the objects required to be presented to a chief as his due; banishment befell him who neglected this duty. The secrecy with which commoners had to drink if they intended to deceive the chiefs by not making an offering is expressed, in the compressed manner of Ponapean proverbs, by the saying "takai en wel" ("stone of the wilderness"), the implication being that it was necessary to secrete oneself in the woods to achieve this purpose, and the "stone" referring to the pounding muller.

# The Ponapean Polity

Ponapean political and ceremonial life is, as the reader will have seen, marked by great complexity and elaboration. Certain other aspects of the culture, not touched upon in this study, are also of considerable intricacy. But Ponapean life seems to focus particularly on those activities that we have labeled political. The time and energies of the natives of Ponape are especially directed toward maneuvering for enhancement of status, above all in the system of titles, which provides them with a mechanism for expressing their well-developed sense of interpersonal competition. Nature is generous enough to provide ample leisure for noneconomic activities, and the Ponapeans have chosen to use this leisure time for the direction of a great part of their energies into political channels.

The political system that has been the subject of this work is one which is perpetually in a fluid state, yet at the same time in balance. There is a kind of dualism in Ponapean society, which has been described in the various kinds of prestige competition, and which is seen again in the two lines of titles. These lines provide the system with a dynamic symmetry. They are united by ties of marriage and kinship and by a host of mutual obligations and privileges. The (formerly exclusive) intermarriage between them, combined with the operation of matrilineal principles, mean that husband and wife, father and son, brothers-in-law, and other pairs of relatives find themselves in opposite lines, but these are relationships that draw the two lines together, not apart. Political solidarity is cemented by the need for the two sides to perform reciprocal services and duties for each other, as in the promotion activities, in the kava ceremonies, in serving, and in propitiation rites. At the same time there is jockeying for position between them, so that when a Nahnmwarki is weak the Nahnken may move in and seize the reins, and vice versa, much depending on the individual personalities of the leaders of the two lines. In this kind of manipulation a new balance is then achieved. The part that the Nahnken plays as intercessor with the Nahnmwarki for the people and his function as a kind of prime minister or even a "talking-chief" (somewhat comparable to Samoa or Tonga) have no exact parallel in the A-line (although the Nahnmwarki will sometimes also function as a mediator); but the political advantages that a Nahnken might derive from these roles are offset by the deference paid to and the special prerogatives that adhere to the Nahnmwarki alone. In dealing with public affairs the two principal chiefs usually present one face to the world.

On lower levels in the tribe and in the sections a similar kind of maneuvering for position goes on, especially in the various forms of prestige competition. Rank due to birth determines limits, but industry, skills, and other personal qualities enable a man to assume his natural position in competition with his fellows, and an outstanding person of low birth may sometimes surmount barriers erected by rules of descent. The equilibrium that results is constantly being eroded as men strive for and achieve advancement but is as rapidly reestablished. If a person becomes disaffected he may resign his title or seek self-exile; but disharmonies are most commonly resolved through the formal feast of propitiation, which, because of the power ascribed to kava to achieve reconciliation, is a powerful stabilizing mechanism.

Public opinion is a deterrent to self-aggrandizement. A vacancy in the title series is filled by the Nahnmwarki and Nahnken, and the opportunity for these two men to serve selfish purposes would seem great. But unilateral decisions are seldom made; lower titleholders are consulted, public opinion is sounded, and deference is paid to the principle of a fair distribution of titles among the sub-clans of the ruling clans, or, for titles held by commoners, among all the common clans. Also the threat of war once kept the rulers from ignoring custom, just as they seldom rode roughshod over their tenants, despite the native theory that they owned all the land.

Conflicts did occur, as noted previously throughout this study. Their causes were several but the most significant is the inherent contradiction between the rules of matrilineal seniority and the various other principles that are incorporated into the political system. We have seen how the expressed native theory that older brother is followed by younger brother, then by oldest sister's oldest son, fails to be borne out in practice for many reasons, among them the just noted deference to fair distribution among families and other kinship groups, personal traits and abilities, achievement in war, etc. In the descent group seniority of birth has no relation to relative age, but in the practicalities of native politics a child is obviously not capable of being a ruler and a junior must often be placed ahead of his senior. Again, in a strictly matrilineal group the position of the father has no bearing on seniority of blood, but with two lines of intermarrying chiefly groups the rank of both sides must count in determination of one's hierarchical position. Thus, when an informant relates the theory of political advancement he is essentially giving the rules of descent-group seniority; but the case histories related in this work reveal how these rules must be accommodated and compromised in applying them to a complex political system. And it is the application of them and their delicate balancing against all the other principles previously mentioned that result in a flexible but stable and workable state.

The Ponapean polity may profitably be compared with that of other parts of the Pacific. Micronesia, in which Ponape is one of the largest and most populous islands, is usually neglected when such comparisons are made—for the very good reason that it has been, until recent years, much less well described in the anthropological literature than either Polynesia or Melanesia. These two areas are often contrasted with each other as being at opposite extremes in the scale of political development. Polynesia is characterized by ranked and stratified classes or social levels, with power concentrated in the hands of men of title, and with chiefs or kings exercising authority over sometimes large areas. Melanesia, on the other hand, although much less homogeneous culturally than Polynesia (or even Micronesia) is for the most part described as classless, lacking in hereditary rank and position, democratic, egalitarian, and segmented.

In aboriginal Polynesia the senior members of the various descent groups (which are generally not unilinear but do have a patrilineal bias) constitute the ruling class. Social position and succession are determined through descent. With rank goes a great number of prerogatives and privileges, honorific forms, and deferential etiquette. Control over economic resources, power of life and death over commoners, tribute giving, and confiscatory rights are frequently occurring Polynesian phenomena.

On the other hand, in most of Melanesia political institutions are vastly simpler and uncentralized. A leisure class and specialized functions are lacking. Hereditary chiefs are found in only a few places; instead, opportunity to achieve prestige is generally open to all, by means of diligence, skills of various kinds, military ability, or other personal traits. Privileges, deferential patterns, and exploitation of other men's economic activities give way to egalitarian principles. The kin-group dominates social situations. Societies are small, usually confined to the level of the village.

In this kind of comparative survey, Micronesia is usually placed by students of the subject with Polynesia. But actually Micronesia is extremely varied in political complexity. In the center of the chain of islands running east and west that comprise the Caroline Islands is the complex atoll of Truk. This group, which lies nearly 400 miles west of Ponape, can be characterized in very much the same sweeping terms just used to describe Melanesia, with local village headmen, absence of central authority, and lack of hierarchical stratification. West of Truk, extending 600 miles nearly to Yap, is a string of atolls and coral islets that includes among others Puluwat, Woleai, and Ulithi. Here again at each of these places there exists a simple, Melanesian-type political structure. In contrast, at the western end of the chain and close to the Philippines, are Palau with two major political groupings and with high and lesser chiefs, and Yap with two caste levels subdivided into nine endogamous strata; both correspond more nearly to the Polynesian characterization. Likewise, Kusaie, a high island 300 miles east of Ponape, and the Marshall Islands, still farther east, possess intricately developed governmental organizations.

Ponape would seem, at least at first glance, also to have the complex coloring of Polynesian political institutions. Here too we encounter ruling classes, status ascribed through descent, centralized power, royal prerogatives, elaboration of honorific usages and language (and here the honorific forms are not limited to vocabulary, as in Polynesia, but are woven into the structure of the language itself), involuted etiquette, economic control by chiefs, tributary rights, power of confiscation and banishment, etc. We also find at the same time, however, a certain degree of social mobility, with status achieved through individual skills and industry, prowess in war, and prestige competition, as in most of Melanesia. We get an impression of two major principles in conflict with one another, the Polynesian and Melanesian ones, which however become compatible in a pliable yet well-functioning organization through the operation of a set of checks and balances.

A thoroughgoing Polynesian system, with succession of office, title, and power through the male line, would seem to require a patrilineal emphasis, since its efficiency would be enhanced by father-to-son inheritance. In Ponape, however, a "Polynesian" polity (no implication of historical connection is intended) wears the aspect of a superimposition on a "Melanesian" social structure, one based on matrilineal clans. The conflict possibly inherent in such a situation is ameliorated by the device of two intermarrying clans ruling together, with division of political function between them and serving to check each others' authority; and it is further resolved by the previously described Melanesian egalitarian traits that function to create a state of balance between the ruling lines and the mass of the people. The effect is a flexible and harmonious political organization, which avoids both the excesses of power of Polynesia and the fragmentation of Melanesia.

## LITERATURE CITED

ABCFM. (American Board of Commissioners for Foreign Missions.)
Letters and journals from the year 1852 on, written by missionaries and others from Ponape: Gulick, Sturges, Doane, Roberts, Pierson, and Snow. (At Houghton Library, Harvard University, Cambridge.)

BAKER, ROLLIN H.
1951. The avifauna of Micronesia, its origin, evolution, and distribution. Univ. Kansas Publ., Museum of Natural History, vol. 3, no. 1.

BASCOM, WILLIAM R.
1948. Ponapean prestige economy. Southwestern Journal of Anthropology, vol. 4, pp. 211–221.
1949. Subsistence farming on Ponape. New Zealand Geography, vol. 5, pp. 115–129.
1965. Ponape: A Pacific economy in transition. Anthropological Records, vol. 22, Univ. California, Berkeley and Los Angeles.

BENNIGSEN, RUDOLF VON
1900. Bericht über seine Reise zum Zwecke der Ubernahme des Inselgebietes der Karolinen, Palau und Marianen in deutschen Besitz. Deutsches Kolonialblatt, vol. 11, pp. 100–112.

BLAKE, P.L.
1924. Untitled reports comprising pp. 12–28 and 654–673 in Historical Records of Australia, Series I, Governors' Despatches to and from England, vol. 20, February 1839–September 1840. The Library Committee of the Commonwealth Parliament.

CABEZA PEREIRO, A.
1893. La Isla de Ponape, Conferencia dada en Reunion Ordinaria de la Sociedad Geografia de Madrid el 24 de Noviembre de 1891. Boletin de la Sociedad Geografica de Madrid, XXXIV.
1895. La Isla de Ponape. Manila.

CAMPBELL, DR.
1836. Ascension. The Colonist, New South Wales, vol. 2, no. 78, June 22, 1836, pp. 193–194.

CHEYNE, ANDREW
1852. A description of the islands in the western Pacific Ocean, north and south of the Equator. London.

CHRISTIAN, F. W.
1899. The Caroline Islands. New York.

DOANE, E. T. See under ABCFM.

EAGLESTON, CAPT. J. H.
1832–33. Journal of the bark *Peru*. (Manuscript at Essex Institute, Salem, Mass.)

FINSCH, OTTO
1880. Ueber die Bewohner von Ponape. Zeitschrift für Ethnologie, vol. 12, pp. 301–332.
1893. Ethnologische Erfahrungen und Belegstücke aus der Südsee. Vienna.

FISCHER, J. L.
n.d. Unpublished Ponapean field notes, 1951–1953.
1958. Contemporary Ponape Island land tenure. *In* Land Tenure Patterns, Trust Territory of the Pacific Islands, vol. 1, office of the Staff Anthropologist, Guam, part 2, pp. 77–160.

FISCHER, JOHN L., with the assistance of Ann M. Fischer
1957. The Eastern Carolines. Behavior Science Monographs, Pacific Science Board, in association with Human Relations Area Files, New Haven.

FRASER, CAPTAIN
1834. Discovery of William the Fourth Group of Islands, Pacific Ocean. Nautical Magazine, vol. 3, 1834, p. 74.

FRITZ, GEORG
1912. Ad majorem Dei gloriam. Leipzig.

GARVIN, PAUL, and RIESENBERG, SAUL H.
1952. Respect behavior on Ponape: An ethnolinguistic study. American Anthropologist, vol. 54, no. 2, pp. 201–220.

GIRSCHNER, MAX
1906. Grammatik der Ponape-Sprache. Mitteilungen des Seminars für Orientalische Sprachen zu Berlin, vol. 9, pp. 73–126.

GLASSMAN, SIDNEY F.
1952. The flora of Ponape. Bernice P. Bishop Museum, Bulletin 209.

GOMEZ, JUAN GUALBERTO
1885. Las Islas Carolinas y las Marianas. Madrid.

GRESSITT, J. LINSLEY
1954. Insects of Micronesia, Introduction. Bernice P. Bishop Museum, Insects of Micronesia, vol. 1.

GULICK, ADDISON
1932. John Thomas Gulick, Evolutionist and Missionary. Chicago.

GULICK, LUTHER HALSEY
1852. Article in *The Friend,* December 17, 1852.
1853. Article in *The Friend,* March 1853, p. 19.
1857. Article in the *Missionary Herald,* vol. 53, pp. 41–48.
1858a. The fauna of Ponape, or Ascension Island, of the Pacific Ocean. *The Friend,* March 1858, p. 18.
1858b. The Climate and Production of Ponape or Ascension Island, one of the Carolines, in the Pacific Ocean. American Journal of Science and Arts, ser. 2, vol. 26, pp. 34–49.
1858c. The flora of Ponape, or Ascension Island. *The Friend,* April 1858, pp. 26–27.
1859. The Ruins of Ponape, or Ascension Island. Journal of the American Geographical and Statistical Society, vol. 1, no. 5, 1859, pp. 129–137.
1862. Micronesia. Nautical Magazine and Naval Chronicle, vol. 31, pp. 169–182, 237–245, 298–308, 358–363, 408–417.
1872. A vocabulary of the Ponape dialect, Ponape-English and English-Ponape, with a grammatical sketch. Journal of the American Oriental Society, vol. 10, pp. 1–109.
See also under ABCFM.

HAHL, ———.
1901. Mittheilungen über Sitten und rechtliche Verhältnisse auf Ponape. Ethnologisches Notizblatt, vol. 2, part 2, pp. 1–13.
1902. Feste und Tänze der Eingeborenen von Ponape. Ethnologisches Notizblatt, vol. 3, part 2, pp. 95–104.
1904. Ein Beitrag zur Kenntnis der Umgangsprache von Ponape. Mitteilungen des Seminars für Orientalische Sprachen, vol. 7, pp. 1–30.

HALE, HORATIO
1846. Ethnology and Philology. *In* United States Exploring Expedition during the Years 1838–1842, under the Command of Charles Wilkes, U.S.N., vol. 6.

HAMBRUCH, PAUL
1917. Die kava auf Ponape. Studien und Forschungen zur Menschen- und Völkerkunde, vol. 14, pp. 107–113.
1932–1936. Ponape. Ergebnisse der Südsee-Expedition 1908–1910, ed. G. Thilenius. II.B.vii. 3 vols. Berlin. vol. 1 by Hambruch alone, vol. 2 by Hambruch with A. Eilers, vol. 3 by Eilers from Hambruch's notes. (Cited as Hambruch 1932, I, II, and III).

HERNSHEIM, FRANZ
1884. Südsee-Erinnerungen (1875–1880). Berlin.

JAMES, HORTON
1835. Notes on the Island of Ascension, Pacific. Nautical Magazine, vol. 4, 1835, p. 708.

JORE, LEONCE

1953. Captain Jules Dudoit, the first French consul in the Hawaiian Islands, 1837–1867, and his brig-schooner, the *Clementine.* 64th Annual Report of the Hawaiian Historical Society, Honolulu.

KITTLITZ, F. H. VON

1858. Denkwürdigkeiten einer Reise nach dem russischen Amerika, nach Mikronesien und durch Kamtschatka. Gotha. 2 vols.

KNIGHT, JOHN B.

1834. Letter to S. C. Phillips, dated January 18, 1834, at Peabody Museum, Salem, Mass.

1925. A journal of a voyage in the brig "Spy," of Salem (1832–1834). Pp. 168–207 of The Sea, the Ship, and the Sailor, Publ. no. 7 of the Marine Research Society, Salem.

KOLONIALAMT, GERMANY

1911, 1912, 1913, and 1914. Die deutschen Schutzgebiete in Afrika und der Südsee. (Four successive years). Berlin.

KUBARY, J. S.

1874. Weitere Nachrichten von der Insel Ponape. Journal des Museum Godeffroy, vol. 3, part 8, pp. 261–267.

LHOTSKY, JOHN

1835. Ruins of an ancient town in one of the South Sea Islands. New South Wales Literary, Political and Commercial Advertiser, February 1835.

LUTKÉ, FRÉDÉRIC

1835–36. Voyage autour du monde executé par ordre de sa Majesté l'Empereur Nicolaus Ier sur la corvette "Le Séniavine," dans les années 1826, 1827, 1828, et 1829. Paris. 3 vols.

MAHLMANN, JOHN JAMES

1918. Reminiscences of an ancient mariner. Yokohama.

MAIGRET, DÉSIRÉ

1837–38. Diary. (Manuscript at Chancery Office, Roman Catholic Diocese of Honolulu.)

1839. A letter, pp. 95–101, of Lettres des premiers missionaires de la congregation des sacres-coeurs, dite "De Picpus."

MARKHAM, CLEMENTS ROBERT

1904. The voyages of Pedro Fernandez de Quiros, 1595 to 1606. Translated and edited by Sir Clements Markham, London.

MICHELENA Y ROJAS, FRANCISCO

1843. Viajes científicos en todo el mundo, desde 1822 hasta 1842. Madrid.

MIGUEL, GREGORIO

1887. Estudio sur las Islas Carolinas. Madrid.

MOSS, FREDERICK J.

1889. Through atolls and islands in the great South Sea. London.

NAVARRETE, MARTIN FERNANDEZ DE

1837. Coleccion de los Viages y Descubrimientos. Vol. 5. Madrid.

O'CONNELL, JAMES F.

1836. A residence of eleven years in New Holland and the Caroline Islands. Boston.

OSBORNE, ALICK

1833. Notes on the present state and prospects of society in New South Wales, with an historical, statistical, and topographical account of Manilla and Singapore. London.

PIERSON, GEORGE. See under ABCFM.

REICHSTAG, GERMANY

1902 through 1911, annually. Denkschrift über die Entwickelung der deutschen Schutzgebiete in Afrika und in der Südsee. Stenographische Berichte über die Verhandlungen des Reichstages. Berlin.

RIESENBERG, SAUL H.

1948. Magic and medicine in Ponape. Southwestern Journal of Anthropology, vol. 4, no. 2, pp. 406–429.

1959. A Pacific voyager's hoax. Ethnohistory, vol. 6, no. 3, pp. 238–264.

ROBERTS, EPHRAIM P. See under ABCFM.

STURGES, ALBERT A. See under ABCFM.

WINN, JOHN D.

1833–35. Log of the ship Eliza. (Manuscript at Essex Institute, Salem, Mass.)

YANAIHARA, TADAO
1940. Pacific Islands under Japanese mandate. London and New York.

YZENDOORN, REGINALD
1927. History of the Catholic Mission in the Hawaiian Islands. Honolulu.

THE FOLLOWING UNSIGNED ARTICLES AND NOTES, IN:
*The Friend,* Honolulu, September 1, 1850; December 17, 1852; May 1853.
*The Hobart Colonial Times,* May 25, 1827.
*The Puritan Recorder,* Boston, vol. 40, no. 38, September 20, 1855, p. 149.
*The Sydney Gazette,* June 15, 1827; May 15, 1830; November 13, 1830; April 8, 1834; May 8, 1834.
*The Sydney Herald,* May 8, 1834; September 4, 7, and 28, 1837.
Article entitled "Wreck of the Harmony," Nautical Magazine, 1838, p. 138.